CAMBRIDGE

D0347588

UNL🔗CK

LISTENING & SPEAKING SKILLS

1

Sabina Ostrowska

CAMBRIDGE
UNIVERSITY PRESS

CAMBRIDGE
UNIVERSITY PRESS

University Printing House, Cambridge CB2 8BS, United Kingdom

Cambridge University Press is part of the University of Cambridge.

It furthers the University's mission by disseminating knowledge in the pursuit of education, learning and research at the highest international levels of excellence.

www.cambridge.org
Information on this title: www.cambridge.org/9781107662117

First published 2014

Printed in the United Kingdom by Latimer Trend

A catalogue record for this publication is available from the British Library

ISBN 978-1-107-67810-1 Listening and Speaking 1 Student's Book with Online Workbook
ISBN 978-1-107-66211-7 Listening and Speaking 1 Teacher's Book with DVD
ISBN 978-1-107-61399-7 Reading and Writing 1 Student's Book with Online Workbook
ISBN 978-1-107-61401-7 Reading and Writing 1 Teacher's Book with DVD

Additional resources for this publication at www.cambridge.org/unlock

CONTENTS

UNLOCK UNIT STRUCTURE

The units in *Unlock Listening and Speaking Skills* are carefully scaffolded so that students build the skills and language they need throughout the unit in order to produce a successful Speaking task.

| **UNLOCK YOUR KNOWLEDGE** | Encourages discussion around the theme of the unit with inspiration from interesting questions and striking visuals. |

| **WATCH AND LISTEN** | Features an engaging and motivating *Discovery Education™* video which generates interest in the topic. |

| **LISTENING 1** | Provides information about the topic and practises pre-listening, while listening and post-listening skills. This section also includes a focus on a pronunciation feature which will further enhance listening comprehension. |

| **LANGUAGE DEVELOPMENT** | Practises the vocabulary and grammar from Listening 1 and pre-teaches the vocabulary and grammar from Listening 2. |

| **LISTENING 2** | Provides a different angle on the topic and serves as a model for the speaking task. |

| **CRITICAL THINKING** | Contains brainstorming, categorizing, evaluative and analytical tasks as preparation for the speaking task. |

| **PREPARATION FOR SPEAKING / SPEAKING SKILLS** | Presents and practises functional language, pronunciation and speaking strategies for the speaking task. |

| **SPEAKING TASK** | Uses the skills and strategies learnt over the course of the unit to produce a presentational or interactional speaking task. |

| **OBJECTIVES REVIEW** | Allows learners to assess how well they have mastered the skills covered in the unit. |

| **WORDLIST** | Includes the key vocabulary from the unit. |

This is the unit's main learning objective. It gives learners the opportunity to use all the language and skills they have learnt in the unit.

UNL?CK MOTIVATION

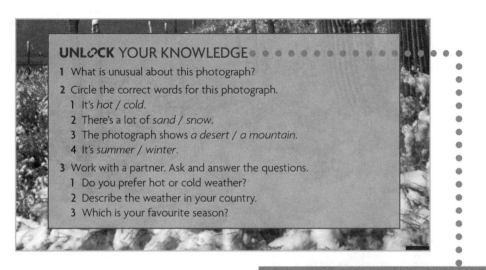

UNL?CK YOUR KNOWLEDGE

1 What is unusual about this photograph?
2 Circle the correct words for this photograph.
  1 It's *hot / cold*.
  2 There's a lot of *sand / snow*.
  3 The photograph shows *a desert / a mountain*.
  4 It's *summer / winter*.
3 Work with a partner. Ask and answer the questions.
  1 Do you prefer hot or cold weather?
  2 Describe the weather in your country.
  3 Which is your favourite season?

PERSONALIZE

Unlock encourages students to bring their own knowledge, experiences and opinions to the topics. This **motivates** students to relate the topics to their own contexts.

DISCOVERY EDUCATION™ VIDEO

Thought-provoking videos from *Discovery Education™* are included in every unit throughout the course to introduce topics, promote discussion and motivate learners. The videos provide a new angle on a wide range of academic subjects.

> The video was excellent! It helped with raising students' interest in the topic. It was well-structured and the language level was appropriate.
>
> Maria Agata Szczerbik, United Arab Emirates University, Al-Ain, UAE

UNLOCK CRITICAL THINKING

BLOOM'S TAXONOMY

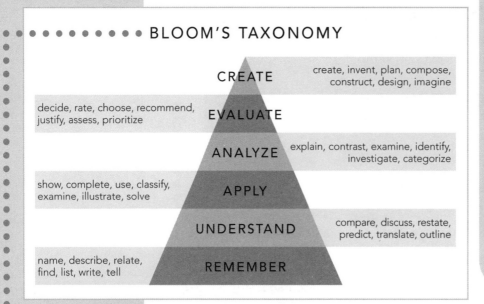

CREATE — create, invent, plan, compose, construct, design, imagine

decide, rate, choose, recommend, justify, assess, prioritize — EVALUATE

ANALYZE — explain, contrast, examine, identify, investigate, categorize

show, complete, use, classify, examine, illustrate, solve — APPLY

UNDERSTAND — compare, discuss, restate, predict, translate, outline

name, describe, relate, find, list, write, tell — REMEMBER

BLOOM'S TAXONOMY

The Critical thinking sections in *Unlock* are based on Benjamin Bloom's classification of learning objectives. This ensures learners develop their **lower-** and **higher-order thinking skills**, ranging from demonstrating **knowledge** and **understanding** to in-depth **evaluation**.
The margin headings in the Critical thinking sections highlight the exercises which develop Bloom's concepts.

LEARN TO THINK

Learners engage in **evaluative** and **analytical tasks** that are designed to ensure they do all of the thinking and information-gathering required for the end-of-unit speaking task.

CRITICAL THINKING

UNDERSTAND

At the end of this unit, you are going to do the speaking task below.

Tell your group about two famous people from your country.

Ideas maps

An ideas map helps you think about the topic and organize information about it. It also helps you to remember key information and vocabulary.

1 Look at the ideas maps below and answer the questions.

1 What is the main topic of each map?
2 What other topics can you find in the maps?
3 What language information can you find in the maps?
4 Which ideas map do you prefer? Why?

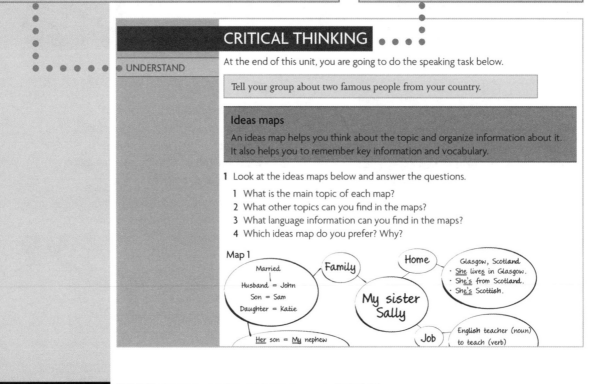

Map 1

Married
Husband = John
Son = Sam
Daughter = Katie
Family

Home
Glasgow, Scotland
· She lives in Glasgow.
· She's from Scotland.
· She's Scottish.

My sister Sally

Her son = My nephew

Job
English teacher (noun)
to teach (verb)

UNLOCK RESEARCH

THE CAMBRIDGE LEARNER CORPUS ◎

The **Cambridge Learner Corpus** is a bank of official Cambridge English exam papers. Our exclusive access means we can use the corpus to carry out unique research and identify the most common errors that learners make. That information is used to ensure the *Unlock* syllabus teaches the most **relevant language**.

THE WORDS YOU NEED

Language Development sections provide vocabulary and grammar-building tasks that are further practised in the UNLOCK ONLINE Workbook. The glossary provides definitions and pronunciation, and the end-of-unit wordlists provide useful summaries of key vocabulary.

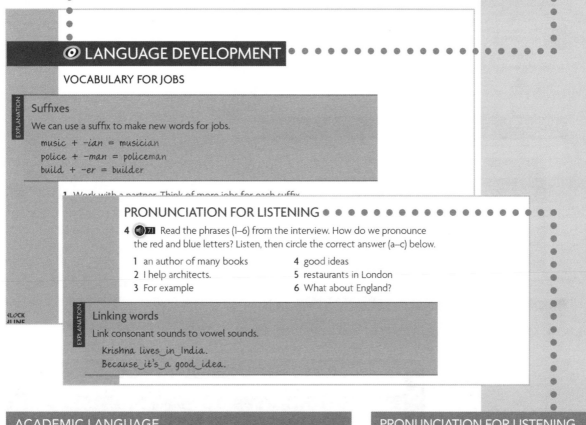

◎ LANGUAGE DEVELOPMENT

VOCABULARY FOR JOBS

EXPLANATION

Suffixes

We can use a suffix to make new words for jobs.

music + –ian = musician
police + –man = policeman
build + –er = builder

1 Work with a partner. Think of more jobs for each suffix.

PRONUNCIATION FOR LISTENING

4 ◀71 Read the phrases (1–6) from the interview. How do we pronounce the red and blue letters? Listen, then circle the correct answer (a–c) below.

1 an author of many books
2 I help architects.
3 For example

4 good ideas
5 restaurants in London
6 What about England?

EXPLANATION

Linking words

Link consonant sounds to vowel sounds.

Krishna lives_in_India.
Because_it's_a good_idea.

ACADEMIC LANGUAGE

Unique research using the **Cambridge English Corpus** has been carried out into academic language, in order to provide learners with relevant, academic vocabulary from the start (CEFR A1 and above). This addresses a gap in current academic vocabulary mapping and ensures learners are presented with carefully selected words which they will find essential during their studies.

PRONUNCIATION FOR LISTENING

This unique feature of *Unlock* focuses on aspects of pronunciation which may inhibit listening comprehension. This means that learners are primed to understand detail and nuance while listening.

> The language development is clear and the strong lexical focus is positive as learners feel they make more progress when they learn more vocabulary.
>
> Colleen Wackrow,
> Princess Nourah Bint Abdulrahman University, Al-Riyadh, Kingdom of Saudi Arabia

FLEXIBLE

Unlock is available in a range of print and digital components, so teachers can mix and match according to their requirements.

UNLOCK ONLINE WORKBOOKS

The UNLOCK ONLINE Workbooks are accessed via activation codes packaged with the Student's Books. These **easy-to-use** workbooks provide interactive exercises, games, tasks, and further practice of the language and skills from the Student's Books in the Cambridge LMS, an engaging and modern learning environment.

CAMBRIDGE LEARNING MANAGEMENT SYSTEM (LMS)

The Cambridge LMS provides teachers with the ability to track learner progress and save valuable time thanks to automated marking functionality. Blogs, forums and other tools are also available to facilitate communication between students and teachers.

UNLOCK EBOOKS

The *Unlock* Student's Books and Teacher's Books are also available as interactive eBooks. With answers and *Discovery Education*™ videos embedded, the eBooks provide a great alternative to the printed materials.

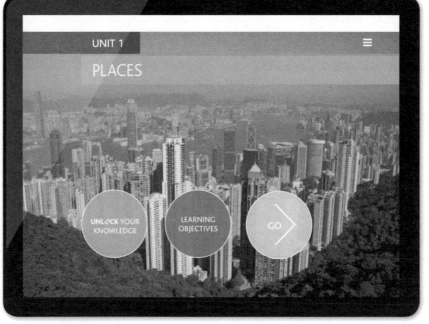

1 Using video in the classroom

The *Watch and listen* sections in *Unlock* are based on documentary-style videos from *Discovery Education*™. Each one provides a fresh angle on the unit topic and a stimulating lead-in to the unit.

There are many different ways of using the video in class. For example, you could ask learners to listen to the audio track of the video without viewing the images and ask learners what the video is about. Then show the whole video and check whether the learners were correct. You could ask learners to reconstruct the voiceover or record their own commentary to the video. Try not to interrupt the first viewing of a new video, you can go back and watch sections again or explain things for struggling learners. You can also watch with the subtitles turned on when the learners have done all the listening comprehension work required of them. For less-controlled listening practice, use the video for free note-taking and ask learners to compare their notes to the video script.

See also: Goldstein, B. and Driver, P. (2014) *Language Learning with Digital Video*, Cambridge University Press, and the *Unlock* website www.cambridge.org/unlock for more ideas on using video in the classroom.

2 Teaching listening skills

Learners who aim to study at university will need to be comfortable listening to long, complex listening texts in a number of different genres. The listening texts in *Unlock Listening & Speaking Skills* provide learners with practice in the different listening sub-skills and also provide topic-related ideas and functional language needed for the *Speaking task*. Every unit focuses on one key listening skill, which is highlighted in a box, as well as various sub-skills, so that learners build on their listening skills throughout.

Before listening for the first time, use the *Preparing to listen* skills boxes to draw on learners' background knowledge and expectations of the listening text. Use the *While listening* skills boxes to focus students on listening sub-skills. Use the *Pronunciation for listening* activities to raise awareness of pronunciation features which can help listeners

decode speech. Learners have an opportunity for reflection on what they have listened to in the *Discussion* activities.

3 Teaching pronunciation

Unlock features *Pronunciation for listening* and *Pronunciation for speaking* sections. In *Pronunciation for listening*, learners focus on aspects of pronunciation which can enhance their listening comprehension, such as linking words, intonation, strong and weak forms in connected speech, homophones, etc. This will help learners to obtain more meaning from the listening text and in real life. Encourage learners to try using these pronunciation features in their own speaking so that they will be primed to hear them.

In *Pronunciation for speaking*, learners focus on aspects of pronunciation which they can put into practice in the *Speaking task*, such as consonant clusters, vowel sounds, connected speech, sentence stress and using intonation and tone. Practise pronunciation with your learners by recording them and giving feedback on the clarity, pace and stress in the *Speaking task*. Encourage your learners to record themselves and reflect on their own pronunciation.

4 Teaching speaking skills

Learners work towards the *Speaking task* throughout the unit by learning vocabulary and grammar relevant for the task, and then by listening to the key issues involved in the topic. Learners gather, organize and evaluate this information in the *Critical thinking* section and use it to prepare the *Speaking task*. *Unlock* includes two types of *Speaking task* – presentational and interactional. In the presentational tasks, learners will be required to give a presentation or monologue about the topic, often as part of a team. The interactional tasks require learners to role-play or interact with another person or persons.

There is an *Additional speaking task* for every unit in the Teacher's Book. This can be used as extra speaking practice to be prepared at home and done in class or as part of an end-of-unit test/evaluation. The *Additional speaking task* is also available on the Online Workbook. See section 8 for more details.

If your learners require IELTS test practice, point out that the discussion questions in the *Unlock your knowledge* sections provide practice of *IELTS Part 1 and 3* and the *Speaking tasks* provide practice of *IELTS Part 2*. Set the *Speaking task* as a timed test with a minimum time of two minutes and grade the learners on their overall fluency, vocabulary and grammar and the quality and clarity of their pronunciation.

5 Managing discussions in the classroom

There are opportunities for free discussion throughout *Unlock Listening & Speaking Skills*. The photographs and the *Unlock your knowledge* boxes on the first page of each unit provide the first discussion opportunity. Learners could be asked to guess what is happening in the photographs or predict what is going to happen or they could investigate the questions for homework in preparation for the lesson.

Throughout the rest of the unit, the heading *Discussion* indicates a set of questions which can be an opportunity for free speaking practice. Learners can use these questions to develop their ideas about the topic and gain confidence in the arguments they will put forward in the *Speaking task*.

To maximize speaking practice, learners could complete the discussion sections in pairs. Monitor each pair to check they can find enough to say and help where necessary. Encourage learners to minimize their use of L1 (their first language) and make notes for any error correction and feedback after the learners have finished speaking.

An alternative approach might be to ask learners to role-play discussions in the character of one of the people in the unit. This may free the learners from the responsibility to provide the correct answer and allow them to see an argument from another perspective.

Task checklists

Encourage your learners to reflect on their performance in the *Speaking task* by referring to the Task checklist at the end of the unit. The checklists can also be used by learners to reflect on each other's performance, if you feel that your learners will be comfortable doing so.

Additional speaking tasks

There are ten Additional speaking tasks in the Teacher's Book, one for each unit. These provide another opportunity to practise the skills and language learnt in the unit.

Model language

Model language in the form of functional expressions and conversation gambits follow the *Additional speaking tasks* to help learners develop confidence in their speaking ability by providing chunks of language they can use during the *Speaking task*. Photocopy the *Model language* and hand this to your learners when they plan and perform their writing task. Make sure learners practise saying them before they begin their task.

6 Teaching vocabulary

The *Wordlist* at the end of each unit includes topic vocabulary and academic vocabulary. There are many ways that you can work with the vocabulary. During the early units, encourage the learners to learn the new words by setting regular review tests. You could ask the learners to choose, e.g. five words from the unit vocabulary to learn. Encourage your learners to keep a vocabulary notebook and use new words as much as possible in their speaking.

7 Using the Research projects with your class

There is an opportunity for students to investigate and explore the unit topic further in the *Research projects* which feature at the end of each unit in the Teacher's Books. These are optional activities which will allow your learners to work in groups (or individually) to discover more about a particular aspect of the topic, carry out a problem-solving activity or engage in a task which takes their learning outside the classroom.

Learners can make use of the Cambridge LMS tools to share their work with the teacher or with the class as a whole. See section 8 for more ideas.

8 Using UNL🔓CK digital components: Online Workbook and the Cambridge Learning Management System (LMS)

The Online Workbook provides:

- additional practice of the key skills and language covered in the Student's Book through interactive exercises. The 🔓 UNL🔓CK ONLINE symbol next to a section or activity in the Student's Book means that there is additional practice of that language or skill in the Online Workbook. These exercises are ideal as homework.

- *Additional speaking tasks* from the Teacher's Books. You can ask your learners to carry out the *Additional speaking tasks* in the

Online Workbook for homework. Learners can record their response to the task and upload the file for the teacher.

- a gradebook which allows you to track your learners' progress throughout the course. This can help structure a one-to-one review with the learner or be used as a record of learning. You can also use this to help you decide what to review in class.
- games for vocabulary and language practice which are not scored in the gradebook.

The Cambridge LMS provides the following tools:

• Blogs

The class blog can be used for free writing practice to consolidate learning and share ideas. For example, you could ask each learner to post a description of their holiday (or another event linked to a topic covered in class). You could ask them to read and comment on two other learners' posts.

• Forums

The forums can be used for discussions. You could post a discussion question and encourage learners to post their thoughts on the question for homework.

• Wikis

In each class there is a Wiki. You can set up pages within this. The wikis are ideal for whole-class project work. You can use the wiki to practise process writing and to train the students to redraft and proofread. Try not to correct students online. Take note of common errors and use these to create a fun activity to review the language in class.

See www.cambridge.org/unlock for more ideas on using these tools with your class.

How to access the Cambridge LMS and setup classes

Go to www.cambridge.org/unlock for more information for teachers on accessing and using the Cambridge LMS and Online Workbooks.

---

9 Using Unlock interactive eBooks

Unlock Listening & Speaking Skills Student's Books are available as fully interactive eBooks. The content of the printed Student's Book and the Student's eBook is the same. However, there will be a number of differences in the way some content appears.

If you are using the interactive eBooks on tablet devices in the classroom, you may want to consider how this affects your class structure. For example, your learners will be able to independently access the video and audio content via the eBook. This means learners could do video activities at home and class time could be optimized on discussion activities and other productive tasks. Learners can compare their responses to the answer key in their eBooks which means the teacher may need to spend less time on checking answers with the whole class, leaving more time to monitor learner progress and help individual learners.

10 Using mobile technology in the language learning classroom

By Michael Pazinas, Curriculum and assessment coordinator for the Foundation Program at the United Arab Emirates University.

The presiding learning paradigm for mobile technology in the language classroom should be to create as many meaningful learning opportunities as possible for its users. What should be at the core of this thinking is that while modern mobile technology can be a 21st century 'super-toolbox', it should be there to support a larger learning strategy. Physical and virtual learning spaces, content and pedagogy all need to be factored in before deciding on delivery and ultimately the technological tools needed.

It is with these factors in mind that the research projects featured in this Teacher's Book aim to add elements of hands-on enquiry, collaboration, critical thinking and analysis. They have real challenges, which learners have to research and find solutions for. In an ideal world, they can become tangible, important solutions. While they are designed with groups in mind, there is nothing to stop them being used with individuals. They can be fully enriching experiences, used as starting points or simply ideas to be adapted and streamlined. When used in these ways, learner devices can become research libraries, film, art and music studios, podcast stations, marketing offices and blog creation tools.

Michael has first-hand experience of developing materials for the paperless classroom. He is the author of the Research projects *which feature in the Teacher's Books.*

1 PEOPLE

Learning objectives

Before you start the *Unlock your knowledge* section, ask students to read the Learning objectives box so that they have a clear idea of what they are going to learn in this unit. Tell them that you will come back to these objectives at the end of the unit when they review what they have learned. Give them the opportunity to ask you any questions they might have.

UNLOCK YOUR KNOWLEDGE

Background note

The photograph shows the jockey Luca Minisini competing during the fifth of six trial horse races in Del Campo square in Siena, Italy, on 1 July 2013. Every year in July and August, ten riders ride bareback around Siena's shell-shaped central square in a bid to win the 'Palio', a silk banner.

Possible answers

1 A crowd of people, someone riding a horse
2 The crowd is watching a horse race. There is one horse galloping around a race track.

Optional activity

👥 👥👥 As a follow-up activity, ask students to work in pairs and think of an event in their country that attracts big crowds. If all the students are from the same country, ask them to think about events in general, e.g. movie premieres, political rallies, sporting events, etc. Allow students about ten minutes to research these events. Students should find a photograph of the event and make basic notes about it, e.g. when it takes place, who attends, etc. Monitor and help with the key words for the internet search. Students then work in groups and tell each other about their chosen event. Students should say what it is, when it takes place and why it is famous. Monitor and help with vocabulary for the task. Ask volunteers to share their answers with the class.

WATCH AND LISTEN

Video script

▶ This is a video about people who make nature films. Let's meet them. This is Glenn Evans. Glenn's a cameraman. He makes films all over the world. Every good cameraman needs a good sound man. This is Jonah Torreano. Jonah likes having fun. And this is Todd Brown. Todd's the assistant, so he helps the team. Jud Cremata's the producer. Jud's job is to plan travel and equipment for the crew.

The crew are in Alaska. They are going to the airport with Jeff Corwin. Jeff is a nature expert. He's also a TV presenter. Film crews have a lot of equipment. You can see all their bags here. They are going from Palmer to Kaktovik. Kaktovik is a small place. Only 300 people live there. The crew take their camera to the ice. They want to film some polar bears. They make camp. The crew start their search for a polar bear. They go by helicopter. They see a seal – food for polar bears – and tracks from the polar bears in the snow. The film crew know they are near. Jeff gets out of the helicopter to look at the polar bears' tracks on the ground. Finally, they see *three* polar bears! The crew film the family of bears from the safety of their helicopter. The film makers make their film and go home happy.

PREPARING TO WATCH

Optional lead-in

👥👥 👥👥👥 Students work in pairs and describe what they can see in the four video stills to each other. Allow a few minutes for discussion, then discuss the video stills as a class. Elicit where the video is taking place, i.e. Alaska /əˈlæskə/.

UNDERSTANDING KEY VOCABULARY

1 👤 👥👥 Students complete the task individually, then check their answers with a partner. Encourage students to use the Glossary at the back of the book. Allow students no more than ten minutes for the task, then check the answers as a class. Check the understanding of the new words and elicit the pronunciation.

Answers

1 tracks /træks/ 2 seal /siːl/ 3 equipment /ɪˈkwɪpmənt/
4 helicopter /ˈhelɪkɒptə/

2 👥👥 Students complete the task in pairs. Give them about five minutes. Allow them to use the Glossary at the back of the book. Check the answers with the class.

Answers

1 takes pictures /teɪks ˈpɪktʃəs/
2 records /rɪˈkɔːdz/ what he can hear /hɪə/
3 helps /helps/
4 buys /baɪz/
5 speaks /spiːks/ to the camera /ˈkæmrə/
6 making /ˈmeɪkɪŋ/

WHILE WATCHING

UNDERSTANDING MAIN IDEAS

3 ▶ 👥 Before you play the video, ask students to read the three questions and guess possible answers in pairs. Students watch the video and write their answers. They then check their answers with a partner. Check the answers as a class.

Answers

1 They travel by plane.
2 They want to film polar bears.
3 They see polar-bear tracks.

UNDERSTANDING DETAIL

4 ▶ 👥 Ask students to read the sentences and make predictions about the answers. Students watch the video one more time and select the correct answers. Ask students to compare their answers with other classmates. Discuss the correct answers as a group.

Answers

1 All over the world 2 Three hundred 3 A lot 4 Three
5 From the helicopter

DISCUSSION

5 👤👥 Students work individually and make notes about the questions. Allow no more than five minutes for note-making and brainstorming. Then students work in small groups and discuss their ideas. Monitor and give feedback on vocabulary and pronunciation. Allow about ten minutes for discussion, then ask the groups to present their ideas to the class. Write down any common mistakes. At the end of the task, write them on the whiteboard or say them aloud and elicit the correct answers from the class.

LISTENING 1

PREPARING TO LISTEN

Skills box

👥 Draw students' attention to the box. Allow them a minute to read it, then check understanding of *key vocabulary*. As a class, ask students to predict what kind of key vocabulary they will hear in Listening 1. By skimming the page, students should notice vocabulary related to families, occupations and countries.

UNDERSTANDING KEY VOCABULARY

1 👥 Students complete the task in pairs. With a mixed-ability class, match the weaker students with the stronger ones. Elicit the first answer from the class. Encourage students to use the Glossary at the back of the book. Monitor and check understanding of the new vocabulary. At the end, display the table on an interactive whiteboard and complete it as a class. Check understanding and the pronunciation of the new vocabulary.

Answers

topic	key vocabulary
family /ˈfæm(ə)li/	brother /ˈbrʌðə/, sister /ˈsɪstə/, mother /ˈmʌðə/, father /ˈfɑːðə/
occupations /ɒkjuˈpeɪʃənz/	student /ˈstjuːdənt/, doctor /ˈdɒktə/, manager /ˈmænɪdʒə/
countries /ˈkʌntriz/	Saudi Arabia /saʊdɪ əˈreɪbiə/, China /ˈtʃaɪnə/

Optional activity

👥 👥👥 With a stronger class, ask students to add more vocabulary to the table. Each pair should add three more words in each topic. Allow about five minutes for the task, then ask students to compare their vocabulary with another pair. Encourage them to use the Glossary at the back of the book. Display the table on an interactive whiteboard and complete it with the new words. Ask for volunteers to write; their partners spell the new words out for them.

PRONUNCIATION FOR LISTENING

2 🔊 1.1 👤👥 Students work alone and write the number of syllables before they listen. If necessary, elicit the meaning of *syllable*, i.e. a sound unit organized around a vowel. Words

like *cat* or *dog* consist of one syllable. Other words, like *sister*, *mother* or *brother*, consist of two syllables; *manager* has three syllables. Students listen and check their answers. Allow them a couple of minutes to compare answers with a partner, then check the number of syllables as a class.

> **Answers**
>
> **Exercise 2 and 3:** 1 introduce (3) /ɪntrəˈdjuːs/
> 2 please (1) /pliːz/ 3 Peru (2) /pəˈru/
> 4 Turkey (2) /ˈtɜːki/ 5 twenty (2) /ˈtwenti/
> 6 eighteen (2) /eɪˈtiːn/ 7 study (2) /ˈstʌdi/
> 8 business (2) /ˈbɪznɪs/ 9 computer (3) /kəmˈpjuːtə/
> 10 producer (3) /prəˈdjuːsə/

Explanation box

👥 👥👥 Ask students to read the Explanation box. Check their understanding of *stress*. Discuss the examples in the box. Ask students to work in pairs and mark the word stress in the words in Exercise 1. Allow about five minutes for the task, then check answers as a class.

3 (◀)) **1.1** 👤 Students complete the task individually, then listen and check their answers. Allow a few minutes to compare answers with a partner. Display the words on an interactive whiteboard and ask for volunteers to mark the stress. If necessary, play the words one more time and drill the pronunciation.

> **Answers**
> See above.

WHILE LISTENING

> **Optional activity**
>
> 👤👥 As an alternative, with a stronger group, ask students to close their books while they listen for the first time. Tell them to take notes about the different speakers and write down details about them. Then students compare their notes with a partner and discuss Exercise 4 in pairs. Students can then use the notes to answer Exercise 5 before listening again to check their answers.

LISTENING FOR MAIN IDEAS

4 (◀)) **1.2** 👤 👥👥 Ask students to look at the pictures and read the questions in Exercise 5. Ask students who the speakers in the programme are, and which countries they might be from. Students should be able to predict that the speakers are students and that they come from Peru, Japan, Turkey and the UAE. Students complete the task individually, then compare their answers with a partner. Check the answers as a class.

> **Answers**
>
> 1 Hussain: United Arab Emirates 2 Nehir: Turkey
> 3 Carlos: Peru 4 Koko: Japan

5 (◀)) **1.2** 👤 👥👥 Ask students to predict the answers. Then they listen again and compare answers with a partner. Check answers as a class.

> **Answers**
> 1 b 2 a 3 c

LISTENING FOR DETAIL

6 (◀)) **1.2** 👥👥 Students read the sentences and discuss in pairs whether they are true or false. They then listen and check their answers. Ask students to correct the false statements. Discuss the answers and the corrections to the false statements. If necessary, ask students to scan the script on page 210 and underline the correct answers. Display the script on an interactive whiteboard and check the answers as a class.

> **Answers**
> 1 T
> 2 F (Her father is a teacher.)
> 3 T
> 4 F (He has two younger sisters and one younger brother.)
> 5 T
> 6 T
> 7 F (He is 19.)
> 8 F (His mother is a doctor.)

7 👥👥 Model the task by asking the class about one of the students from Exercise 4. Students complete the task in pairs. Monitor and give feedback on the pronunciation of the key vocabulary.

DISCUSSION

8 and 9 👤 👥 👥👥 Allow students a few minutes to make notes about themselves. Elicit the meaning of *occupation* /ˌɒkjʊˈpeɪʃən/ (a person's job) and *hometown* /ˈhəʊmtaʊn/ (the town or city where the person is from). Students then complete the task in pairs. If possible, have them work with a new partner. Allow about eight minutes for discussion, then model Exercise 9. Draw students' attention to the useful expressions, and model switching from first to third person singular. Students work with another pair and tell the group members about their partner. Monitor and give feedback on the pronunciation of the key words. Make sure students use the third person singular correctly. Note any common mistakes you hear during monitoring and write them on the whiteboard at the end. Elicit the correct answers from the class.

👁 LANGUAGE DEVELOPMENT

PERSONAL PRONOUNS AND POSSESSIVE ADJECTIVES

Explanation box

👥👥 Pronouns are used in place of a noun. Personal pronouns (*I, you, he, she, it, we* and *they*) are used in the subject position in a sentence.

Possessive adjectives, like *my, your, his, her, its, our* and *their,* are used to show ownership or belonging.

Display the Explanation box on an interactive whiteboard and ask the class to identify which words in the example sentences are possessive adjectives and which ones are personal pronouns. Explain the difference using the example sentences from the Explanation box.

Optional activity

🔊 1.2 👥👥 Divide the class into teams. Play Carlos's part from audio 1.2. Ask the teams to write down all the pronouns and possessive adjectives they hear. With a more advanced class, play the whole track again. Each team should write the words on a piece of paper. The team who has all the words from the audio wins. Write them on the whiteboard as a class and check understanding.

Answers

Personal pronouns: I, I, you, she, she, she, she
Possessive adjectives: our, her, her

1 👥 👥👥 Allow about five minutes for students to do this in pairs, then ask them to compare their answers with another pair. Monitor to make sure all the groups have the correct answers. At the end, draw students' attention to words with the same pronunciation, e.g. *there* /ðeə/ and *their* /ðeə/, *our* /aʊə/ and *hour* /aʊə/, and *your* /jɔː/ and *you're* /jɔː/.

Answers

1 my 2 your 3 its 4 we 5 their

Language note

Students may ask about the difference between *my* and *mine, your* and *yours, her* and *hers, our* and *ours,* and *their* and *theirs*. A simple explanation is that *my, your, her, our* and *their* are possessive adjectives and are used before nouns, e.g. *her phone, our house* or *your book*. *Mine, yours, hers, ours* and *theirs* are possessive pronouns and are used at the end of a sentence or after the verb, e.g. *This phone is hers, This house is ours, This book is yours.*

2 and 3 👤 👥👥 Students complete these exercises individually, then check their answers with a partner. Allow no more than ten minutes for both tasks. Display the exercises on an interactive whiteboard and ask for volunteers to write the answers.

Answers

Exercise 2: 2 his 3 her 4 their 5 our
Exercise 3: 1 Her 2 your 3 it 4 He 5 Their 6 Its
7 I; my 8 We; our

THE VERB *BE*

4 🔊 1.3 👤 👥👥 Students read the two dialogues in pairs and check the meaning of any unknown vocabulary. Encourage them to use the Glossary at the back of the book. Monitor and check understanding of the new vocabulary. Students listen and complete the task individually. Check the answers as a class. Elicit the pronunciation of the contracted forms. Drill the pronunciation as a class. Allow students a few minutes to practise the dialogues in pairs.

Answers

1 That's /ðæts/ 2 It's /ɪts/ 3 What's /wɒts/ 4 isn't /ˈɪzənt/ 5 She's /ʃiːz/ 6 I'm not /aɪm ˈnɒt/ 7 I'm /aɪm/ 8 aren't /ɑːnt/ 9 They're /ðeə/ 10 We're /wɪə/

Explanation box

👥 Display the Explanation box on an interactive whiteboard and allow students a couple of minutes to read the information. Elicit the meaning of *I'm*, *it's*, *we're* and *they're*. Check understanding of the negative and question forms. Ask for original example sentences from students. Write the sentences on the whiteboard, then ask the class to underline the verb *be* in each one.

5 and 6 👤👥 Students complete Exercise 5 individually, then check their answers with a partner. Encourage them to use the Glossary to check the meaning of any new vocabulary. Monitor and check the answers. Students then practise the dialogue in pairs. Monitor and make sure they use the contractions of the verb *be*. At the end, ask for volunteers to demonstrate their dialogue to the class.

Answers

Exercise 5: 2 am not / 'm not 3 am/'m 4 are 5 Are 6 are/'re 7 are/'re 8 is/'s 9 is/'s 10 Are 11 are/'re

LISTENING 2

PREPARING TO LISTEN

UNDERSTANDING KEY VOCABULARY

1 👥 Display the photographs on an interactive whiteboard. Students discuss the questions in small groups. Allow four or five minutes for discussions, then ask the groups to share their ideas with the class.

Answers

It is not important whether the students recognize or know the people in the photographs.
Who can you see in the photographs?
famous people
What are their jobs?
scientist, fashion designer, businesswoman, businessman, basketball player, sportswoman
Where are they from?
Britain and the US

Background note

The people in the photographs are:

a Sir Harry Kroto, British scientist (won the Nobel Prize for Chemistry in 1996)

b Victoria Beckham, British fashion designer (formerly known as one of the Spice Girls, but now best known for her fashion label and being married to David Beckham)

c Ursula Burns, American businesswoman (CEO of Xerox)

d Larry Page, American businessman (co-founder of Google)

e Kobe Bryant, American basketball player (plays for the Los Angeles Lakers)

f Jessica Ennis-Hill, British sportswoman (gold medallist at the London 2012 Olympics)

2 👤👥 Students complete the task individually, then check their answers with a partner. Encourage them to use the Glossary at the back of the book. At the end of the task, check answers as a class and elicit the pronunciation of the key vocabulary.

Answers

1 b 2 f 3 c 4 d 5 e 6 a

3 🔊 1.4 👤👥 Review the meaning of *syllable* and check understanding. Students listen and individually mark the syllables. Then they check their answers with a partner. Allow them a minute or two to compare their answers, then check as a class. Tap on a desk at the syllable boundaries. Students listen again and mark the most stressed syllables in each word. Allow students a couple of minutes to compare answers with a partner. Check the answers as a class. Drill the pronunciation of the key vocabulary as a class. Allow students a couple of minutes to practise in pairs.

Answers

1 fashion (2) /ˈfæ.ʃən/ designer (3) /dɪˈzaɪ.nə/
2 sportswoman (3) /ˈspɔːts.wʊ.mən/
3 businesswoman (4) /ˈbɪz.nɪs.wʊ.mən/
4 businessman (3) /ˈbɪz.nɪs.mən/
5 basketball (3) /ˈbɑː.skɪt.bɔːl/ player (2) /ˈpleɪ.ə/
6 scientist (3) /ˈsaɪ.ən.tɪst/

WHILE LISTENING

LISTENING FOR MAIN IDEAS

4 (🔊 1.5) 👤👥 Students listen and complete the task individually. Then they compare their answers with a partner. Go through the answers with the class.

> **Answers**
> 1 the US 2 d, c 3 the UK 4 f, a

LISTENING FOR DETAIL

5 (🔊 1.5) 👤👥 Students work individually and match the sentences with the people. While they read the sentences, encourage them to use the Glossary and check the meaning of any new vocabulary. Before the listening, check understanding of *scientist* /ˈsaɪəntɪst/ (an expert who studies or works in one of the sciences), *medal* /ˈmedl/ (a small metal disk given as a reward for winning a competition), and *Nobel Prize* /nəʊˈbel ˈpraɪz/ (an international prize given each year to people who make important discoveries). Then they listen and check their answers. Go through the answers with the class.

> **Answers**
> Marie's person 1: 3, 9
> Marie's person 2: 4, 7
> Clare's person 1: 1, 5, 8
> Clare's person 2: 2, 6, 10

DISCUSSION

6 👤👥 Divide the class into Students A and B. If possible, make sure that students work with new partners. Ask Student As to follow the instructions on page 195. Student Bs follow the instructions on page 197. Allow them a couple of minutes to read the information on their cards and check any new vocabulary in the Glossary. Monitor and check pronunciation of the key vocabulary. Make sure students use the third person singular forms correctly; if necessary, write down mistakes and discuss them at the end of the task. At the end of the activity, ask for volunteers to demonstrate the dialogue to the class.

> **Optional activity**
> 👥 Prepare ten flashcards with photographs of famous people and a very brief description of who they are, where there are from, what they do and what they are famous for. Choose famous people who are familiar to students, i.e. currently in the news or of historical importance. A volunteer chooses a flashcard and reads the information about the famous person. Help the student with any unknown vocabulary. The rest of the class ask 'yes/no' questions about the famous person. Model simple questions, e.g. *Is it a man?*, *Is he an actor?*, *Is he American?*, etc. The student with the card can only answer *yes* or *no*. The student who correctly guesses the identity of the famous person wins. To make it more competitive, you can put students into teams and assign points for each correct guess.

CRITICAL THINKING

👥 At this point in each unit, students are asked to begin to think about the speaking task that they will do at the end of the unit (*Tell your group about two famous people from your country*). Give them a minute to look at the box. As a class, brainstorm ideas for the speaking task. Elicit some famous people whom students would like to talk about. Ask them why they would like to talk about these people.

UNDERSTAND

Skills box

👥 Draw students' attention to the box and allow them a couple of minutes to read the information and look at the examples of ideas maps on the page. Check understanding by asking students: *What is an ideas map?*, *Why do we make ideas maps?*, *When do we use ideas maps?* and *What is at the centre of an ideas map?* Elicit answers from the whole class.

1 👥👥 Students discuss the questions in pairs. Then they compare their answers with another pair. Encourage students to use the Glossary at the back of the book. Monitor and help with the vocabulary for the task.

Answers

1 Map 1: My sister Sally
  Map 2: uncle (Abdullah)
2 family, home, job
3 Map 1: grammar
  Map 2: syllables and stress
4 Map 2
5 Answers will vary. Allow students to explain why
  they like one map more than the other, and highlight
  the positive features of both ideas maps, i.e. images
  and attractive design, organization and details.

2 👥 👥 Students complete the exercise in pairs,
then compare their answers with another pair.
Allow about five minutes for the task, then
discuss the answers as a class.

CREATE

3 and 4 👤 👥 Students work individually and
prepare an ideas map about somebody from
their family. In sensitive situations, expand the
task and ask students to prepare an ideas map
about a relative, a friend or somebody they
like. Allow about ten minutes to complete
the ideas maps. Monitor and help with the
vocabulary for the task and check the spelling.
Then match students into new pairs. Students
ask and answer questions about the person
in their ideas map. If necessary, model the
task with a stronger student to ensure that all
students speak in complete sentences.

5 and 6 👥 Students complete the activities in
small groups. Students take turns to explain
their ideas maps to the group. Monitor and
give feedback on the pronunciation of the
key vocabulary, third person singular forms
and contractions. Allow a couple of minutes
for each student to explain their ideas map.
Then students discuss the strengths and
weaknesses of their maps. At the end, ask for
volunteers to present their ideas maps to the
class. If possible, display all the ideas maps on
a classroom board.

Optional activity

👤 As a follow-up, ask students to think of two famous
people from their country and do internet research
about them. Students should find photographs of
these people and basic information similar to the
model ideas maps. Students then prepare ideas maps
with the information from the internet.

SPEAKING

PREPARATION FOR SPEAKING

COUNTRIES AND NATIONALITIES

1 👥 Divide the class into Students A and B.
Student As go to page 194 and spell out
the nationalities to Student Bs. Emphasize
the point that students should not look at
each other's books, so as to allow them to
practise writing spelled-out words. If possible,
ask students to sit back to back with each
other. When Student As are finished spelling
out the nationalities, Student Bs should go
to page 196 and spell their nationalities to
their partners. At the end of the activity, ask
students to check if the way they spelled the
nationalities is the same as they are spelled in
the Student's Book on pages 194 and 196.

Answers

1 Mexican /'meksɪkən/ 2 Omani /əʊ'mɑːni/
3 Egyptian /ɪ'dʒɪpʃən/ 4 Emirati /emɪ'rɑːti/
5 Japanese /dʒæpə'niːz/ 6 Turkish /'tɜːkɪʃ/

2 👤 👥 Students complete the task individually,
then check their answers with a partner.
Check the answers as a class and elicit the
pronunciation of the nationalities. Drill the
pronunciation as a class, then allow students
a couple of minutes to practise saying the
sentences in pairs. Monitor and correct
the pronunciation of the key words. At the
end, check understanding of the difference
between *countries* and *nationalities*.

Answers

1 Omani /əʊ'mɑːni/ 2 Mexico /'meksɪkəʊ/ 3 Egyptian
/ɪ'dʒɪpʃən/ 4 Japan /dʒə'pæn/ 5 Chinese /tʃaɪ'niːz/
6 Emirati /emɪ'rɑːti/

Optional activity

👥 Play *Hangman*. Divide the class into teams.
Prepare a list of countries and nationalities to be
used in the game. With a more advanced class, add
more countries and nationalities to the ones in the
unit. Choose one word from the list and then draw
a row of dashes on the whiteboard to represent the
number of letters in the word. Teams take turns and
guess the missing letters. If a team guesses the correct
letter, they can repeat their turn. If they guess wrong,
draw an element of the hanged-man figure on the
whiteboard. Teams can only guess the whole word
during their turn. The team that guesses the most
words wins.

INTRODUCING AND STARTING A TALK

3 🔊 1.6 👤👥👥 Students complete the exercise individually, then listen to check their answers. Play the audio one more time and ask students to repeat the sentences as they hear them in the recording. Allow two or three minutes for students to practise saying the sentences in pairs.

> **Answers**
> 1 b 2 a 3 b 4 c 5 c

> **Optional activity**
> 👥 Students work in pairs and use the sentence structures from Exercise 3 to make new sentences about famous people they know. Students don't have to write these down. Ask students to make as many sentences as they can in three minutes. As a class, ask each pair to demonstrate their best sentences to the other students.

KEY VOCABULARY FOR PEOPLE

4 👤👥👥 Students complete the table individually by scanning for other jobs that were introduced in the unit. Encourage students to use the Glossary to check the meaning of any new words. Students compare their ideas with a partner. Display the table on an interactive whiteboard and complete it as a class. Nominate a writer and ask the rest of the class to spell out the job titles. Drill the pronunciation of the job titles as a class.

> **Answers**
> verb + -er/-r: producer, presenter, player, designer, teacher
> noun + -ist: scientist

PRONUNCIATION FOR SPEAKING

Explanation box

In spoken English, we don't stress all the words in a sentence. Usually only content words, like nouns, verbs, adjectives and adverbs, are stressed. Functional words, like pronouns, auxiliary verbs, articles and prepositions, are usually pronounced in their weak form. Notice the stressed syllables in these examples: *I'm <u>going</u> to <u>tell</u> you about two <u>famous people</u> from <u>Britain</u>* and *<u>Ana García</u> is a <u>famous Mexican chef</u>*.

👥👥 Write the words *He's a famous footballer* on the whiteboard. Work with the class and divide

the sentence into syllables: *He's–a–<u>fa</u>–mous–foot–ball–er*. You can encourage students to clap their hand for each syllable. Discuss which syllables in the sentence are stressed. Elicit that only two syllables are stressed and drill the sentence with the class to practise the rhythm. As you drill the sentence, you may emphasize the stressed syllables by tapping the palm of your hand on a desk. Ask students to come up with similar sentences, e.g. *She's a famous singer, He's a famous dancer*, etc. Again, divide the new sentences into syllables, then assign the stress.

5 🔊 1.7 👤👥👥 Students listen and repeat the syllables after the recording. Allow students a couple of minutes to practise in pairs. Monitor and give feedback on the word stress.

6 and 7 🔊 1.8 👤👥👥 Play the audio and ask students to repeat the sentences as a class. Allow a couple of minutes for students to practise saying the sentences in pairs. Students complete Exercise 7 in pairs, then listen again to check their answers. Check the answers as a class. Drill the sentence stress by saying the sentences as a group and tapping on the desk on the stressed syllables.

> **Answers**
> **Exercise 7**
> 2 Ka<u>rim</u> <u>Ab</u>del <u>A</u>ziz is a <u>fa</u>mous <u>ac</u>tor.
> 3 <u>Car</u>men Su<u>lei</u>man's a <u>fa</u>mous <u>sing</u>er.
> 4 Ka<u>rim's</u> <u>fa</u>ther is Mo<u>ham</u>med <u>Ab</u>del <u>A</u>ziz.
> 5 He's a <u>film</u> di<u>rec</u>tor.
> 6 Ka<u>rim's</u> <u>aunt</u> is Sa<u>mi</u>ra <u>Muh</u>sin.
> 7 She's an <u>ac</u>tor.

8 and 9 👤👥👥 Students work alone and write their own sentences about famous people from their country. Monitor and help with vocabulary for the task, and check grammar. Students compare their answers with a partner. Allow six to eight minutes to prepare. Students then practise saying their sentences in pairs. Monitor and give feedback on the pronunciation of the key vocabulary and the grammar. Write down any common mistakes that you hear during monitoring and discuss them with the class at the end.

SPEAKING TASK

Introduce the speaking task by telling students that they have to tell their groups about two famous people from their country. In a monocultural class, ask students to talk about two famous people they admire – they don't have to be from one country. As a class, discuss what kind of people they may want to consider, e.g. not only celebrities like actors or singers. They can include writers, scientists, politicians, businesspeople, sportspeople, etc.

PREPARE

1 👤👥 Students prepare ideas maps about the famous people they want to talk about. Allow them time to search the internet. Ask students to find photographs of the famous people they want to talk about. Tell students to show their completed ideas maps to their partners and ask each other for feedback on how they can improve them. Monitor and check vocabulary and grammar for the task.

2 and 3 👤👥 Students complete the tasks individually, then compare their answers with a partner. Ask students to close their books and practise their presentations in pairs.

PRACTISE/DISCUSS

4 and 5 👥 Students work in groups of three or four. Remind them not to read their presentations, but to say them from memory. The other group members listen and complete notes about each famous person. Monitor and write down any common grammar or pronunciation mistakes that you hear. Elicit the correct answers at the end.

Optional activity

With a stronger class, you may want to assign job titles to students to encourage them to do more research. Write down different job titles on pieces of paper, e.g. writer, politician, chef, TV presenter, movie maker, actor, etc. Put the pieces of paper in a bag and ask students to pick out two pieces of paper. Students have to think of two famous people within the two disciplines they picked.

OBJECTIVES REVIEW

See Teaching tips, pages 10–11, for ideas about using the Objectives review with your students.

WORDLIST

See Teaching tips, pages 10–11, for ideas about how to make the most of the Wordlist with your students.

REVIEW TEST

See pages 106–107 for the photocopiable Review test for this unit and Teaching tips, pages 10–11, for ideas about when and how to administer the Review test.

ADDITIONAL SPEAKING TASK

See page 126 for an additional speaking task related to this unit.

Allow students a minute to make notes about themselves. Students then work in pairs and interview each other. Allow five or six minutes for the interaction, and monitor to make sure students take notes about their partners' personal details. Students then introduce their partners to the class. Write down any common mistakes in the use of personal pronouns and possessive adjectives and discuss them as a class at the end.

RESEARCH PROJECT

Create a documentary about a famous person

Divide the class into groups and ask each group to pick a famous person. Tell them that they have to find out about that person's childhood, career and personal life, including video clips and photos. They could search for that person's website or look for information in online newspapers. Social networking sites often also have pages about famous people. Students could use tools on the Cambridge LMS to record and share their research.

Students then use this information to film or record a documentary about that person. To plan the documentary, students will need to create a script or storyboard. They will also have to think about who will direct and record the video, who will do the editing and who will do the presenting.

2 SEASONS

UNLOCK YOUR KNOWLEDGE

1, 2 and 3 👥 Display the photograph on an interactive whiteboard. Students work in pairs and discuss the questions. Allow about five minutes for discussion. Encourage students to use the Glossary at the back of the book to check the meaning of any new words. At the end, students share their ideas with the class. Check understanding and pronunciation of key vocabulary, i.e.

unusual /ʌnˈjuːʒəl/	different from others of the same type
sand /sænd/	very small grains of rock
snow /snəʊ/	small, soft, white pieces of ice that fall from the sky
desert /ˈdezət/	an area, often covered with sand or rocks, where there is very little rain and not many plants
mountain /ˈmaʊntən/	a raised part of the Earth's surface, much larger than a hill, the top of which might be covered in snow
hot /hɒt/	having a high temperature
cold /kəʊld/	having a low temperature, not warm
weather /ˈweðə/	the conditions in the air above the Earth, such as wind, rain or temperature
season /ˈsiːzən/	the period of the year when something that happens every year happens

Answers

1 There's snow in the desert. Snow is unusual in hot countries, even in winter.
2 1 cold 2 snow 3 a desert 4 winter

WATCH AND LISTEN

Video script

▶ Around the world, the seasons and the weather are different. Why is this? Why are there two seasons in some countries – a dry season and a rainy season – but four seasons in others – summer, autumn, winter and spring? This red line is the equator. Above and below the equator are two zones: the Tropic of Cancer and the Tropic of Capricorn. Countries that are on the equator or in these two zones have hot weather. Parts of Kenya are on the equator. They have two seasons. It is hot all year round, but it rains from April to June and October to December. Egypt is in the Tropic of Cancer. The wet season is from December to April. Above and below the tropics, the weather is different.

In this video, we're going to look at seasons in the United States and Canada. Spring in the United States and Canada is from March to May. The weather is warm and wet. In Alaska, the rainfall is over 400 centimetres a year, but in Arizona, it is only eight centimetres a year. There's a lot of rain and sun. Plants and flowers grow at this time. After spring comes summer. The summer months are June, July and August. It is hot and sunny. There's no school in the summer, so children play outside. You can sometimes see storms in the summer, but usually there are blue skies. In summer, the plants and trees have lots of green leaves and fruit, and vegetables grow. Autumn is between September and November. The weather is cold and it can be misty in the morning and evening. Many people like the autumn because the leaves on the trees change colour and fall. It can be very beautiful. Winter is from December to February. Winter is cold and there can be a lot of snow. It can be as cold as minus 60 degrees Celsius. You can see snow in the cities and in the country. Snow can be dangerous for cars, but children like it, and many people go skiing. Some people hate the cold weather; they travel south to the tropics for the sun and hot weather. Do you like hot or cold seasons?

PREPARING TO WATCH

Optional lead-in

👥 Before students start working on the vocabulary, ask them to look at the four video stills. Students describe the photographs to each other. Allow three or four minutes for pair discussions, then discuss the photographs as a class.

UNDERSTANDING KEY VOCABULARY

1 🧍🧍🧍 Students complete the task individually, then compare their answers with a partner. Encourage students to use the Glossary at the back of book. Check answers as a class. Check understanding and the pronunciation of the key vocabulary.

> **Answers**
>
> a flowers /ˈflaʊəz/ (the parts of plants which are often brightly coloured with a pleasant smell)
> b a storm /stɔːm/ (an extreme weather condition with very strong wind, heavy rain and often thunder and lightning)
> c snow /snəʊ/ (the small, soft, white pieces of ice which sometimes fall from the sky when it is cold)
> d fruit /fruːt/ (the usually sweet-tasting part of a tree or bush which holds seeds and which can be eaten)
> e vegetables /ˈvedʒtəblz/ (plants, roots, seeds or pods that are used as food)
> f plants /plɑːnts/ (living things which grow in earth or in water)

2 🧍🧍 Students discuss the questions in pairs. Monitor and encourage students to answer the questions in complete sentences. With more advanced classes, encourage students to develop their answers by giving examples. Give feedback on the pronunciation of the key vocabulary. Allow three or four minutes for discussion, then ask students to share their answers with the class.

USING VISUALS TO PREDICT CONTENT

3 🧍🧍 🧍🧍🧍 Display the diagram on an interactive whiteboard. To facilitate the task, ask students to point to the north and the south on the diagram. If possible, ask students to point to the general areas where their country/countries are located. Allow students to read the example sentence, then ask them whether they agree with it. Students then complete the task in pairs. Remind them to use the Glossary to check any new words. Allow about five minutes for the task, then ask students to compare their answers with another pair. Check the answers as a class.

> **Answers**
>
> 2 a, e   3 b, c, d   4 a, e

WHILE WATCHING

4 ▶️🧍🧍🧍 Students watch the video and complete the task individually. Then they compare their answers with a partner. Check the answers as a class and model the pronunciation of *equator* /ɪˈkweɪtə/, *Tropic of Cancer* /ˈtrɒpɪk əv ˈkænsə/ and *Tropic of Capricorn* /ˈtrɒpɪk əv ˈkæprɪkɔːn/.

> **Answers**
>
> 1 c   2 b   3 d

UNDERSTANDING DETAIL

5 ▶️🧍🧍 Before you play the video again, ask students to read the statements and discuss possible answers in pairs. Remind them that we can often use our background knowledge to predict answers. Students then watch the video and check their answers. If necessary, encourage them to use the Glossary at the back of the book. With a weaker class, ask students to find the answers in the video script on page 211. Check the answers as a class. Check understanding and pronunciation of *grow* /grəʊ/ (to increase in size or amount), *dangerous* /ˈdeɪndʒərəs/ (describes a person, animal, thing or activity that could harm you) and *tropics* /ˈtrɒpɪks/ (the hottest area of the Earth).

> **Answers**
>
> 1 f, i
> 2 a, c, e, h
> 3 b
> 4 d, g, j

DISCUSSION

6 🧍🧍 Students work in pairs, ideally with someone they have not worked with before. Allow them a couple of minutes to make notes about the questions. Then give them about five minutes to discuss the questions. Monitor and encourage students to give their answers in complete sentences. Check the pronunciation of the key vocabulary. Discuss students' ideas with the whole class.

> **Answers**
>
> 2 Yes – man-made (artificial) skiing (e.g. Ski Dubai)

LISTENING 1

PREPARING TO LISTEN

UNDERSTANDING KEY VOCABULARY

1 👤👥 Before students begin the task, elicit example words and their antonyms to help students understand the matching exercise, e.g. *white–black, day–night, happy–sad*. Students complete the exercise individually, then check their answers with a classmate. Encourage students to check the meanings of words they don't know using the Glossary at the back of the book. Go over the answers as a class and elicit the pronunciation of the key vocabulary.

> **Answers**
>
> 1 b sky /skaɪ/ sea /siː/
> 2 e inside /ɪnˈsaɪd/ outside /aʊtˈsaɪd/
> 3 a cold /kəʊld/ hot /hɒt/
> 4 f summer /ˈsʌmə/ winter /ˈwɪntə/
> 5 c beautiful /ˈbjuːtɪfəl/ ugly /ˈʌɡli/
> 6 d natural /ˈnætʃərəl/ man-made /mænˈmeɪd, ˈmænmeɪd/

2 👤👥 Students complete the exercise individually, then check their answers with a classmate. Remind them to use the Glossary to check the meaning of any new words. Allow about five minutes for the task. Display the sentences on an interactive whiteboard and complete them as a class.

> **Answers**
>
> 1 hot 2 winter 3 man-made 4 cold 5 ugly 6 outside
> 7 sky 8 beautiful 9 natural 10 inside 11 sea
> 12 winter

USING VISUALS TO PREDICT CONTENT

Skills box

👥 Draw students' attention to the Skills box. Allow them a minute to read it, then check understanding of *photographs* /ˈfəʊtəɡrɑːfs/, *pictures* /ˈpɪktʃəz/, *graphs* /ɡrɑːfs/ and *tables* /ˈteɪblz/. Check understanding of *predict* /prɪˈdɪkt/ and ask students whether they try to predict the content before they listen, and how it can help them in listening comprehension.

3 👥👥👥 Display the photographs on an interactive whiteboard. Students discuss the questions in pairs. Allow three or four minutes

for discussion, then ask students to compare their answers with another pair. At the end, share ideas as a class. Draw students' attention to the caption on each photo.

> **Answers**
>
> 2 photographs a and c
> 3 photograph c
> 4 photograph a: summer; photograph b: winter;
>   photograph c: summer
> 5 photograph b
> 6 photographs a and b
> 7 photographs a and c

PRONUNCIATION FOR LISTENING

> **Language note**
>
> Not all the words in a sentence are equally stressed in spoken English. Functional words, like articles, prepositions, pronouns and auxiliary verbs, are usually weak and unstressed, whereas content words, like nouns, verbs and adjectives, are stressed.

Explanation box

👥 Ask students to read the Explanation box. Check understanding of *noun, verb* and *adjective*. Elicit additional examples of nouns, adjectives and verbs from the class. Check understanding of *stress* /stres/ (when a word or syllable is pronounced with greater force than the other words in the same sentence).

4 ◀) 2.1 👤👥 Students listen to the recording and underline the stressed words in each sentence. Then they check their answers with a partner and sort out the underlined words into nouns, verbs and adjectives, changing the underlining to highlighting or a circle as necessary. Check the answers as a class. Play the audio one more time and pause after each sentence. Ask students to repeat the sentence together, following the stress pattern from the recording. If necessary, tap on your desk to emphasize the stressed syllables. Allow students a couple of minutes to practise saying the sentences in pairs. Monitor and give feedback on sentence stress.

> **Answers**
>
> 1 Today, I want to look at something new.
> 2 Take a look at photograph 1.
> 3 There's a beautiful beach next to a blue sea.
> 4 It's winter and there's a mountain.
> 5 It's hot and there's sand and there are rocks.

Answers

1 Dubai's hot in July.
2 Canada has a lot of snow in winter.
3 Cities are man-made places.
4 We get snow when it's cold here.
5 I don't like cities. I think they are ugly places.
6 I like to stay at home when there is snow outside.
7 There are no clouds in the sky today.
8 'This is a photograph of my house.'
  'Oh! It's lovely – it's really beautiful.'
9 Mountains and forests are natural places.
10 It's starting to rain and I don't want to get wet – I think we should go inside.
11 Many people like to swim in the sea.
12 They have the World Skiing Championships in winter every four years.

WHILE LISTENING

LISTENING FOR MAIN IDEAS

5 and 6 🔊 2.2 👤👥 Display the three photographs on an interactive whiteboard. Students listen and complete the task individually. Then they check their answers with a partner. Students discuss Exercise 6 in pairs. Allow a couple of minutes for discussion, then ask the pairs to share their ideas with the class.

Answers

Exercise 5: a 3 b 2 c 1
Exercise 6: *Possible answers*: They are man-made places. / They are inside (outside the season is different).

LISTENING FOR DETAIL

7, 8 and 9 🔊 2.2 👤👥 Students listen and complete Exercises 7 and 8 individually. Encourage them to use the Glossary. Then they compare their answers with a partner. Play the audio one more time to allow students to

check their answers. Check the answers as a class and check the pronunciation of the key vocabulary. With a weaker class, ask students to check their answers in the audio script on page 211.

Answers

Exercise 7: 1 it's winter 2 Ocean; Japan 3 inside; outside 4 Snow; London 5 hot; sand 6 United States
Exercise 8: 1 winter 2 man-made 3 inside; hot

DISCUSSION

10 👥👥 Display the box of phrases on an interactive whiteboard and discuss it with the class. Check which parts of speech can be used to complete the expressions and elicit examples (see answers below). Allow students a couple of minutes to make notes about their photographs. Students then work in small groups and tell each other about the photographs. Other group members listen, then guess which photograph was described. Ask students to allow the speakers to finish their description before they guess the answers. Monitor and check the pronunciation of the key vocabulary and the grammar in the model expressions. Write down any grammar mistakes that you hear and discuss them as a class at the end.

Possible answers

It's winter/summer/spring/autumn.
It's a hot/cold/rainy/sunny day.
This place is (*name of the place*) / in (Japan).
There is the sea / a beach / a forest / the sand / etc.
There are mountains/clouds/houses/rocks.

⊙ LANGUAGE DEVELOPMENT

MONTHS AND SEASONS

Lead-in

Start this section with a quick discussion about the differences between the seasons around the world. It may be useful to prepare slides with photos of the different seasons and show *spring* /sprɪŋ/, *summer* /'sʌmə/, *autumn* /'ɔːtəm/ and *winter* /'wɪntə/, *rainy* /'reɪni/ and *dry* /draɪ/ *season* /'siːzən/.

Language note

Autumn /'ɔːtəm/ is used in British English. *Fall* /fɔːl/ is more commonly used in the US and Canada. Both *autumn* and *fall* describe the season that comes between summer and winter.

1 ◀) 2.3 👥 Students work in pairs and guess the answers. Remind them to use their background knowledge to complete the task. If possible, ask students to find a map of the world online and find the location of the countries in the exercise (Thailand, Russia, Brazil, England, Japan, Australia, Nigeria). Encourage them to use the Glossary. Students then listen and check their predictions. Check understanding of the vocabulary for the seasons and elicit the pronunciation. Drill the pronunciation as a class. Play the recording again and ask students to repeat the sentences as they heard them on the recording. Allow two or three minutes for students to practise saying the sentences in pairs.

Answers

a 7 b 4 c 5 d 1 e 3 f 2 g 6

2 👤👥 Students complete the task individually, then check their answers with a partner. Check the answers as a class and elicit the fact that the names of the months always start with a capital letter.

Answers

2 February 3 March 5 May 10 October
12 December

3 ◀) 2.4 👥 Students complete the task in pairs. Then play the audio and ask students to check their answers. Ask students to underline the stressed syllable in each word. Play the audio again and ask students to check their answers. Go over the answers and drill the pronunciation as a class. Allow a couple of minutes for students to practise saying the names of the months in pairs.

Answers

1 January (4) /'dʒænjuəri/ 2 February (4) /'februəri/
3 March (1) /mɑːtʃ/ 4 April (2) /'eɪprəl/ 5 May (1) /meɪ/
6 June (1) /dʒuːn/ 7 July (2) /dʒuˈlaɪ/ 8 August (2)
/'ɔːgʌst/ 9 September (3) /sepˈtembə/ 10 October
(3) /ɒkˈtəʊbə/ 11 November (3) /nəʊˈvembə/
12 December (3) /dɪˈsembə/

Language note

Native speakers sometimes pronounce *January* and *February* with three syllables: /'dʒænjori/ /'februri/.

Optional activity

👥 The names of the months are often misspelled by students. To improve their accuracy and to practise the names of the months, ask students to write them down on a separate piece of paper. Tell students to close their books and work with the notes. Students work in pairs. Ask them to take turns and spell out the names of the months to each other, starting with January. When they have completed the task, ask them to check their spelling with their notes.

4 👤👥 Allow students a couple of minutes to complete the phrases in the box individually. Monitor and check the grammar. Students ask and answer the questions in pairs. Monitor and give feedback on the pronunciation of key vocabulary. Ask for volunteers to demonstrate their answers to the class.

Optional activity

👥 With a more advanced class, ask students to work in pairs and ask each other questions about their lives. Generate a list of possible questions as a class and write them on the whiteboard. Questions may include: *When is your birthday?*, *When do you go on holiday?*, *When do you start school?*, etc. Elicit the fact that we use the preposition *in* when we talk about months, e.g. *in January*. Students take turns and ask each other questions. Monitor and make sure students use the correct preposition before the names of the months. If necessary, give feedback on the pronunciation of the names of the months.

WEATHER

Language note

We can form adjectives using the –y suffix, like *sunny*, *rainy*, *stormy*, etc. Adjectives are used to describe nouns. They can be placed before a noun, e.g. *sunny day*, *windy weather*, or after the verb *be*, e.g. *It is sunny*, *It is windy*.

5 👤👥 Students complete the task individually, then check their answers with a partner. Encourage students to check the meanings of the new words in the Glossary. Go over the answers as a class. Check understanding and the pronunciation of the adjectives. Elicit the difference between *sun–sunny*, *wind–windy*, etc. Draw students' attention to which words are nouns and which are adjectives.

Answers

picture	noun	adjective
3	sun /sʌn/	sunny /ˈsʌni/
6	snow /snəʊ/	snowy /ˈsnəʊi/
2	wind /wɪnd/	windy /ˈwɪndi/
5	rain /reɪn/	rainy /ˈreɪni/
1	cloud /klaʊd/	cloudy /ˈklaʊdi/
4	storm /stɔːm/	stormy /ˈstɔːmi/

6 👤👥 Before the task, check understanding of the difference in use between nouns and adjectives. Ask students to underline the nouns related to weather in the example sentences from Exercise 1: *There's a lot of rain in Thailand* and *Russia gets a lot of snow*. Then ask the class to complete these sentences: *Thailand is ...* and *Russia is ...* . Elicit *rainy* and *snowy*. Students complete the task individually, then check their answers with a partner. Encourage them to use the Glossary to check the meaning of any new vocabulary. Check the answers as a class. Drill the sentences as a class, then allow a couple of minutes for students to practise saying them in pairs.

Answers

1 sunny 2 cloud 3 rainy 4 storms 5 windy

Optional activity

👤👥👥 Prepare a worksheet with questions like: *Do you like to stay inside when it's sunny?*, *Do you like to go outside when it's windy?*, *Do you like to stay at home and read when it's rainy?*, *Are you afraid when it's stormy?*, etc. Students mingle with the rest of their classmates and ask them the questions. Allow about five minutes for the task, then ask students to share their findings with the class.

COLOURS

7 👤👥 Students complete the task individually, then check their answers with a partner. Go over the answers as a class. Display the colour wheel on an interactive whiteboard and elicit the pronunciation of the key vocabulary. If necessary, drill the pronunciation as a class. With a more advanced class, use additional photographs and ask students to name the colours that they see. Elicit additional words, like *brown* /braʊn/, *pink* /pɪŋk/, *violet* /ˈvaɪələt/, *purple* /ˈpɜːpl/ and *grey* /greɪ/.

Answers

1 white /waɪt/ 2 red /red/ 3 blue /bluː/
4 yellow /ˈjeləʊ/ 5 green /griːn/ 6 orange /ˈɒrɪndʒ/
7 black /blæk/

8 👥 Draw students' attention to the phrases in the box and provide model questions and answers (see *Possible answers* below). Check understanding of the difference between *is* and *are*. Students complete the task in pairs. Monitor and make sure students answer in complete sentences using the language from the box. Give individual feedback on the grammar, i.e. *is* and *are*, and the pronunciation of the key vocabulary. With a more advanced class, encourage students to add more nouns to the list and then ask about them.

Possible answers

Sample questions: *What colour are tomatoes? / What colour is snow? / What colour are trees?*
Sample answers: *They can be red or green. / It is white. / They are green.*
Allow any colour as an answer that students can justify.
1 red (yellow, orange or green) 2 white (blue) 3 green (yellow, red) 4 yellow (orange) 5 white, black

LISTENING 2

PREPARING TO LISTEN

USING VISUALS TO PREDICT CONTENT

> **Lead-in**
>
> 👥 👥👥 Display the photographs from Exercise 2 on an interactive whiteboard. Ask students to brainstorm where the pictures could have been taken. Allow two or three minutes for discussion, then ask the pairs to share their ideas with the class. Tell students that they will find out from the listening where two of the photographs were taken.

1 👥👥 Before the task, pre-teach the word *landscape* /ˈlændskeɪp/ (a view or picture of the countryside) and point to examples in the unit. Students discuss the questions in small groups. Encourage students to use complete sentences and to use the vocabulary for weather and colours from the *Language development* section. At the end, display the photographs on an interactive whiteboard and discuss the questions as a class.

> **Answers**
>
> 1 a autumn b spring/summer c summer
> 2 It is sunny in all the photographs.
> 3 blue, green, orange, yellow, white

2 👤 👥👥 Students complete the task individually and then check their answers with a partner. Encourage them to use the Glossary. Go over the answers as a class and elicit the pronunciation of the key vocabulary. If necessary, drill the pronunciation as a class.

> **Answers**
>
> 1 mountains /ˈmaʊntɪnz/ 2 town /taʊn/ 3 sea /siː/
> 4 island /ˈaɪlənd/ 5 forest /ˈfɒrɪst/ 6 desert /ˈdezət/
> 7 sky /skaɪ/

WHILE LISTENING

LISTENING FOR MAIN IDEAS

3 🔊 2.5 👤 👥👥 Students listen to the audio and complete the task individually. Then they check their answers with a partner.

> **Answers**
>
> 1 Photograph b 2 Photograph a 3 Photograph c

> **Optional activity**
>
> 👤 With a more advanced class, ask students to close their books and take notes while they listen. Students then use their notes to answer the questions.

LISTENING FOR DETAIL

4 🔊 2.5 👤 👥👥 Ask students to read the sentences and check the meaning of any new vocabulary in the Glossary. Before the listening task, elicit the meaning of *beautiful* /ˈbjuːtɪfəl/ (very attractive), *ugly* /ˈʌgli/ (unpleasant to look at; not attractive) and *park* /pɑːk/ (a large area of land with grass and trees, surrounded by fences or walls, which is specially arranged so that people can walk in it for pleasure or children can play in it). Ask students to predict the answers or, if they have been taking notes, use their notes to answer the questions. Students listen again and check their answers. Go over the answers as a class. If necessary, display the audio script from page 212 on an interactive whiteboard and underline the correct answers in the script.

> **Answers**
>
> 1 a spring /sprɪŋ/ b Turkey /ˈtɜːki/ c park d beautiful
> 2 a another /əˈnʌðə/ b autumn /ˈɔːtəm/ c park
> d cold /kəʊld/

DISCUSSION

5 and 6 👤 👥👥 To model the task, display an attractive photograph of a place in your country or a country you have visited. Tell students to ask you questions from Exercise 5. Answer them using the expressions from the box in Exercise 6. Allow students between six and eight minutes to prepare for the task, i.e. find an attractive photograph on the internet and make notes about the place. Monitor and help with the internet search and note-making. Remind students to use the questions in Exercise 5 to make notes. Students then work in pairs and discuss their photographs. Allow about seven minutes for discussion. Monitor and write down any grammar mistakes that you hear. At the end, write the mistakes on the whiteboard and correct them as a class.

CRITICAL THINKING

At this point in each unit, students are asked to begin to think about the speaking task they will do at the end of the unit (*Describe photographs of a landscape*). Give them a minute to look at the box.

UNDERSTAND

1 Students complete the task in pairs. Then they work with another pair and explain their opinions to each other. Monitor and encourage students to support their opinions.

2 Divide the class into Students A and B. Students first work in small groups and use the questions from Exercise 1 to take notes. Student As take notes about the photographs in Listening 1, and Student Bs take notes about the photographs in Listening 2. Allow up to ten minutes for note-taking. Monitor and help with this. Students then work in A+B pairs and complete the task. Allow up to ten minutes for this. Monitor and give individual feedback on vocabulary and pronunciation of the key words.

APPLY

Skills box

Draw students' attention to the box and allow a minute to read it. As a class, discuss what kind of photographs they should look for. Elicit ideas about what makes a photograph interesting and what kind of topic or vocabulary the photograph for the task should illustrate.

3 and 4 Tell students that they are going to search for an interesting photograph of a landscape for their speaking task. Before they begin the internet search, ask them to complete Exercise 3 and choose the features that they want in their photograph. Encourage them to use the Glossary to check the meaning of any new words. Students then search the internet for an interesting photograph of a landscape. Monitor and help with the internet search. Allow up to ten minutes for this, then ask students to show their photographs to the class and explain why they like them. If there is no internet access in the class, allow students to search for the photograph at home or in the library, and bring it to the next class.

Optional activity

Allow students to select a few photographs before they choose the one for the speaking task. Students then work in small groups and use the questions from Exercise 1 to evaluate the photographs. Students discuss which photograph is the most interesting; they can help each other select the best photograph for the task.

SPEAKING

PREPARATION FOR SPEAKING

1 ◄) **2.6** Students work in pairs and predict the answers. Then they listen to the audio and check their answers.

> **Answers**
> 1 b 2 g 3 d 4 f 5 a 6 e 7 c

PRONUNCIATION FOR SPEAKING

2 and 3 ◄) **2.6** Students complete the task in pairs. If necessary, review the sentence-stress principles on page 37 (Listening 1). Then play the audio and ask students to check their answers. Play the audio one more time. Pause after each sentence and ask the class to repeat. Emphasize the rhythm of the stressed words by tapping gently on a desk. Allow students a couple of minutes to practise saying the sentences. Monitor and give feedback on sentence stress.

> **Answers**
> a OK, so, good <u>morning, everybody</u>.
> b OK, so I'm going to <u>talk</u> about <u>two</u> <u>photographs</u> of a <u>place</u> in <u>spring</u>.
> c OK, so <u>here's</u> my <u>first</u> <u>photograph</u>.
> d <u>Hello, everybody</u>! OK, so, I'm <u>Altan</u>.
> e I'm from <u>Samsun</u>. <u>Samsun</u> is in <u>Turkey</u>.
> f Here's my <u>first</u> <u>photograph</u>.
> g Here's <u>another</u> <u>photograph</u> of the <u>park</u>.

4 Display the photographs on an interactive whiteboard. Students discuss the photographs in pairs. Model the task by giving one or two examples, e.g. *There is snow* or *There are people*. Allow three or four minutes for discussion. Monitor and give feedback on key vocabulary. Lead group discussion at the end and elicit vocabulary, e.g. *snow, sky, clouds, trees, mountain, path*, etc.

5 ◀) 2.7 Students listen to the audio and complete the task individually. Then ask them to check their answers with a partner. With a more advanced class, ask students to predict the answers before they listen. Play the audio one more time, then ask students to practise saying the sentences in pairs. Allow two or three minutes for practice and give feedback on sentence stress and pronunciation of the key vocabulary.

Answers

1 f 2 c 3 e 4 a 5 b 6 d

6 Divide the class into Students A and B. If possible, ask them to work with a new partner. Assign the photographs in Exercise 4 to Students A and B. Give them up to eight minutes to work individually and make notes about their photograph without looking at Exercise 5. If necessary, play recording 2.7 one more time. Students take turns and describe the photographs to each other. Monitor and give individual feedback on sentence stress, making sure students have changed the details to personalize the descriptions.

THERE IS … / THERE ARE …

Explanation box

Display the box on an interactive whiteboard and allow students a minute to read the first sentence and the three related examples. Check their understanding of *noun*. Elicit when we use *there is* and *there are,* and point out the nouns that follow each expression. To check understanding, make two or three incorrect sentences, e.g. *There are snow in the mountains**, *There is a lot of children on the beach** and *There are a forest**, and ask students to correct them as a group. Check understanding of *a lot of* /əˈlɒt əv/ (a large amount or number). Point out that the short form *there's* is pronounced /ðeəz/.

7 Students complete the task individually, then compare their answers with a partner.

Answers

1 there's a lot of snow
2 there's a big mountain, There's a path
3 there are trees, there are people, There are a lot of white clouds

8 ◀) 2.8 Students work in pairs and predict their answers. Then they listen and check. Go over the answers as a class, and check understanding of when we use plural and singular nouns with *there is* and *there are*.

Answers

1 park 2 forest 3 trees 4 mountain 5 a lot of

Explanation box

Display the box on an interactive whiteboard again and draw students' attention to the negative and question forms. Allow students a minute to read the examples. Check understanding by dividing the class into two groups. Group A asks questions and Group B answers in negative forms. Write different nouns on the whiteboard as prompts, e.g. *sand, snow, clouds, trees, mountains, sea*, etc. Use the key vocabulary from the unit. Group A asks *Is there sand there?*, and Group B answers *There's no sand* or *There isn't any sand*. Give feedback on the pronunciation of the contractions, e.g. *There aren't any* /ðeər ˈɑːnt ˈeni/ and *There isn't any* /ðeər ˈɪzənt ˈeni/.

9 Model the task by using one of the photographs from Exercise 4. Display the photograph on an interactive whiteboard and ask students questions from the table in this exercise. Elicit the answers from students using the expressions from the table. Students then complete the activity in pairs. Monitor and give feedback on the grammar of *there is* and *there are* and the pronunciation of the contractions (see above).

10 and 11 ◀) 2.9 Before listening, students complete the sentences individually, then compare their answers with a partner. Students listen to the recording and check their answers.

Answers

1 There's a 2 There's 3 There are 4 There are
5 There's a 6 There's a 7 There are

Optional activity

◀) 2.9 Ask students to underline the stressed words in the sentences in Exercise 10. Students listen again and check their answers. Play each sentence one by one and practise the sentence stress as a class. Gently tap on a desk to emphasize the stressed words. Ask students to work in pairs. Allow a couple of minutes for students to practise saying the sentences.

Answers

1 There's a <u>river</u> in the <u>photograph</u>.
2 There's <u>snow</u> on the <u>mountains</u>.
3 There are <u>people</u> on the <u>beach</u>.
4 There are <u>trees</u> in the <u>garden</u>.
5 There's a <u>small</u> <u>town</u> in the <u>mountains</u>.
6 There's a <u>red</u> <u>car</u> in the <u>desert</u>.
7 There are <u>black</u> <u>clouds</u> in the <u>sky</u>.

12 Students correct the sentences individually, then check their answers with a partner. Go over the answers as a class.

Answers

1 **There's** a park. / There are **parks**.
2 **There is** a mountain in the photograph. / This **is** a mountain in the photograph.
3 There's a **car** by the houses. / **There are** cars by the houses.
4 **There's** a big tree there.
5 **There's** snow on the mountains.

ADJECTIVES

Explanation box

 Display the box from page 47 on an interactive whiteboard and ask students which words in the example sentences are adjectives. Allow the students a minute to read the box, then check understanding of where we put adjectives in a sentence. As a class, draw arrows from the adjectives to the nouns that they describe.

13 Students complete the task individually, and then check with a partner. Monitor and check understanding of the use of adjectives. Go over the answers as a class.

Answers

1 The <u>clouds</u> are <u>black</u>.
2 The <u>trees</u> are <u>red</u> and <u>yellow</u>.
3 It's a <u>windy</u> <u>day</u>.
4 It's a <u>famous</u> <u>place</u> in <u>Thailand</u>.
5 There are <u>small</u> <u>islands</u> in the <u>sea</u>.
6 There's a <u>white</u> <u>mountain</u> in the <u>photograph</u>.
7 You can <u>see</u> there's a <u>big</u> <u>house</u> in the <u>park</u>.
8 You can <u>see</u> there are <u>young</u> <u>people</u> on the <u>path</u>.

Optional activity

 Students work in pairs and underline the stressed words in each sentence. Check their answers as a class. Allow students a couple of minutes to practise saying the sentences by stressing only the content words. Monitor and give feedback on sentence stress.

Answers

See answers for Exercise 13.

14 Students correct the mistakes, then check them with a partner. To provide more practise with sentence stress, ask students to underline the most stressed words in each sentence. Check the answers as a class and drill the sentence stress as a group. Allow students a couple of minutes to practise saying the sentences. Monitor and give feedback on sentence stress.

Answers

1 It's **sunny** in the <u>photograph</u>.
2 It's <u>windy</u>. / **It's** a <u>windy</u> **day**.
3 There's a **big** <u>mountain</u>.
4 The <u>people</u> **are** <u>happy</u>.
5 **There's** a <u>big</u> <u>forest</u>.
6 It's a **rainy** <u>day</u>.

15 Students complete the task in pairs. If possible, change their partners to provide more interaction. If necessary, model the task using one of the photographs from Exercise 4. Monitor and give feedback on grammar and sentence stress. Write down any grammar mistakes on the whiteboard and discuss them as a class. At the end of the activity, ask for volunteers to talk about their photograph in front of the class.

SPEAKING TASK

Tell the students that they are going to talk about an interesting photograph of a landscape.

PREPARE

1, 2, 3 and 4 Students answer questions 1–4 in Exercise 1 and make notes before the internet search. Encourage students to use the key words from Critical thinking Exercise 3 (page 43) in their search. Monitor and help with note-making and later with the internet search. Students complete the checklist from Critical thinking Exercise 1 and make notes with key vocabulary. Monitor and elicit the pronunciation of the key words written down by students. Students then complete the model presentation. Monitor closely and check the grammar.

PRACTISE

5 👤👥 Students complete the task individually, then practise their sentences with a partner. Encourage students to give each other constructive feedback on grammar and pronunciation. Most of the stressed words will be the gapped words in Exercise 4.

PRESENT

6 👥 Before the task, elicit how to ask about the spelling of the names of foreign places, countries or unknown words. Students complete the task in groups of three or four. If possible, make sure they work with new partners. Each group member talks about their photograph while the others take notes. At the end, students exchange tables and check that Students 1 and 2 have written down correct information.

Optional activity

👤 To change the interaction, ask students to make videos in which they talk about their photographs. Students show the videos to the class, and their classmates complete notes about each video.

OBJECTIVES REVIEW

See Teaching tips, pages 10–11, for ideas about using the Objectives review with your students.

WORDLIST

See Teaching tips, pages 10–11, for ideas about how to make the most of the Wordlist with your students.

REVIEW TEST

See pages 108–109 for the photocopiable Review test for this unit and Teaching tips, pages 10–11, for ideas about when and how to administer the Review test.

ADDITIONAL SPEAKING TASK

See page 127 for an additional speaking task related to this unit.

If necessary, check understanding of the expressions in the Model language section and elicit additional examples as a class. Allow students a couple of minutes to make notes to answer the questions in the box. Monitor and help with vocabulary for the task. Make sure students use key words in their notes, not complete sentences. Students then give their presentations in pairs or small groups. Ask the listeners to write down any mistakes they hear during the presentation and to discuss them in their pairs or groups after each turn. Display a clock to help students monitor the length of their presentations. At the end, ask for volunteers to tell the class about their partners' presentations.

RESEARCH PROJECT

Become a weather forecaster

Divide the class into groups and ask them to research ways to monitor the weather in different places around the world. For example, one group could do an internet search for 'weather in London', another group could search for 'weather in Sydney' and another group 'weather in Mumbai'. Students could note down information on how hot/cold the weather is, how windy it is, and whether it is raining/snowing, etc.

Each group could present the information they have found to the rest of the class as a weather forecast. They can see examples of weather forecasts on video-sharing websites, and could film and upload their own forecasts to the same or a similar website. Each group could also create a blog on the Cambridge LMS with the weather report for their chosen place and update this daily over the course of a week.

3 LIFESTYLE

UNLOCK YOUR KNOWLEDGE

1 and 2 🧑🧑 🧑 Display the photograph on an interactive whiteboard. Students work in pairs and describe the photograph. Allow a couple of minutes for discussion, then ask students to answer the questions about themselves. Encourage them to check the meaning of unknown words in the Glossary. Monitor and check understanding of new vocabulary, e.g.

busy /ˈbɪzi/	doing a lot of things
lifestyle /ˈlaɪfstaɪl/	the way that you live
laptop /ˈlæptɒp/	a small computer that you carry around
tablet /ˈtæblət/	a small, thin computer controlled by touching the screen

3 🧑🧑🧑 Students mingle and interview each other. Before the task, model the questions and answers as a class. Ask students to make a question about *have a busy lifestyle* using the verb *do*, and elicit the correct question form, i.e. *Do you have a busy lifestyle?* Encourage students to answer in complete sentences, i.e. *Yes, I have a busy lifestyle* or *No, I don't have a busy lifestyle.* Allow about five minutes for the task. Monitor to check that students use complete sentences. At the end, ask students to share their findings with the class.

Optional activity

🧑🧑🧑 With a more advanced class, develop Exercise 3 above. Introduce *why* questions and model them using examples from Exercise 2, e.g. *Why do/don't you like to study outside?* Model the answers using *Because ...* Students interview their classmates using

the expressions from Exercise 2 and then asking for explanations. Monitor and encourage students to answer in complete sentences. Allow students up to eight minutes, then ask volunteers to demonstrate their questions and answers to the class.

Possible answers

'Do you have a busy lifestyle?' 'Yes, I do.'
'Why do you have a busy lifestyle?' 'Because I have a lot of exams.'

WATCH AND LISTEN

Video script

▶ Sinai in Egypt is a land of mountains and desert. It's difficult to live here, but for thousands of years, people – called the Bedouin – have lived here. For the Bedouin, the desert provides everything they need. They follow their camels through the desert. They only use what their camels can carry. Once, there were around 300,000 Bedouin in the desert, but today there are only 22,000. Doctor Ahmed is the last Bedouin healer in Sinai. He uses plants from the desert to make traditional medicines. He helps people who cannot reach a hospital. Now that Doctor Ahmed is old, he wants to give his knowledge of traditional medicine to a new generation. His six pupils have learnt many things, like making medicine. He takes the boys 160 kilometres into the desert – but they will have to get home on their own. For a journey through the desert, the Bedouin need a camel. Doctor Ahmed shows them how to choose a good one. Ahmed watches the boys start for home. Doctor Ahmed waits for them at his clinic. The boys arrive back tired, but safe. A very proud moment for their Bedouin teacher.

PREPARING TO WATCH

Optional lead-in

🧑🧑 🧑🧑🧑 Display the four video stills on an interactive whiteboard. Students work in pairs and describe the stills to each other. Ask them to make a list of things (nouns) that they see in the video stills. Encourage them to use the Glossary. Allow a couple of minutes for the task, then ask students to compare their lists with another pair. At the end, elicit the words from the class and check understanding by pointing to the objects in the photographs.

UNDERSTANDING KEY VOCABULARY

1 👤👥 Students work individually, then compare their answers with a partner. Encourage students to use the Glossary to find the meaning of unknown words. Go over the answers as a class and check understanding of *journey* /ˈdʒɜːni/ (trip), *medicine* /ˈmed(ɪ)sən/ (treatment for an illness) and *pronounce* /prəˈnaʊns/ (to say a word in a particular way). Elicit the meaning of the key vocabulary and the pronunciation.

> **Answers**
>
> 1 traditional /trəˈdɪʃənəl/ 2 safe /seɪf/ 3 happy /ˈhæpi/
> 4 difficult /ˈdɪfɪkəlt/ 5 easy /ˈiːzi/
> 6 important /ɪmˈpɔːtənt/

2 👤👥 Students complete the sentences individually, then check their answers with a partner. Encourage students to use the Glossary. Check the answers as a class.

> **Answers**
>
> 1 Traditional 2 easy 3 important 4 safe 5 difficult
> 6 happy

USING YOUR KNOWLEDGE TO PREDICT CONTENT

> **Background note**
>
> *Bedouin* /ˈbeduɪn/ is a term used to describe desert-dwelling tribes who live or used to live a mostly nomadic lifestyle. Depending on the region, students may be more or less familiar with this lifestyle. When teaching in the Middle East and Northern Africa, you should remember that there are different Bedouin tribes across the region, and that many local students may be affiliated with them. It is advisable not to make broad generalizations about this lifestyle, but rather allow students to discuss it.

3 👥 Students discuss questions about the video stills in pairs. Allow three or four minutes for discussion, then ask the pairs to share their ideas with the class. Explain to students that we can improve our understanding of a video if we use our background knowledge of the subject. Ask students to predict the topic of the video (*Bedouin lifestyle*).

> **Answers**
>
> 1 In the desert 2 camel 3 Students' own answers (but probably *traditional*)

WHILE WATCHING

UNDERSTANDING MAIN IDEAS

4 ▶👤👥 Students watch and complete the task individually. Then they check their answers with a partner. Check the answers as a class.

> **Answers**
>
> 1 c 2 a 3 b

UNDERSTANDING DETAIL

5 👥👤 Students work in pairs. Ask them to read the sentences and guess their answers before they watch the video again. Then they watch the video and check their answers. Provide class feedback and discuss why the false statements are incorrect. Check understanding of *proud* /praʊd/ (feeling pleasure and satisfaction because you or people connected with you have done something good). If necessary, ask students to scan the video script on page 212 and check their answers.

> **Answers**
>
> 1 T (*It's difficult to live here …*)
> 2 T (*They follow their camels through the desert. They only use what their camels can carry.*)
> 3 F (*He uses plants from the desert to make traditional medicines.*)
> 4 F (*His six pupils have learnt many things …*)
> 5 T (*He takes the boys 160 kilometres into the desert …*)
> 6 F (*A very proud moment for their Bedouin teacher.*)

DISCUSSION

> **Optional lead-in**
>
> 👥 To help students prepare for the discussion task, prepare sets of flashcards that illustrate traditional and modern lifestyles. Make sure that the flashcards are labelled with expressions like *living in an apartment*, *using the internet*, *growing vegetables*, *making fire*, *living in a tent*, etc. Some flashcards can be ambiguous to initiate discussion, like *working in a garden* or *cooking dinner*. Students work in small groups and sort out the flashcards into 'modern' and 'traditional' lifestyles. At the end, ask students to share their ideas with the class.

6 👥 👥👥 Students discuss the questions in pairs. Monitor and help with vocabulary for the task. Allow four or five minutes for pair discussions, then discuss the questions as a class. Encourage students to explain their opinions and give examples to support them.

LISTENING 1

PREPARING TO LISTEN

UNDERSTANDING KEY VOCABULARY

1 and 2 👥 Students work in pairs and discuss the four questions, filling in the table as they do so. Allow about five minutes, then ask students to discuss Exercise 2. Ask students to use the Glossary to check the meaning of *healthy* /ˈhelθi/ (good for your health) and *unhealthy* /ʌnˈhelθi/ (not good for your health). Check understanding. At the end, ask students to share their answers with the class. Check understanding and pronunciation of key vocabulary: *gym* /dʒɪm/, *exercise* /ˈeksəsaɪz/, *smoke* /sməʊk/ and *chocolate biscuit* /ˈtʃɒklət ˈbɪskɪt/.

> **Answers**
> Healthy: go to a gym, do exercise
> Unhealthy: smoke, eat a lot of chocolate biscuits

PRONUNCIATION FOR LISTENING

> **Language note**
>
> Intonation in statements and questions can vary, depending on the English dialect, but the general rule in Standard English is that intonation rises in *yes/no* questions, whereas it falls in open questions, e.g. *Wh-*questions. In a statement, the intonation falls at the end of a sentence.

3 🔊 3.1 👥 Draw students' attention to the Explanation box and allow them a minute to read the information and the examples. Check understanding of *intonation* /ɪntəˈneɪʃən/ and ask for volunteers to read the example sentences following the indicated intonation pattern. Play the recording and ask students to repeat the intonation as they hear it. If necessary, play the audio a few times and pause after each sentence. Allow students to work in pairs and practise the dialogue

following the intonation pattern on the recording. Monitor and help students imitate the pattern on the audio.

4 👤 👥 Before the task, ask students which of the four sentences are questions, i.e. *What's your name?* and *Are you from New York?*. Then elicit the difference between the two types of questions, i.e. *yes/no* questions and *Wh-* questions. If necessary, give examples of *yes/no* questions and *Wh-* questions and ask students to guess what type they are. Students then complete the task individually and check the answers with their partners.

> **Answers**
> 1 down 2 down 3 up

5 🔊 3.2 👥 👥👥 Students work in pairs and predict the intonation in the six sentences. Then play the audio and allow students to check their answers. Go over the answers as a class and ask for volunteers to repeat the sentences, using the intonation pattern from the recording. If necessary, play the audio again, pausing after each sentence and drilling the intonation pattern with the class. Give students two minutes to practise saying the sentences in pairs. Monitor and give feedback on intonation.

> **Answers**
> 1 up 2 down 3 down 4 up 5 down 6 down

WHILE LISTENING

LISTENING FOR MAIN IDEAS

Skills box

👥👥 Display the Skills box on an interactive whiteboard and allow students a minute to read it. Elicit that *where* is for place, *who* is for people, and *why* asks about reasons.

6 🔊 3.3 👤 👥 Before listening, ask students to read the questions and check the meaning of unknown words in the Glossary. Check understanding of *lecture* /ˈlektʃə/, *lecturer* /ˈlektʃərə/ and *conversation* /kɒnvəˈseɪʃən/. Students listen and complete the task individually. Then they check their answers with a partner. Go over the answers as a class. Some students may confuse *coffee* /ˈkɒfi/ (a drink made of coffee beans) with *café* /ˈkæfeɪ/ (a type of small restaurant).

Write the two words on the whiteboard and elicit the difference in meaning and pronunciation.

Answers

1 in a café: C; in a lecture: B; on the phone: A
2 a lecturer and a student: B; a son and his father: A; two students in the same class: C
3 for information about a video: C; somebody for money: A; for information about lifestyle: B

LISTENING FOR DETAIL

7 (◀) 3.3 👤👥 With a stronger class, ask students to discuss the questions before listening again. Students complete the task individually. Then they compare their answers with a classmate. Check the answers as a class. If necessary, display the audio script from page 213 and ask students to scan for the answers.

Answers

1 in the park
2 to go to the gym / for a gym
3 the United States
4 lifestyles (of people in Canada)

Optional activity

👥 With a weaker class, ask students to look at the audio script on page 213 and follow it as they listen. Then divide the class into three groups (A, B and C). The students in each group work on one of the dialogues (A, B or C) from the listening. Students work in pairs and practise saying the dialogues. Monitor and give feedback on sentence stress and intonation. Allow about five minutes for practice, then ask for volunteers from each group to present the dialogues to the class.

DISCUSSION

8 👥👥👥 Students work in pairs and discuss the questions. Allow three or four minutes for pair discussion, then ask students to share their ideas with the class. As a class, discuss the advantages and disadvantages of students living alone. Draw a table on the whiteboard with columns labelled '+' (advantages) and '–' (disadvantages). Elicit ideas from the class and write them on the whiteboard.

Possible answers

Advantages: do what you want, can eat junk food, don't need to clean up
Disadvantages: have to cook for yourself and do your own washing, feel lonely, be afraid at night

Optional activity

👥👥👥 With a more advanced class, discuss the advantages and disadvantages of studying abroad. Give students ten minutes to brainstorm the pros and cons in pairs, then elicit the opinions from the whole class. Write the advantages and the disadvantages on the whiteboard, or nominate a stronger student to write them up. At the end, ask students to raise their hands if they prefer studying in their home country to studying abroad.

◉ LANGUAGE DEVELOPMENT

DAYS OF THE WEEK

Optional lead-in

👥👥👥 Write the names of the days of the week on separate slips of paper. Prepare enough slips so that students can work in pairs or small groups. Cut each day of the week into smaller pieces according to the syllables in each word, i.e. *Sun-day* (2), *Mon-day* (2), *Tues-day* (2), *Wednes-day* (2), *Thurs-day* (2), *Fri-day* (2) and *Sa-tur-day* (3). Ask students to work in pairs or small groups and unscramble the pieces to make names of the days of the week. Then ask students to put the days in chronological order, starting from *Sunday*. Point out that the names of the days are always spelled with capital letter.

1 (◀) 3.4 👤👥 Students listen to the audio and write out the number of syllables for each day. Then ask students to work in pairs and underline the stressed syllable in each word. Play the audio one more time and allow students to check their answers. Drill the stress pattern as a class.

Answers

<u>Sa</u>-tur-day /ˈsætədeɪ/ (3)
<u>Wednes</u>-day /ˈwenzdeɪ/ (2)
<u>Fri</u>-day /ˈfraɪdeɪ/ (2)
<u>Tues</u>-day /ˈtjuːzdeɪ/ (2)
<u>Sun</u>-day /ˈsʌndeɪ/ (2)
<u>Thurs</u>-day /ˈθɜːzdeɪ/ (2)
<u>Mon</u>-day /ˈmʌndeɪ/ (2)

2 👥 Students complete the task in pairs. Before they begin, model the answers to ensure that students answer in complete sentences, e.g. *I go to school on Mondays and Wednesdays.* Elicit what preposition is used before weekdays, i.e. *on*. Monitor and make sure students answer in complete sentences and use the correct preposition. Give feedback on the pronunciation of the days of the week.

Optional activity

👥 👥👥 The days of the week are often misspelt by students. To improve students' accuracy and to practise spelling the names, prepare a running dictation. Print out sheets of paper with the rhyme below, or another text that has the key vocabulary. Post the pieces of paper in different locations around the classroom or, if possible, somewhere outside the classroom. They should be posted far enough away so that students have to walk away from their desks to read them. Students work in pairs. One is a writer and the other is a runner. The runner memorizes a line at a time of the poem, then dictates it to the writer from memory. Model the game before students begin. The runners can walk/run to the poem as many times as they need to. After two or three minutes, ask students to change their roles. Set a time limit for the game, e.g. ten minutes. Students submit their texts, and the pair with the least number of spelling mistakes wins. Alternatively, ask students to count their own mistakes and report to you. Make sure students spell the names of the days with capital letters.

Work on Monday,

Study on Tuesday,

Clean on Wednesday,

Watch movies on Thursday,

Sleep on Friday,

Play football on Saturday,

Drink coffee on Sunday.

TIME EXPRESSIONS

3 👤👥 Students complete the task individually, then check their answers with a partner. To facilitate the task, draw students' attention to the example answer. Ask them what *6.30* (time) and *morning* (part of the day) in the sentence refer to. Allow two or three minutes for the task and check the answers as a class. Elicit the meaning of *every* /ˈevri/ (shows that something is repeated regularly), *morning* /ˈmɔːnɪŋ/ (the time of the day when the sun rises until the middle of the day), *afternoon* /ɑːftəˈnuːn/ (the period between 12 o'clock and about six o'clock), *evening* /ˈiːvnɪŋ/ (the part of the day between the end of the afternoon and night) and *dinner* /ˈdɪnə/ (the main meal of the day, usually eaten in the evening).

Answers

2 Chen and Wang watch films every <u>Tuesday evening</u>.
3 My sister makes my lunch on <u>Wednesdays</u>.
4 I play football with my friends every <u>Saturday</u>.
5 Faisal goes home at <u>3.00</u> in the <u>afternoon</u>.
6 Tania gets up at <u>6.00</u> in the <u>morning</u>.
7 Abdullah has English class at <u>7.30</u> in the <u>evening</u>.
8 Fatima has coffee with her friends every <u>day</u>.
9 Hakan goes to work at <u>8.30</u> in the <u>morning</u>.
10 Kerry has dinner at <u>6.30</u> in the <u>evening</u>.

4 👥 Students complete the task in pairs. Before they begin, draw their attention to the example answer. Ask them which sentences in Exercise 3 have the same structure as the example expression (2 (*every Tuesday evening*), 4 (*every Saturday*) and 8 (*every day*)). Elicit that the missing words are prepositions and check understanding of *preposition* /prepəˈzɪʃən/, i.e. words usually placed before nouns or pronouns which are used to help us locate things in time and space. At the end, check answers as a class. Ask students which sentences in Exercise 3 demonstrate the rules presented in this exercise.

Answers

2 in (sentences 1 (*in the morning*), 5 (*in the afternoon*), 6 (*in the morning*), 7 (*in the evening*), 9 (*in the morning*) and 10 (*in the evening*))
3 at (sentences 1 (*at 6.30*), 5 (*at 3.00*), 6 (*at 6.00*), 7 (*at 7.30*), 9 (*at 8.30*) and 10 (*at 6.30*))
4 on (sentence 3 (*on Wednesdays*))

5 and 6 🔊 3.5 👤👥 Students complete the gaps individually, then check their answers with a partner. Students then listen to the audio and check their answers. Monitor and, if necessary, go over the answers as a class.

Answers

1 at 2 at 3 at 4 on 5 at 6 at 7 in 8 on

THE PRESENT SIMPLE

7 👥 Model the answers by asking students questions about Élodie (from Exercise 5), e.g. *What time does she arrive at school? –She arrives at school at 8.30. What time does she have a biology lecture? –She has a biology lecture at nine.* Elicit the answers from the class and, if necessary, write them on the whiteboard to discuss. Make sure that students use *-s* in third person singular forms. Check understanding of the contracted forms *where's* /weərz/ (where is) and *she's* /ʃiːz/ (she is). Students complete the task in pairs. Monitor and write down any grammar mistakes in the Present simple. At the end, write them on the whiteboard and correct as a class.

Answers

1 She's from <u>France</u>.
2 She goes to <u>university</u>.
3 The bus comes at <u>7.30</u>.

4 No, she has <u>a biology lecture</u>. / No, she doesn't.
5 She has English class at <u>three o'clock in the afternoon</u>.
6 She <u>goes to the cinema with her family</u>.

Optional activity

🔊 3.5 👥 Students listen to the recording about Élodie one more time and follow the text as they listen. Students then practise saying the sentences in pairs. Allow a couple of minutes for practice. Monitor and give feedback on the pronunciation of the time expressions.

8 👥 Students complete the task in pairs. Remind them to use the Glossary to check the meaning of unknown words. Allow about eight minutes for the task, then check the answers as a class. Check understanding and the pronunciation of the new vocabulary, i.e. *breakfast* /ˈbrekfəst/, *dinner* /ˈdɪnə/, *tennis* /ˈtenɪs/, *basketball* /ˈbɑːskɪtbɔːl/, *computer games* /kəmˈpjuːtə geɪmz/, *university* /juːnɪˈvɜːsɪti/, *morning* /ˈmɔːnɪŋ/, *bus* /bʌs/, *taxi* /ˈtæksi/ and *train* /treɪn/. Check understanding of the collocations by asking students whether these sentences are correct or not: *I take lunch at 12 every day* (incorrect), *I take a taxi to school every morning* (correct), *I have basketball every evening* (incorrect).

Answers

1 have /hæv/ 2 watch /wɒtʃ/ 3 make /meɪk/
4 play /pleɪ/ 5 go /gəʊ/ 6 get /get/ 7 take /teɪk/

Explanation box

👥 Display the Explanation box on an interactive whiteboard and allow students a couple of minutes to read it. Elicit when we use the Present simple form, i.e. to talk about regular activities, to talk about habits and facts. Ask volunteers to write example sentences about their daily routine on the whiteboard using phrases from Exercise 8. Encourage students to write sentences about their classmates' daily routine to practise using third person singular forms. Elicit when we use *-s* at the end of the verb and correct students' sentences if necessary. Check understanding of the negative contractions *don't* /dəʊnt/ (do not) and *doesn't* /ˈdʌzənt/ (does not). Ask students to make negatives of the sentences they wrote on the whiteboard. Then ask students to make questions using phrases from Exercise 8, e.g. *Do you go to university?*, *What time do you get up in the morning?*, *What time do you have lunch?*,

When does he play football?, etc. Model the questions and correct if necessary.

9 👥 Draw students' attention to the examples and check understanding of the question form. Students complete the task in pairs. Monitor and correct question forms and statements if necessary. Make sure students answer in complete sentences. Write down any common mistakes in the Present simple that you hear while monitoring and write them on the whiteboard at the end. Elicit the correct answers from the class.

10 👥 Before students begin, draw their attention to the example sentences and elicit the third person singular verb forms. Monitor and give feedback on third person singular forms. Write down any grammar mistakes and correct them as a class at the end. Ask for volunteers to tell the class about their partner.

LISTENING 2

PREPARING TO LISTEN

UNDERSTANDING KEY VOCABULARY

1 and 2 🔊 3.6 👥👥 Students read the dialogues and choose the answers that they think are correct. Then they listen to the audio and check their answers. Play the audio again, pausing after each speaker's turn. Students repeat after each turn. Draw their attention to the intonation and ask them to repeat each turn as it is on the recording. Students then work in pairs and practise saying the dialogues. Monitor and give feedback on intonation. At the end, choose two or three pairs to demonstrate the dialogues to the class.

Answers

1 I don't have time, I'm sorry.
2 Yes, sure.
3 Nice to meet you!
4 No, not really.
5 Really?
6 I see.

WHILE LISTENING

LISTENING FOR MAIN IDEAS

3 🔊 3.7 👥👥 Before students begin, ask them to read the questions and check the meaning of new vocabulary in the Glossary. If necessary, explain the words: *stranger* /'streɪndʒə/ (someone you do not know), *journey* /'dʒɜːni/ (trip) and *information* /ɪnfə'meɪʃən/ (facts about a situation). Students listen to the audio and complete the task individually. Then they check their answers with a partner.

Answers

1 c 2 a 3 a

LISTENING FOR DETAIL

4 (◀ 3.7) 👤 👥 Ask students to guess the answers before they listen. Encourage them to use the Glossary to check the meaning of unknown words. Students check their predictions in pairs. Then play the audio and allow students to check their answers in pairs. Display the survey on an interactive whiteboard and complete it as a class. Elicit the meaning of *relax* /rɪ'læks/ (to calm down, to become less stressed), *scientist* /'saɪəntɪst/ (a person who does research and studies science) and *biology* /baɪ'ɒlədʒi/ (the study of nature).

Answers

A1 Y B1 study C1 Y C2a (goes to a) gym C2b Y
C2c Y C2d N C3a (on) Saturday (afternoon)
C3b a café

PRACTICE

Optional lead-in

(◀ 3.7) 👥 Play the audio one more time and draw students' attention to the 'Asking' and 'Answering' boxes. Ask students to follow the expressions as they listen and complete the sentences with gaps. Check answers as a class or, with a more advanced class, ask students to check their answers in the audio script on pages 213–214. Allow students a couple of minutes to practise saying the sentences as they heard them on the recording. Monitor and give feedback on intonation.

Possible answers

I'm a student at the university.
I'm asking people questions about their lifestyle.
OK, do you live with your parents?
OK, do you work or study?
OK, do you have a busy lifestyle?

5 👤 👥 Students complete the questionnaire for themselves and check the meaning of

unknown words in the Glossary. Allow about five minutes to prepare for the task. Check understanding of the expressions in the boxes. Divide the class into Students A and B. Student As ask questions about the survey and Student Bs answer. Tell Student Bs to close their books when they answer the questions. Student As take notes about their partners. Allow about five minutes for the task, then ask students to change roles.

6 👥 Put students into new pairs. Ask them to take turns to tell each other about the student they interviewed in Exercise 5. Monitor and write down any common mistakes with the Present simple. At the end, write them on the whiteboard and elicit the answers from the class.

CRITICAL THINKING

👥👥 At this point in each unit, students are asked to begin to think about the speaking task they will do at the end of the unit (*Interview students for a survey*). Give them a minute to look at the box.

CREATE

Skills box

👥👥 Display the Skills box on an interactive whiteboard and allow students a minute or two to read it. Ask students to look at the survey in Listening 2 again. Elicit what kind of text it is (a questionnaire). Ask them whether they have ever filled out a survey and, if so, what it was about. Ask students in what situations and for what purpose we use questionnaires/surveys, i.e. to find out a customer's opinion in a shop or a restaurant, to find out students' opinion about a course, etc. Practise the pronunciation of *survey* /'sɜːveɪ/ and *questionnaire* /ˌkwestʃə'neə/.

1 👥 👥👥 Remind students that ideas maps are a visual way of making notes that help in brainstorming a topic. Draw students' attention to the ideas map and point out that the main topic (*Student survey*) is in the middle, with sub-topics coming off it and related vocabulary/ideas coming off each sub-topic. Tell students to work in pairs and decide what the missing topics might be, based on the related vocabulary. Give them a few minutes to decide, then go through the answers as a class.

Answers

a work b study c food d lifestyle

Optional activity

Ask students to think of other ideas they could add to the ideas map.

REMEMBER

2 👥 👥👥 Students complete the task in pairs, then check their answers with another pair. Check answers as a class.

Answers

The correct order: 5, 2, 3, 4, 1

Optional activity

👤👥👥 Allow students a few days for this task. As a class, brainstorm places where you can often find small paper-based surveys, e.g. restaurants, hotels, beauty salons, shops, car dealers, health clinics, etc. Ask students to find a survey outside college and bring it to the class. They present their surveys to the class and explain where they got them and what questions they ask. Each student has to teach three new words they have learnt from the survey to the class.

SPEAKING

PREPARATION FOR SPEAKING

COLLOCATIONS FOR LIFESTYLE

Skills box

👥👥👥 Draw students' attention to the Skills box and allow them a minute to read it. Check understanding of *collocation* /kɒləˈkeɪʃən/. Use the examples from the box to demonstrate that collocations are fixed expressions, e.g. we say *go out with friends* and not *walk out with friends**, or *download apps* and not *take apps**.

Optional lead-in

👥👥 👥👥👥 Prepare paper slips with these collocations from the table: *send texts, post a video online, chat online, eat out at restaurants, have coffee with friends, have dinner with friends, go out with friends, go to the cinema* and *play computer games*. Prepare enough slips for several pairs or groups. Cut the slips into halves and ask each pair or group to match the collocations. At the end, ask each pair to say one collocation and write it on the whiteboard. To make it more competitive, ask the groups to work quietly and raise a hand when they think they are finished. The group that correctly completes all the collocations first wins.

---

1 and 2 👥👥 👥👥👥 Students work in pairs and complete the task. Encourage them to use the Glossary to check the meanings of the new words. Then they work with another pair and compare their answers. Check the answers as a class and elicit the meaning and the pronunciation of the new vocabulary.

Answers

Exercise 1: 2 download /daʊnˈləʊd/ 3 write /raɪt/
4 cook /kʊk/ 5 eat /iːt/ 6 order /ˈɔːdə/
7 watch /wɒtʃ/ 8 do /duː/ 9 go /gəʊ/
Exercise 2: a technology /tekˈnɒlədʒi/ b food /fuːd/
c free time /friː taɪm/

PRESENT SIMPLE QUESTIONS

3 👤 👥👥 Students complete the task individually, then check their answers with a partner. Check answers as a class and allow a minute for the pairs to practise saying the questions.

Optional activity

👥👥 To review the intonation skills from Listening 1, ask students to work in pairs and decide which questions have a falling intonation and which ones have a rising intonation. Check answers and model the questions with the class. Ask students to work in pairs and practise asking the questions. Monitor and give feedback on intonation.

Answers

1 Do you watch TV in the evening? (rising)
2 Do you cook food for your family? (rising)
3 Do you eat out at restaurants? (rising)
4 Do you write a blog? (rising)
5 Which computer games do you play? (falling)
6 How many texts do you send every day? (falling)

4 (◀) 3.8 👤 👥👥 Students complete the task individually, then check their answers with a partner. Play the audio to check their answers.

Answers

1 b 2 d 3 f 4 a 5 e 6 c

5 and 6 Students work in pairs and practise the sentences following the stress pattern in the recording. Students then change partners and ask and answer the questions from Exercise 3 about themselves. Monitor and give feedback on the Present simple if necessary.

◄) 3.8 👥👥 👥 Play the audio one more time and pause after each sentence. Ask students to repeat each sentence as they hear it on the recording. Emphasize the stressed words by tapping on a desk.

Answers

1 A: Do you watch <u>TV</u> in the <u>evening</u>?
   B: <u>No</u>, not <u>really</u>. I <u>go</u> to the <u>gym</u> in the <u>evening</u>.
2 A: Do <u>you</u> cook <u>food</u> for your <u>family</u>?
   B: <u>No</u>! I <u>can</u> order <u>pizza</u> but I <u>can't</u> <u>cook</u>!
3 A: Do <u>you</u> eat <u>out</u> at <u>restaurants</u>?
   B: <u>Yes</u>. I <u>go</u> with my <u>family</u> every <u>Monday</u> <u>evening</u>.
4 A: Do <u>you</u> write a <u>blog</u>?
   B: <u>No</u>, but I <u>follow</u> one. It's about <u>football</u>.
5 A: Which <u>computer</u> games do you <u>play</u>?
   B: I <u>like</u> NBA *Basketball*. I <u>play</u> it on my <u>PC</u>.
6 A: How many <u>texts</u> do you <u>send</u> every <u>day</u>?
   B: I'm not <u>sure</u>. I <u>send</u> a <u>lot</u> of them – <u>40</u> or <u>50</u>, maybe?

7 and 8 👤👥 Students complete the tasks individually, then check their answers with a partner. Check the answers as a class.

Allow students two or three minutes to work in pairs and ask each other the questions in Exercise 7. With a more advanced class, ask students to develop the answers in Exercise 8 into complete sentences (see below).

Answers

Exercise 7
1 Do you cook food for your family?
2 Do you eat out at restaurants?
3 Do you have coffee with friends?
4 What do you eat at home?
5 Where do you have dinner with friends?
6 What kind of fast food do you like?
Exercise 8
1 d (I go to a café with my friends.)
2 a (I study biology.)
3 b (They are friends.)
4 f (Because they need information.)
5 c (I take the number 3.)
6 e (I go out with my friends on Saturday.)

PRONUNCIATION FOR SPEAKING

9 and 10 ◄) 3.9 👥👥 👥 Play the audio and drill the intonation patterns that are used in the questions. Pause after each question and ask students to repeat the question, following the intonation pattern they hear. Then ask students to work in pairs and complete

Exercise 10. Allow them about five minutes for the task, then tell them to compare their answers with another pair. Play the audio one more time and check the answers as a class. At the end, elicit the pronunciation of *do you* /dəjuː/. Explain that in connected speech, *do you* is weak. Drill *do you* questions from the exercise using the weak form.

Answers

Exercise 10: 1 down 2 up 3 up 4 down 5 up 6 down

11 ◄) 3.10 👥👥 Play the audio, then ask students to repeat the words as they hear them on the recording. Elicit the difference between the long vowel /uː/ as in *true*, *room* and *computer*, and the short vowel /ʊ/ as in *good*, *would* and *pull*.

12 ◄) 3.11 👥 Students complete the task in pairs. Then play the audio and ask them to check their answers. Drill the pronunciation of the words as a group.

Answers

/uː/	/ʊ/
tr<u>ue</u> /truː/	g<u>oo</u>d /gʊd/
r<u>oo</u>m /ruːm/	w<u>ou</u>ld /wʊd/
comp<u>u</u>ter /kəmˈpjuːtə/	p<u>u</u>ll /pʊl/
f<u>oo</u>d /fuːd/	b<u>oo</u>ks /bʊks/
y<u>ou</u> /juː/	f<u>oo</u>tball /ˈfʊtbɔːl/
n<u>ews</u> /njuːz/	c<u>oo</u>k /kʊk/
sch<u>oo</u>l /skuːl/	

13 👥 👥👥 Students complete the task in pairs. Monitor and give feedback on grammar, intonation and pronunciation. Ask for volunteers to present their dialogue to the class. If possible, ask the pairs to record their dialogues. Students then work with another pair and play their dialogues to each other. Ask students to give each other feedback on grammar and pronunciation.

14, 15 and 16 👤👥 Students write their questions individually, then check their answers with a partner. With a weaker class, write example questions on the whiteboard. Then ask students to work in pairs and practise saying the questions using the intonation patterns introduced in the unit. Ask them to give each other feedback. Allow about five minutes for this task, then ask students to change partners and practise asking and answering the questions. Monitor and correct any mistakes with the Present simple and intonation if necessary.

SPEAKING TASK

PREPARE

1 👥👥👥 Divide the class into Students A and B. Student As work together in small groups and Student Bs work together in small groups. Students make notes and write down questions for their interview. Tell students to practise asking their questions in the groups. Monitor and give feedback on grammar and pronunciation, but encourage students to correct each other. If necessary, address any common mistakes during group feedback at the end. Write down the mistakes on the whiteboard or say them aloud. Elicit the correct answers from the class.

PRACTISE/DISCUSS

2, 3 and 4 👥👥👥 Allow students 10–15 minutes to complete the interviews. Remind them to record or write down the information that they hear. Then allow 10–15 minutes for students to share their information with their groups. Monitor and help with grammar and vocabulary for the task. Ensure that students use Present simple forms correctly, especially the -s ending in the third person singular. If necessary, discuss any common mistakes as a class. Then ask students to work with a partner from another group and tell them the information they learnt from the interviews.

> **Optional activity**
>
> 👥👥👥 Students make videos or record their interviews. Then they edit the video or the audio recording and show it to the group. Students work in small groups. Tell them to listen to or watch the recording and correct any mistakes that they hear. At the end, students retell the information from the video or audio to the class.

OBJECTIVES REVIEW

See Teaching tips, pages 10–11, for ideas about using the Objectives review with your students.

WORDLIST

See Teaching tips, pages 10–11, for ideas about how to make the most of the Wordlist with your students.

REVIEW TEST

See pages 110–111 for the photocopiable Review test for this unit and Teaching tips, pages 10–11, for ideas about when and how to administer the Review test.

ADDITIONAL SPEAKING TASK

See page 128 for an additional speaking task related to this unit.

Students work in groups of three or four and write down questions for the task. Monitor and give feedback on Present simple questions. Allow students four or five minutes to write the questions. Students compare their questions with another group. They then mingle with other classmates and ask questions to find out at least one person for each category in the prompt. Allow 10–12 minutes for the activity. Students then go back to their groups and tell the group members about other students. Monitor and make sure students speak in complete sentences and use the Present simple. At the end, ask students to share their findings with the class.

RESEARCH PROJECT

Create a lifestyle podcast

Explain to students that they are going to create a lifestyle podcast. Different groups in the class could think about a different topic, e.g. sports and exercise, technology use, holiday destinations or food. Students can use the tools on the Cambridge LMS to share the information that they find with the rest of their group.

Each group should create a short (two-minute) podcast about their chosen topic. The podcast could include interviews with teachers or other students, a discussion, or advice (e.g. learners recommend hobbies that they enjoy). Students will need to plan the recording, record the podcast and then edit it. They can find editing software by searching for 'free audio-editing software/apps'. They could then upload their podcast to the Cambridge LMS (podcasts should be saved as mp3 files for this) or a media-library application.

4 PLACES

Learning objectives

Before you start the *Unlock your knowledge* section, ask students to read the Learning objectives box so that they have a clear idea of what they are going to learn in this unit. Tell them that you will come back to these objectives at the end of the unit when they review what they have learnt. Give them the opportunity to ask you any questions that they might have.

UNLOCK YOUR KNOWLEDGE

Background note

The photograph shows the Palm Jumeirah in Dubai, a collection of man-made islands with very exclusive houses built on them.

1, 2 and 3 👥 Display the photograph on an interactive whiteboard and ask students to discuss the questions in pairs. Allow students three or four minutes for discussion. Monitor and help with vocabulary for the task. If students have a similar place in their country, ask them to find a photograph of that place on the internet. At the end, discuss the photograph as a class and ask students to tell the class about similar places in their countries.

Optional activity

👤👥 Ask students to think of a place they would like to visit. Allow them about five minutes to make notes about the place, i.e. its name, location, what can people do there, etc. Ask them to find a photograph of that place on the internet. Students then work in small groups and tell each other about the place they would like to visit. Model the first sentence *I would like to visit ...* Monitor and write down any vocabulary used by students that is related to places. At the end, write the vocabulary on the whiteboard and elicit the meaning from the class.

WATCH AND LISTEN

Video script

▶ The Great Barrier Reef is the Earth's largest living thing. It lies off the coast of Australia. The Great Barrier Reef started to grow about 10,000 years ago, and it is huge. It is made up of 900 islands. It is larger than Italy and it can be seen from space. The Great Barrier Reef is home to 400 kinds of coral and 1,600 kinds of fish. Fishing is not allowed here, but

tourism is very popular. It is big business for Australia and brings in five billion dollars a year. People love seeing the different kinds of fish. There are more species per cubic metre than in any other place on the planet; for example, more fish varieties live on a single reef than in the entire Caribbean. And these are humpback whales that spend the winter here in the warm water. And there are sharks, too. Small dog sharks and the great white on the Great Barrier Reef.

PREPARING TO WATCH

Optional lead-in

👥 👥 Display the video stills on an interactive whiteboard. Ask students to describe them to each other. Ask them to write down nouns used to describe the photographs. As a group, elicit new vocabulary from students and write it on the whiteboard. Practise pronunciation of the words. Make sure to elicit key vocabulary items, i.e. *island* /ˈaɪlənd/, *sea* /siː/, *fish* /fɪʃ/, *lagoon* /ləˈɡuːn/, *reef* /riːf/, *shark* /ʃɑːk/ and *coral* /ˈkɒrəl/.

UNDERSTANDING KEY VOCABULARY

1 👤👥 Students complete the sentences individually, then check their answers with a partner. Encourage students to use the Glossary. Check the answers with the class. Check understanding and the pronunciation of the new vocabulary.

Answers

1 scuba diver /ˈskuːbə ˈdaɪvə/ 2 underwater /ʌndəˈwɔːtə/ 3 bright /braɪt/ 4 coral /ˈkɒrəl/ 5 Tourists /ˈtʊərɪsts/ 6 famous /ˈfeɪməs/ 7 shark /ʃɑːk/ 8 dangerous /ˈdeɪndʒərəs/

2 👥 Students complete the task in pairs. Before they begin, model the task. For example, ask them: *What's a shark?* and elicit the answer *It's a fish*. Monitor and make sure that students' questions are grammatically correct and that they answer in complete sentences. At the end, ask a few questions about the key vocabulary to check understanding.

USING YOUR KNOWLEDGE TO PREDICT CONTENT

3 👥 Students complete the task in pairs. Encourage students to use their background knowledge about geography.

Optional activity

👥👥 To help activate background knowledge, ask students to look at the photographs on the page and ask them if they have ever been to the ocean. Ask them about the experience, what they did there, what animals they saw, etc. If no one in the class has ever been to the ocean, ask them about movies or documentaries about the ocean. As a class, discuss what animals live in the ocean and what activities people usually do there, e.g. scuba diving, sailing, fishing, etc. Ask students if they would like to visit the places in the photographs and encourage them to explain why.

WHILE WATCHING

UNDERSTANDING MAIN IDEAS

4 ▶️ 👤 Students watch the video and check their answers from Exercise 3. Check the answers as a class and ask students to explain them. With a weaker class, refer to the video script on page 214 while checking the answers. Check understanding of *grow* /grəʊ/ (increase in size and amount), *coast* /kəʊst/ (the land next to or close to the sea), *space* /speɪs/ (the empty area outside the Earth's atmosphere) and *allowed* /əˈlaʊd/ (permitted).

Answers

1 b (*It lies off the coast of Australia.*)
2 c (*The Great Barrier Reef started to grow about 10,000 years ago …*)
3 c (*It is made up of 900 islands. It is larger than Italy and it can be seen from space.*)
4 c (*Fishing is not allowed here, but tourism is very popular.*)
5 a (*… these are humpback whales that spend the winter here …*)

UNDERSTANDING DETAIL

5 ▶️ 👥 👤 Before the listening task, ask students to work in pairs and practise saying the numbers. Allow a couple of minutes for this. Monitor and give individual feedback on the pronunciation of the numbers. At the end,

elicit the pronunciation of the figures from the class. Ask students to predict the answers. Then play the video one more time and ask students to check their answers. Go over the answers as a class or ask students to scan for the answers in the video script on page 214.

Answers

1 d 2 e 3 b 4 a 5 c

DISCUSSION

6 👤 👥👥 Allow students a couple of minutes to make notes about the questions. Students then discuss the questions in pairs. Allow about five minutes for this. Monitor and help with vocabulary for the task. Make notes and write down any common mistakes you hear during monitoring. At the end, write the mistakes on the whiteboard or say them aloud and ask students to correct them.

Optional activity

👥 With a more advanced class, prepare a role play. Divide the class into Students A and B. Allow students two or three minutes to make notes and prepare for the tasks individually (see the prompts below). Student As and Student Bs should work in small groups and help each other with the language. Monitor and help with grammar and vocabulary. Students then work in A+B pairs and role-play a short conversation between a tourist and a tourist agent. At the end, ask for volunteers to present their role play to the class.

Student A	Student B
You are a tourist. You would like to go to the reef in the video. Ask Student B questions, using the ideas below. Begin like this: *Hello. I'd like to go to Australia. Can you tell me about the reef?* *Where / reef / ?* *How many fish / on / reef / ?* *When / whales / ?*	You work for a tour company in Australia. Answer Student A's questions about the reef in the video. Use the answers to Exercises 3 and 5 to help you.

LISTENING 1

PREPARING TO LISTEN

PRONUNCIATION FOR LISTENING

> **Language note**
>
> Students may have problems distinguishing the meaning of the word pairs in the table. Make sure they understand that *this* and *that* are used with singular nouns, and *these* and *those* are used with plural nouns.

> **Optional lead-in**
>
> 👥 Prepare between three and five slides with photographs of objects, both singular and plural, and close and far away. Display each slide and describe the objects using sentences starting with *this*, *that*, *these*, *those*, *here* and *there*. Then display the slides again and elicit the sentences from students.

1 ◀4.1 👥👤👥 Draw students' attention to the words in the table and allow them a minute to read the Explanation box. Elicit the difference in meaning between *this* and *that*, *these* and *those*, and *here* and *there* (see the Language note above). Play the audio. Students complete the sentences individually, then check their answers with a partner. Go over the answers as a class and drill the pronunciation of the key vocabulary.

> **Answers**
>
> 1 this /ðɪs/ 2 these /ðiːz/ 3 here /hɪə/; there /ðeə/
> 4 that /ðæt/ 5 Those /ðəʊz/ 6 here /hɪə/

2 ◀4.1 👥 Play the audio again. Students work in pairs and answer the questions. Check answers as a class. If necessary, play the audio again, pausing after each sentence to discuss the stress and intonation of the words from the gaps. Drill the sentences with the class. Then ask students to work in pairs and practise the sentences as they heard them on the recording.

> **Answers**
>
> 1 Yes, the words in the gaps are stressed.
> 2 They have falling intonation, i.e. the voice goes down.

UNDERSTANDING KEY VOCABULARY

> **Optional lead-in**
>
> 👥 Prepare sets of cards with photographs of famous places (use the cities and countries from Exercise 3), e.g. the Eiffel Tower in Paris, Big Ben in London, Red Square in Moscow, the Real Madrid Stadium in Spain, the Leaning Tower of Pisa in Italy, etc. Do not label the photographs. Prepare slips of paper with the names of the cities/countries where these famous places are. Students work in small groups and match the places with the cities/countries. Allow them to use the internet. Set a time limit for the task. The group that has the most correct matches wins. Display a map of Europe and ask students to identify the countries from the task on the map. As a class, discuss which of these places students have visited or would like to visit.

3 👥 👥👥 Students complete the task in pairs, then check their answers with another pair. Encourage students to use the internet to find the locations of the places. Display a world map (use an interactive whiteboard, the overhead projector or a paper map) and ask students to locate on the map the places listed in the box. Elicit the pronunciation of the place names. Show the places on the map and ask for volunteers to pronounce them. Check that students understand the difference between *cities* and *countries*. Check the meaning of *region* /ˈriːdʒən/ (part of a country or the world) and *direction* /dɪˈrekʃən/ (a position toward which someone is facing or moving).

> **Answers**
>
> Regions: Australia /ɒsˈtreɪliə/, Asia /ˈeɪʒə/, America /əˈmerɪkə/, the Arab /ˈærəb/ world, Europe /ˈjʊərəp/
> Countries: Turkey /ˈtɜːki/, Tunisia /tjuːˈnɪziə/, Holland /ˈhɒlənd/, Italy /ˈɪtəli/, Spain /speɪn/
> Capital cities: Riyadh /riˈyæd/, Ankara /ˈæŋkərə/, London /ˈlʌndən/, Madrid /məˈdrɪd/, Moscow /ˈmɒskəʊ/, Paris /ˈpærɪs/
> Cities: Shanghai /ˈʃæŋhaɪ/, Istanbul /ɪstænˈbʊl/, Rotterdam /ˈrɒtədæm/
> Directions: north /nɔːθ/, east /iːst/, south /saʊθ/, west /west/

USING YOUR KNOWLEDGE

4 👥 👥👥 Display the map on an interactive whiteboard. Students work in pairs and answer the questions. Then they compare their answers with another pair. Monitor and check answers with the groups. Students are not expected to know all the countries on the map, as they will hear most of them in the recording. However, it would help if they can identify a few countries as points of reference to help them understand the lecture.

Answers

1 Europe
2 *Students are not expected to know the answers to this, as they will hear the audio* (A London/England/UK; B Rotterdam/Holland; C Paris/France; D Madrid/Spain; E Moscow/Russia; F Rome/Italy; G Istanbul/Turkey)
3 *Students are not expected to know the answers to this, as they will hear the audio* (blue: England/UK, Holland, Germany, Austria, Italy; yellow: Italy, France, Spain)

WHILE LISTENING

LISTENING FOR MAIN IDEAS

5 (◀) 4.2) 👥 Students work in pairs and predict their answers. Encourage them to use the Glossary to check the meaning of any new vocabulary before they listen. Students then listen and check their answers. Go over the answers as a class and refer to the sections of the audio script on page 214 to make sure students understand the answers.

Answers

1 b (… *mega* means 'big', 'very big'.)
2 b (What are these red circles? […] Yes, that's right. These are big cities.)
3 c (main idea question)

LISTENING FOR DETAIL

6 (◀) 4.2) 👤👥 Draw students' attention to the Skills box and allow them a minute to read it. Elicit the difference between *main ideas* and *details*. Check understanding of *road* /rəʊd/ (a long surface on which vehicles travel), *example* /ɪɡˈzɑːmpl/ (something that is typical of a group), *business* /ˈbɪznɪs/ (an activity of buying and selling goods and services) and *economy* /ɪˈkɒnəmi/ (the system of trade and industry in a country or region). Ask students to predict the answers to the questions, then play the audio again. Tell students to correct the false statements. Students check their answers with a partner, then check answers

as a class. With a weaker class, ask students to look at the audio script on page 214 and follow it as they listen to the audio one more time.

Answers

1 F (It's Europe at night.)
2 T (… here at 'C' is Paris …)
3 F (The blue one here and the yellow one there? These show megaregions.)
4 F (So can you give me an example of a mega*city*? […] Istanbul. […] Shanghai.)
5 T (… a megaregion is a group of important cities. They're important for business …)
6 F (… the 'blue banana'. It's the name for a group of cities that go from north to south in Europe.)
7 T (The economy is good here. That's at 'B', here on the map.)

DISCUSSION

7 👤👥 Students work individually and make notes about the questions. Encourage them to explain their answers and give examples. Allow four minutes to prepare. Students discuss the questions in pairs. Monitor and help with vocabulary for the task. Take notes and write down any common mistakes you hear during monitoring. At the end, write the mistakes on the whiteboard or say them aloud and ask students to correct them.

⊙ LANGUAGE DEVELOPMENT

VOCABULARY FOR PLACES

Optional lead-in

👥👥 Prepare sets of flashcards with different places, e.g. *bank, shop, street, road, park, library, mosque, port, airport, train station, hotel, restaurant, river, mountains, bus stop, hospital, health club, school, university, supermarket, market, cinema, theatre, swimming pool, stadium, bridge*, etc. Add places that are related to the city or town in which students are living. Ask them to come up with categories which can be used to group these places. At the end, ask each group to present their ideas and explain their categories to the class. The task is open-ended and aims to develop critical thinking. Ensure that students understand this and encourage them to use the Glossary. With a weaker class, ask students to match photographs of the places with the labels. The winner is the group that completes the task correctly first.

1 👥 Students complete the task in pairs. Encourage students to use the Glossary. Check answers as a class. Check understanding and pronunciation of the new vocabulary.

> **Answers**
>
> 1 port /pɔːt/ 2 mosque /mɒsk/ 3 library /ˈlaɪbrəri/ 4 bridge /brɪdʒ/ 5 supermarket /ˈsuːpəmɑːkɪt/ 6 bank /bæŋk/ 7 park /pɑːk/ 8 station /ˈsteɪʃən/

2 (◀)4.3 👤👥 Students listen to the audio and complete the sentences individually. Then they check their answers with a partner. If necessary, play the audio one more time. Display the task on an interactive whiteboard and ask students to spell the missing words out while you write them.

> **Answers**
>
> 1 supermarket 2 hotel 3 Mosque 4 library 5 restaurant 6 train station 7 bus 8 park

3 (◀)4.3 👥 Students work in pairs and match the questions from Exercise 2 with the answers in this exercise. It is not possible to match all the sentences without listening, but encourage students to make predictions based on what they remember from Exercise 2. Then they listen to the audio again and check their answers.

> **Answers**
>
> 1 g 2 b 3 e 4 f 5 a 6 h 7 d 8 c

> **Optional activity**
>
> (◀)4.3 👥 Play the audio again and pause after each conversation. Ask students to repeat the questions and answers as they hear them on the recording. Students work in pairs and practise the short dialogues from the audio. Monitor and give feedback on the pronunciation of the key vocabulary.

PREPOSITIONS OF PLACE

4 👤👥 Elicit the meaning of *preposition* /prepəˈzɪʃən/, i.e. a word usually placed before a noun or pronoun which is used to help us locate something in time and space. Students complete the task individually and check their answers with a partner. Go over the answers as a class and check understanding of the meaning of the different prepositions. For example, draw a box or a square on the whiteboard and ask volunteers to draw a dot

or a small animal in different places around the box to represent the meaning of the prepositions from the task.

> **Answers**
>
> a between b next to c on; behind d at e in f opposite; on g behind h in front of; on

5 👤👥 Students complete the gaps individually, then check their answers with a partner. Encourage them to use the Glossary. Display the pictures on an interactive whiteboard and check answers as a class. Elicit pronunciation of the prepositions in the task.

> **Answers**
>
> 1 in front of /ɪn ˈfrʌnt əv/ 2 next to /ˈnekst tə/ 3 behind /bɪˈhaɪnd/ 4 opposite /ˈɒpəzɪt/ 5 between /bɪˈtwiːn/ 6 on the left/right /ɒn ðə ˈleft/raɪt/ 7 at /æt/ 8 in /ɪn/

LISTENING 2

> **Optional activity**
>
> 👥 Prepare cards or slides with questions and multiple-choice answers. The questions should be about the campus and places in the city where students are taking their course. If possible, organize the questions into categories like sport, nature, entertainment, education, etc. Divide the class into teams. Ask each team to come up with a name for themselves. Keep a score on the whiteboard. Decide on a time limit or a number of rounds. The team that scores the most points wins.

PREPARING TO LISTEN

USING YOUR KNOWLEDGE

1 and 2 👥 Display the map on an interactive whiteboard. Students work in pairs and complete Exercises 1 and 2. Encourage students to use the Glossary. Check answers as a class and elicit the meaning of new vocabulary: *international airport* /ɪntəˈnæʃənəl ˈeəpɔːt/, *campus* /ˈkæmpəs/, *building* /ˈbɪldɪŋ/ and *hospital* /ˈhɒspɪtəl/. Draw students' attention to the university departments marked on the map and check understanding of the subjects taught there, i.e. Physics /ˈfɪzɪks/ (study of matter and energy), Language /ˈlæŋgwɪdʒ/ (study of languages), Arts /ɑːts/ (study of history, language and literature), History /ˈhɪstəri/ (study of past events or events of a particular period) and

Chemistry /ˈkemɪstri/ (study of the basic characteristics of substances).

| Answers
| **Exercise 1:** b (a map of a university campus)
| **Exercise 2:** 1 F 2 T 3 F 4 F 5 F 6 T 7 T 8 F

WHILE LISTENING

LISTENING FOR MAIN IDEAS

3 4.4 Students work in pairs and predict the answers before listening. Then play the audio and ask students to check their answers. Go over the answers as a class.

| Answers
| 1 c 2 a 3 a

LISTENING FOR DETAIL

4 4.4 Ask students to work in pairs and predict the answers before listening. Students listen and complete the task individually. Check answers as a class.

| Answers
| 1 A 2 F 3 G 4 C 5 E

PRACTICE

5 Put students into new pairs to work with Map 2. Students take turns and ask and answer questions. Monitor and help with vocabulary. Make sure students use the prepositions from the unit. Encourage students to answer in complete sentences. Write down any common grammar or pronunciation mistakes and discuss them at the end with the class.

Optional activity

Ask students to draw maps with the directions from the college/school to where they live. Students present their maps to the class and explain how to get from the college/school to where they live.

DISCUSSION

6 Students complete the task in pairs, then check their answers with another pair. Discuss their answers as a class.

| Answers
| 1 a street map
| 2 *Suggested answers:* (a) a climate map, a population map (b) a street map, an interactive map
| 3 a street map

CRITICAL THINKING

At this point in each unit, students are asked to begin to think about the speaking task they will do at the end of the unit (*Ask for and give directions*). Give them a minute to look at the box.

UNDERSTAND

1 Tell students that they are going to practise asking for and giving directions using prepositions of place. Ask them to work in pairs and check the meaning of any new vocabulary in the Glossary. Before the task, check understanding of the key vocabulary and, if possible, prepare slides to illustrate it. Drill the pronunciation of the key vocabulary. Students complete the task in pairs. Display the map on an interactive whiteboard and refer to it when you check the answers as a class.

| Answers
| 1 out of /aʊt əv/ 2 left /left/ 3 along /əˈlɒŋ/ 4 up /ʌp/
| 5 around /əˈraʊnd/ 6 down /daʊn/ 7 over /ˈəʊvə/
| 8 across /əˈkrɒs/ 9 through /θruː/ 10 under /ˈʌndə/
| 11 right /raɪt/ 12 into /ˈɪntu/

APPLY

2 Students work in pairs. Encourage them to take turns to give directions.

SPEAKING

PREPARATION FOR SPEAKING

ASKING FOR DIRECTIONS

1 4.5 Students complete the task individually, then listen to the audio to check their answers. Ask students to work in pairs and take turns to ask and answer. Encourage them to give real answers about the places on their campus, in their school or in their city. Ask for volunteers to present their dialogues to the class.

Answers

1 Where's the gym?
2 Is there a café near here?
3 How do I get to the Language Centre?
4 Can you tell me the way to the train station?
5 I'm looking for the library. Is it near here?

2 (◀ 4.6) 🔒👥 Students listen to the audio and complete the task individually. Then they check their answers with a partner.

Answers

a 4 b 2 c 3

PRONUNCIATION FOR SPEAKING

3 (◀ 4.7) 🔒👥 Students work in pairs and predict the stress. Before listening, discuss their answers as a class. Play the audio and allow students to check their predictions. Play the audio one more time and drill the stress pattern with the class. Gently tap on the desk to emphasize the stressed syllables. Ask students to work in pairs and practise.

Answers

1 Ex-<u>cuse</u> me! <u>Where</u>'s the <u>bank</u>, please?
2 Ex-<u>cuse</u> me! I <u>think</u> I'm <u>lost</u>. <u>How</u> do I <u>get</u> to the <u>gym</u>?
3 Ex-<u>cuse</u> me! Can you <u>tell</u> me the <u>way</u> to the <u>ca</u>-fé?

4 and 5 (◀ 4.7) 👥 Play the audio again. Students answer the questions in pairs. Check the answers as a class and ask for volunteers to repeat the sentences using the same intonation as in the recording. Students work in pairs and practise the intonation pattern from the audio. If necessary, play the audio one more time before the practice.

Answers

Exercise 4
1 1 up 2 up 3 up
2 down
3 1 down 2 up
4 up

6 and 7 👥 Divide the class into pairs of Student A and B. Student B asks for directions for the places from the map on page 76. Student A answers in complete sentences. Allow up to eight minutes for the task. Monitor and write down any common grammar or pronunciation mistakes and discuss them with the class at the

end. Then ask students to change partners. Students change their roles. Student A asks for directions and Student B answers. Monitor and give individual feedback on grammar and pronunciation.

GIVING DIRECTIONS

8 and 9 (◀ 4.8) 👥 Students work in pairs and complete the gaps with the missing prepositions. Allow about five minutes, then play the audio. Students listen and check their answers. Play the audio one more time and pause after each sentence. Ask the class to repeat. Students work in pairs and practise saying the sentences as they heard them on the recording. Allow five minutes for the practice session, then ask students to complete Exercise 9. Check answers as a class.

Answers

Exercise 8: 1 opposite 2 in 3 through 4 in; on 5 at 6 along; over 7 to 8 on; behind
Exercise 9
a 1, 2, 4, 5, 7, 8
b 3, 6

10 🔒👥 Students complete the task individually, then check their answers with a partner. Display the map on an interactive whiteboard and refer to it while checking the answers.

Answers

1 behind 2 left 3 along 4 left 5 on 6 next to 7 opposite 8 on

Explanation box

👥 Draw students' attention to the Explanation box. Ask them to read the example sentences. Explain that we use imperatives to give instructions or directions. Elicit that we don't use personal pronouns before imperatives.

Optional activity

👥 To practise listening to and using the imperatives, play *Simon Says* with the class. In the game, one player takes the role of 'Simon' and gives instructions using imperatives, e.g. *Pick up your pen, Stand up, Turn around, Close your book*, etc. The other players follow the commands only if they are preceded by the phrase *Simon says …* Students are eliminated from the game if they do not follow the instructions immediately, misunderstand the instructions or follow instructions that are not preceded by the phrase *Simon says … .* The last student in the game wins. Model the game first, then allow volunteers to take over.

SPEAKING TASK

PREPARE

1 👤 Divide the class into Students A and B. Tell Student As to open the book on page 194 and Student Bs to open it on page 196. Tell students that they are going to ask and give directions to places on their maps and that they have different maps to describe. Allow students about five minutes to study their maps. Encourage them to make notes about directions to the different places on the map. Before they begin, model the task. Tell students to ask you for directions to a place on their map. Look at the map and give the directions using the imperatives and the prepositions practised in the unit.

PRACTISE

2 👥 Put students into A/B pairs. Students do the role play. Monitor and write down any common mistakes you hear. Allow 10–15 minutes for the activity, then give group feedback. Write the grammar mistakes on the whiteboard or say them aloud and elicit the correct answers from the class.

> **Answers**
> 1 D 2 E 3 A 4 C 5 B

3 and 4 👥 Students change roles. Monitor and write down the grammar mistakes that you hear. At the end, write them on the whiteboard. Divide the class into two groups and allow time to correct the mistakes in groups. Ask the teams to write their answers down before correcting them as a class. Award 1 point for each correct answer. Students then look at their partner's map and check whether their directions were correct.

> **Answers**
> 1 E 2 C 3 B 4 D 5 A

OBJECTIVES REVIEW

See Teaching tips, pages 10–11, for ideas about using the Objectives review with your students.

WORDLIST

See Teaching tips, pages 10–11, for ideas about how to make the most of the Wordlist with your students.

REVIEW TEST

See pages 112–113 for the photocopiable Review test for this unit and Teaching tips, pages 10–11, for ideas about when and how to administer the Review test.

ADDITIONAL SPEAKING TASK

See page 129 for an additional speaking task related to this unit.

Check the use of imperatives and check understanding of the verbs used to give directions. Ask students to work individually and prepare maps illustrating their route from the college/school to where they live. Monitor and check that the maps are clearly labelled with landmarks. Students work in pairs and give each other directions to their house. At the end, ask for volunteers to explain the directions to their partner's house to the class.

RESEARCH PROJECT

Create a TV advertisement for a city in your country

Ask students to think about a city in their or a different country which is good to visit. They will need to find out about this city, e.g. what you can do there, famous buildings you can visit. They could do an internet search, use their own knowledge or talk to people who know about the city. In some cases, a city's tourism pages give the visitor the option to 'follow' them on social networking sites, and you could encourage students to do this.

Tell the class that they will be filming a TV advertisement to appeal to tourists visiting the city. They could do this as a whole class or you could divide the class into groups. Ask them to plan the advertisement by creating a script and/or storyboard. They will also have to think about who will direct and record the video, who will do the editing and who will present or narrate the advertisement. If different groups are creating advertisements, the class could vote on which city they would most like to visit. There are free online voting systems which allow you to do this. Search for 'voting software' to view some of these.

5 SPORT

UNLOCK YOUR KNOWLEDGE

1, 2 and 3 👥 Display the photograph on an interactive whiteboard. Students discuss the photograph in pairs. Monitor and help with the vocabulary for the task. Encourage students to answer in complete sentences. Allow three or four minutes for the task, then discuss their answers as a class. Elicit the name of the sport on the photograph, i.e. *skiing* /ˈskiːɪŋ/.

Optional activity

👤 👥 Students research on the internet about their favourite sport. Ask them to find photographs of the sport and some basic facts, e.g. *Is it a team sport?*, *What are the rules?*, *Where can you play it?* Allow up to ten minutes for research, then ask students to work in small groups and tell each other about their favourite sport. Monitor and check that students use the sports vocabulary correctly. At the end, ask for volunteers to tell the class about their sport and write down any new sports-related vocabulary on the whiteboard. Check understanding of the new vocabulary as a class.

WATCH AND LISTEN

Video script

▶ Europe. Italy. The island of Sicily. Sicily is the biggest island in the Mediterranean Sea. Today, it is home to five million people. Sicily has many old traditions. One of Sicily's oldest traditions is fishing. Today, there are not many jobs for fishermen in Sicily. Meet 24-year-old Sicilian, Michaele Ralo. Michaele wants to be a free diver. Free diving is when you dive without oxygen tanks. Free diving is a modern sport, but it is also an ancient tradition in Sicily.

Michaele trains every day. Each time he dives, he swims faster, dives deeper and stays under water longer. He is training for a competition, but also because he wants to be a professional diver. To become a professional, Michaele must dive to more than 50 metres. Free diving is a dangerous sport.

Today, there is a free-diving competition. The town wakes up to a beautiful morning.

Fans come to wish Michaele good luck. The divers go out to sea. Safety divers go down before the free divers to help in an emergency. Then it's time! The older divers go first. They dive deep and stay down for four minutes. These divers are good. They are better than the others that Michaele knows. Michaele waits for his turn. He sees the dive in his mind, going faster and deeper. He's off! It's a good start, swimming fast and deep. It's a long dive. The older men are worried. But Michaele returns. He's happy. He knows it's a good dive. The dive is over 56 metres – Michaele can become a professional!

PREPARING TO WATCH

Optional lead-in

▶ 👥 Play *20 Questions* as a class. Before the task, model the game with a different topic. Think of a place, e.g. library, bank, school, and tell students that they have to guess the place by asking *yes/no* questions. Divide the class into Students A and B. Student As watch the video without the sound and learn about the sport in the video, i.e. free diving /ˈfriː ˈdaɪvɪŋ/. Student Bs have to guess the sport by asking 20 *yes/no* questions. While Student As watch the video, give Student Bs time to write questions they want to ask. Monitor and help with the questions. Student As can only answer *yes* or *no*. The student who guesses the sport wins.

USING YOUR KNOWLEDGE TO PREDICT CONTENT

1 and 2 ▶ 👤 👥 Play the video, but mute the sound. Students complete the task individually, then check their answers with a partner. Allow up to eight minutes to compare the answers. Encourage students to use the Glossary to check the meaning and the spelling of the new vocabulary.

3 👥 👥 Students complete the task in pairs. Display the exercise on an interactive whiteboard and complete the table as a class. Ask students to spell the words as you write. Check the meaning and the pronunciation of the new words. Encourage students to use the Glossary.

Answers

people (e.g. *an old woman*)	places (e.g. *a school*)
a free diver /ˈdaɪvə/ old men /əʊld men/ a young man /jʌŋ mæn/ scuba divers /ˈskuːbə/	the sea /siː/ the world /wɜːld/ Italy /ˈɪtəli/ Sicily /ˈsɪsəli/ a city /ˈsɪti/ a town /taʊn/
things (e.g. *a car*)	**times of day (e.g. *afternoon*)**
boats /bəʊts/ a scooter /ˈskuːtə/ rocks /rɒks/ sand /sænd/ a red balloon /bəˈluːn/	evening /ˈiːvnɪŋ/ morning /ˈmɔːnɪŋ/

4 👥 Students answer the question in pairs. Allow them to use the Glossary. Check their answer as a class and discuss why answers a) and b) are incorrect. Elicit the meaning of *equipment* /ɪˈkwɪpmənt/ (the set of necessary tools and clothes needed for a particular purpose) and ask for examples.

Answer

c (diving under water without equipment)

WHILE WATCHING

UNDERSTANDING DETAIL

5 ▶️ 👥 Students work in pairs, read the questions and predict the answers. Then play the video again (this time with the sound) and ask students to check their answers. Check the answers as a class. Display the video script from page 216 on an interactive whiteboard and underline the correct answers. Check understanding of *emergency* /ɪˈmɜːdʒənsi/ (something dangerous or serious, such as an accident, which happens unexpectedly).

Answers

1 c (*... it is home to five million people.*)
2 b (*One of Sicily's oldest traditions is fishing.*)
3 c (*Michaele wants to be a free diver. [...] because he wants to be a professional diver.*)
4 a (*Safety divers go down before the free divers to help in an emergency.*)
5 b (*The dive is over 56 metres ...*)

UNDERSTANDING KEY VOCABULARY

6 👤👥 Students complete the task individually, then check their answers with a partner. Encourage them to use the Glossary. Check the answers as a class. Elicit the meaning and the pronunciation of the new vocabulary.

> ### Optional activity
>
> 👥 Divide the class into teams. Write the new vocabulary on slips of paper and ask the first team to pick a word. Teams take turns saying original sentences using the new words. The team that uses the word correctly in a sentence gets a point. Keep score on the whiteboard.

Answers

1 deep /diːp/ (going, or being, a long way down)
2 fans /fænz/ (people who admire and support a person or sport)
3 million /ˈmɪljən/ (the number 1,000,000)
4 professional /prəˈfeʃənəl/ (related to work that requires special training)
5 competition /kɒmpəˈtɪʃən/ (an event where people try to win a prize)
6 traditional /trəˈdɪʃənəl/ (related to customs that have existed for a long time)
7 ancient /ˈeɪnʃənt/ (of or from a long time ago)
8 important /ɪmˈpɔːtənt/ (necessary or of great value)

DISCUSSION

7 and 8 👥 👥👥 Students work in pairs and prepare a list or an ideas map of dangerous sports that they know. Encourage students to use bilingual dictionaries to find names of the sports. Allow 10–15 minutes to complete the notes. Monitor and check understanding of the new vocabulary and the pronunciation of the sports. Students then work with another pair and discuss the questions in Exercise 8. Monitor and check the pronunciation of new vocabulary. Write down any common mistakes you hear and discuss them at the end.

LISTENING 1

PREPARING TO LISTEN

> ### Optional lead-in
>
> 👥👥 With a more advanced class, prepare pictures of typical sports from different countries around the world, e.g. tae kwon do for Korea, yoga for India, karate for Japan, kung fu for China, basketball for the US, football for Brazil, cricket for the UK, etc. Write

the names of the countries on separate slips of paper. Students work in small groups and match the countries with their typical sports. Students discuss which of these sports they like or have seen, and what other countries are good at these sports. Allow five minutes for discussion, then ask students to discuss which of these sports are good for women and which ones are good for men. Monitor and help with vocabulary for the task. At the end, elicit and explain the importance of fluency and length of turn in speaking, and how class discussions can develop these skills.

UNDERSTANDING KEY VOCABULARY

1 👥 Students work in pairs and discuss the questions. Ask them to check the meaning of the words from the box in the Glossary. Allow about five minutes for the task. Display the photographs on an interactive whiteboard and discuss students' ideas as a class. Check understanding and the pronunciation of the words from the box.

Answers

1 tae kwon do /taɪˈkwɒndəʊ/ (a sport in which people fight with arms, legs and feet); a martial art /ˈmɑːʃəl ɑːt/ (a sport that is a traditional Japanese or Chinese form of fighting)
2 yoga /ˈjəʊgə/ (a set of physical and mental exercises, originally from India)
3 the back /bæk/; a bone /bəʊn/ (any of the hard parts inside a human or animal)

2 👤👥 Students complete the task individually, then compare their answers with a partner. Encourage students to use the Glossary. Allow about seven minutes for the task. Discuss students' answers as a class. Elicit the meaning of the adjectives by asking for synonyms or antonyms. Discuss why students selected different adjectives to describe the sports, for example *Why do you have to be fast and strong in tae kwon do? – Because you have to kick and fight with another person.*

Possible answers

1 fast /fɑːst/, tough /tʌf/, quick /kwɪk/, hard /hɑːd/, strong /strɒŋ/*
2 slow /sləʊ/, good /gʊd/, tough, hard, strong*
3 fast, slow, good
4 tough, hard, strong*
* *Strong* is used to describe people who do this sport/ exercise, not the sport/exercise itself.

3 🔊 5.1 👤👥 Students complete the task individually, then compare their answers with a partner. Play the audio one more time

and check the answers as a class. Drill the pronunciation of the words.

Answers

1 /k/ 2 /ŋ/ 3 /f/

4 🔊 5.2 👥👥👥 Students complete the task in pairs, then listen to the audio to check their answers. Display the table on an interactive whiteboard. Ask for a volunteer to write the words in the table and the rest of the class to spell them for the writer. Play the audio again and drill the pronunciation as a class.

Answers

quick /kwɪk/	**strong** /strɒŋ/	**tough** /tʌf/
country /ˈkʌntri/	evening /ˈiːvnɪŋ/	father /ˈfɑːðə/
mosque /mɒsk/	singer /ˈsɪŋə/	phone /fəʊn/
smoke /sməʊk/	spring /sprɪŋ/	physics /ˈfɪzɪks/

5 👥 Students complete the task in pairs. Monitor and check the pronunciation of the words with /k/, /ŋ/ and /f/. Allow a couple of minutes for a discussion.

Explanation box

👥👥👥 Display the Explanation box on an interactive whiteboard and allow students a couple of minutes to read it. Discuss the example sentences in the box and ask students what two things are compared in each sentence, e.g. *women* and *men*, *zumba* and *walking*, etc. Underline them in each sentence. Elicit how we can tell the difference between regular adjectives and comparative ones, i.e. we add *-er* to short adjectives and *more* to long adjectives.

6 👥 Students answer the questions in pairs. Check the answers as a class. With a more advanced class, elicit sentence stress in the example sentences.

Answers

1 a 2 b

PRONUNCIATION FOR LISTENING

7 🔊 5.3 👤👥 Students listen to the audio and underline the most stressed words in each sentence. Students check their answers with a partner. Check the answers as a class.

Play the audio again, pausing after each sentence. Discuss which words are the most stressed and ask students to repeat the sentences as a class. During practice, tap on the desk to help students notice the most stressed words.

Answers

Running's a <u>tough</u> <u>sport</u>.
<u>Free</u> diving's <u>tougher</u> than <u>ru</u>nning.
<u>Mark</u>'s a <u>strong</u> <u>man</u>.
Lisa's <u>stronger</u> than <u>Steph</u>.
<u>Yoga</u>'s <u>good</u> for you.
<u>Yoga</u>'s <u>better</u> for you than tae <u>kwon</u> do.

WHILE LISTENING

LISTENING FOR MAIN IDEAS

8 (◄) 5.4) 👤👥 Students listen to the audio and complete the task individually. Then they check their answers with a partner. Elicit which words or phrases gave them the answer. Elicit why answers a) and c) are incorrect.

Answers

b (men, women and sport)

LISTENING FOR DETAIL

9 and 10 (◄) 5.4) 👤👥 Students listen to the audio and complete the task individually. Then they check their answers with a partner. Allow students five minutes to compare their answers. Then check their answers as a class.

Answers

1 f 2 e 3 d 4 c 5 b 6 a

Optional activity

👥 With a stronger class, display the script for audio 5.4 on an interactive whiteboard. Students work in pairs and write a few more questions to add to Exercise 9. Monitor and check the accuracy of the questions. Ask students to work with new partners and ask and answer the questions.

PRACTICE

11 👥 Students complete the task in pairs. Monitor and give feedback on sentence stress. At the end, ask for volunteers to present their dialogues to the class.

⊙ LANGUAGE DEVELOPMENT

VOCABULARY FOR SPORT

Background note

Zumba and pilates may not be familiar to students. Zumba is a dance fitness programme which involves dance and aerobic exercise to music (usually with a Latin rhythm). Pilates is a non-aerobic physical fitness routine which helps develop flexibility and muscle strength.

1 and 2 👥 Students work in pairs and complete these two exercises. Encourage students to use the Glossary or a bilingual dictionary. Allow 10–15 minutes for the task. Then tell students to compare their answers with another pair. Check the answers as a class. Check understanding of the names of the sports. Prepare slides or photographs of the sports and display the slides one by one, eliciting the names of the sports and what students know about them. Elicit the pronunciation and drill as a class.

Answers

Exercise 1: baseball /'beɪsbɔːl/, basketball /baːskɪtbɔːl/, football /'fʊtbɔːl/, volleyball /'vɒlibɔːl/
Exercise 2: 2 karate /kəˈrɑːti/ 3 judo /'dʒuːdəʊ/ 4 kung fu /kʌŋˈfuː/

3 👥👥 Students work in pairs and complete the task. Then they compare their answers with another pair. At the end, discuss the answers as a class and check the pronunciation of the key vocabulary.

Answers

1 football, basketball, baseball, volleyball
2 swimming, running, skiing, yoga, pilates
3 karate, judo
4 tennis, judo
5 no
6 (potentially most of them if you include Olympic events but) karate, tennis, judo, football, baseball, basketball, kung fu, volleyball
7 Answers will vary depending on students' country of origin, so allow for student discussion.

Optional activity

👥👥 Prepare flashcards or slips of paper with the sports from Exercises 1 and 2 (except for zumba and pilates). With a more advanced, class, add up to eight more sports names, e.g. golf, diving, fencing, table tennis (ping pong), cycling, badminton, hockey and skating. Students work in small teams. They take turns and draw slips of paper with the word. Students have to act out the sport. The team that guesses the sport scores a point. To gain bonus points, ask the teams to spell the names of the sports they guess. The team with the most points wins. Keep track of the scores on the whiteboard.

COMPARATIVE ADJECTIVES

4 and 5 👤👥 Students complete the exercises individually, then check their answers with a partner. If necessary, ask them to review the Explanation box in Listening 1 on page 91. Check the answers as a class.

> ### Answers
> **Exercise 4:** 1 tall 2 faster than 3 faster than 4 bigger than 5 a better
> **Exercise 5**
> 1 Is football ~~more~~ healthier than yoga?
> 2 Are men tougher than women?
> 3 Are martial arts ~~more~~ easier for men?
> 4 Is swimming more dangerous than judo?
> 5 Is tennis more popular than basketball in your country?
> 6 Is running better than volleyball?

6 👥 Students discuss the questions in pairs. Encourage them to answer in complete sentences by using the comparative adjectives and by explaining their point of view, e.g. *I think football is healthier than yoga because you play it outside.* Make notes during monitoring and write down any common mistakes that you hear, especially in the use of the comparative form. At the end, during feedback, write the mistakes on the whiteboard and elicit the correct answers from the class.

LISTENING 2

PREPARING TO LISTEN

USING YOUR KNOWLEDGE

👥 Draw students' attention to the Skills box. Ask students why thinking about what we already know about the topic is a good listening skill, i.e. it helps us to guess the meaning of new words, it helps us predict the content, and it helps us understand new information.

1 👥 Display the photographs on an interactive whiteboard. Students work in pairs and discuss the questions. Allow up to eight minutes, then check the answers as a class. If students have not completed the Language development section, elicit the names of the sports of the photographs, i.e. *zumba* /ˈzʊmbə/, *kung fu* /kʌŋˈfuː/, *tennis* /ˈtenɪs/, *skiing* /ˈskiːɪŋ/ and *pilates* /pəˈlɑːtiːz/. Ask students what they know about the sports in the photographs. Ask them which of the sports look the most and the least interesting.

> ### Answers
> 1 a zumba b kung fu c tennis d skiing e pilates/yoga
> 2 *Suggested answers:* a fast, quick b tough, fast, quick, hard, strong c fast, quick d fast, quick, hard, tough e slow, good, strong
> 3 Answers will vary. Allow group discussion.

UNDERSTANDING KEY VOCABULARY

2 👤👥 Students complete the task individually, then check their answers with a partner. Remind them to use the Glossary. Check the answers as a class; check understanding and pronunciation of the key vocabulary and understanding of new vocabulary:

healthy /ˈhelθi/	strong and well
thin /θɪn/	slim, not fat
popular /ˈpɒpjʊlə/	liked and enjoyed by many people
fat /fæt/	large, big
unpopular /ʌnˈpɒpjʊlə/	not liked by many people
weak /wiːk/	not strong
unfit /ʌnˈfɪt/	not healthy because you do too little exercise
unhealthy /ʌnˈhelθi/	not in good health, or not strong and well

> ### Answers
> | 2 fitter | e |
> |---|---|
> | 3 thinner | a |
> | 4 faster | g |
> | 5 more popular | c |
> | 6 stronger | d |
> | 7 better | b |
> | 8 happier | f |

WHILE LISTENING

LISTENING FOR MAIN IDEAS

3 (�))5.5 👤👥 Students listen to the audio and answer the questions, then check their answers with a partner. Check the answers as a class and ask students to explain their answers. Teach *lose weight* /luːz weɪt/ (to become lighter and thinner) and *muscle* /'mʌsl/ (one of many tissues in the body that produces movement).

Answers

1 a and e
2 more popular with women

LISTENING FOR DETAIL

4 and 5 (�))5.5 👤👥 With a stronger class, ask students to predict their answers before they listen. Students listen and complete the task individually. Then they check their answers with a partner. Tell students to check their spelling of the adjectives with Exercise 2. Display the task on an interactive whiteboard and ask for volunteers to complete the sentences. Ask the rest of the class to spell the words for the writers. If necessary, ask the students to scan the audio script on pages 216–217 and underline the answers.

Answers

1 unhealthy 2 unhappy 3 fitter 4 slower 5 better
6 stronger

DISCUSSION

6 👥 Students work in pairs and discuss the sports by using comparatives. Use the first pair (zumba and pilates) to model the activity. Elicit sentences from students, e.g. *Zumba is faster than pilates*, *Pilates is healthier than zumba*, *Zumba is more popular than pilates*, etc. Allow five or six minutes for students to make notes and write their sentences. Then students change partners and compare the sports. Monitor and ensure that students are producing correct comparative sentences and make a note of any errors. At the end, discuss the errors and correct them as a class.

Optional activity

👥👥👥 Tell students that they have to decide which of the sports in each pair they would like to do. Students have to explain to each other why one sport is better than the other. Allow five or six minutes, then ask students to change partners and repeat the task. Monitor and make sure students use comparative sentences correctly. Write down any errors you hear and correct them as a class at the end.

CRITICAL THINKING

👥👥👥 At this point in each unit, students are asked to begin to think about the speaking task they will do at the end of the unit (*Compare different kinds of sport and exercise*). Give them a minute to look at the box.

REMEMBER

1 👥👥👥 Students discuss the questions in pairs. Allow about five minutes, then elicit the names of the sports in the photographs. Ask students to share their answers with the class.

Answers

a football /'fʊtbɔːl/ b basketball /'bɑːskɪtbɔːl/
c cycling /'saɪklɪŋ/ d badminton /'bædmɪntən/

APPLY

Optional lead-in

👥👥👥 Bring in examples of 'real' tables used in your school or college. Draw students' attention to the Skills box and allow them a minute to read it. Elicit the meaning of *table* /'teɪbl/ (an arrangement of facts and numbers in rows and blocks). Ask students whether they have used tables before, and why. Divide the class into groups. Give each group a 'real' table and ask them to analyze it. Each group should discuss what information there is in the table and how it is organized. Allow three or four minutes for group discussions, then ask each group to tell the class about their table.

2 👥👥👥 Display the table on an interactive whiteboard. Elicit the organization of the table, i.e. each column represents one sport and each row represents the features of this sport. Students work in pairs and complete the table. Tell students to search the internet for any information they do not know. Students use the names of the sports as key words in their search. Allow 15–20 minutes for the task, then tell students to compare their answers with another pair. Monitor and help students with the internet search. Students complete their tables. At the end, ask for volunteers and complete the table as a class.

Possible answers

Allow all possible answers, e.g. cycling can have winners and losers (e.g. the Tour de France); football can be played inside; basketball can be played outside.

	football	badminton	cycling	basketball
one or many people?	many	many	one	many
two players or teams?	teams /tiːmz/	players or teams	no teams	teams
how many players in a team?	11	2 or 4	no teams	5
winners and losers?	yes	yes	no	yes
score goals or points?	goals /ɡəʊlz/	points /pɔɪnts/	no goals or points	points
inside or outside?	outside	inside	outside	inside
places?	a football pitch /pɪtʃ/	a badminton court /kɔːt/	deserts, forests, mountains, roads, streets	a basketball court

3 👥👥 Students work in small groups and discuss the sports in the table. Tell them to look for similarities and differences. Allow up to eight minutes for this, then lead class discussion. Make sure students explain their opinions.

SPEAKING

PREPARATION FOR SPEAKING

PRONUNCIATION FOR SPEAKING

1 (◄) **5.6** 👤👥👥 Students listen to the audio and complete the task individually. Then they check their answers with a partner before checking as a whole class. Play the audio again and pause after each sentence. Ask the class to repeat the sentence stress as it is on the

recording. Tap on the desk to emphasize the rhythm of each sentence.

Answer
The parts in bold show stress.

2 and 3 (◄) **5.6** 👥👥 Students listen to the audio again and discuss the question in pairs. Discuss the answers as a class. Draw students' attention to the Explanation box and check understanding of *weak vowel* /wiːk vaʊ(ə)l/ (a vowel sound that is not stressed). Ask students whether words like *but*, *than*, *a*, *for* are 'strong' or 'weak' (they're all weak). Play the audio again and ask students to repeat the sentences after the recording.

Answer
The parts in red do not have stress.

4 👥👥 Students work in pairs and discuss whether the statements in Exercise 1 are true or false. Allow three or four minutes for discussion. At the end, lead class discussion and ask students to express their opinions.

Answers
1–2 Students' own opinions
3 True: There are five active players in basketball and 11 in football.
4–5 Students' own opinions

MAKING COMPARISONS

5 and 6 👥👥 Students complete the tasks in pairs, then check their answers with another pair. Encourage them to use the Glossary. Discuss the answers as a class and explain why the selected answers are correct and the others are not (see the explanations below). In Exercise 6, explain that the sentences have to be grammatically correct. If necessary, display the sentence halves on an interactive whiteboard and underline the subject and verb in each sentence.

Answers
Exercise 5
1 c (*Running* and *swimming* are not team games.)
2 a (*Basketball*, *baseball* and *football* are all team games.)
3 b (c) is factually incorrect. In b), *fit* is used to refer to people, not activities.)

4 c *Goals* are specific to football. There are *points* and *players* in badminton.

5 b (In badminton, there are usually two players. In basketball, there are five players. *More* makes the sentence grammatically correct.)

6 b (*Go cycling* is a fixed collocation.)

Exercise 6: 1 e 2 c 3 a 4 d 5 b

> ## Optional activity
>
> 👥 Tell students to mark the most stressed words in the sentences in Exercise 5. Allow about five minutes, then check answers as a class. Model the sentence rhythm of each sentence. Allow students another five minutes to practise saying the sentences in pairs.

Answers

1 <u>Foot</u>ball and <u>bas</u>ketball are <u>sim</u>ilar. They are <u>team</u> games.
2 <u>Foot</u>ball and <u>cy</u>cling are <u>dif</u>ferent.
3 <u>Cy</u>cling is a <u>heal</u>thy <u>sport</u>.
4 There are <u>no</u> <u>goals</u> in <u>bad</u>minton.
5 There are <u>more</u> players in <u>bas</u>ketball than in <u>bad</u>minton.
6 <u>Peo</u>ple go <u>cy</u>cling <u>out</u>side.

7 👤👥 Give students about five minutes to make notes about the sports. Encourage them to use similar sentence structures to the ones in Exercises 1–6. Then students work in pairs and make sentences that compare the three sports. Monitor and help with vocabulary for the task. Write down any common mistakes that you hear, then discuss them at the end with the class. Elicit the correct answers.

SPORTS COLLOCATIONS

8 👤👥 Students complete the task individually, then check their answers with a partner. Encourage them to use the Glossary. Check answers as a class. Ask students to work in pairs and make original sentences using the collocations. Give examples, e.g. *I play football every Friday. I like to go swimming in the morning. My brother does kung fu.* Volunteers present their sentences to the class.

Answers

1/2 baseball /'beisbɔːl/; rugby /'rʌgbi/
3/4 horse-riding /'hɔːs 'raidɪŋ/; running /'rʌnɪŋ/
5/6 judo /'dʒuːdəʊ/; yoga /'jəʊgə/

INTRODUCING A TALK

9 and 10 🔊5.7 👤👥 Give students a minute to read the text and check the meaning of any unknown words. Students listen to the audio and complete the gaps individually. Then they check their answers with a partner. Tell students to complete the gaps with the words from Exercise 10.

Answers

Exercise 10: 1 c 2 f 3 e 4 b 5 d 6 a

> ## Optional activity
>
> 🔊5.7 👥 Play the audio one more time and ask students to follow the text as they listen. Allow a couple of minutes for students to practise saying the introduction in pairs. Monitor and give feedback on sentence stress.

11 and 12 🔊5.8 👤👥 Students complete the task individually, then check their answers with a partner. They then work in pairs and underline the stressed words in each sentence. Play the audio again and check answers as a class. Pause after each sentence and ask the class to repeat by following the stress pattern on the recording. At the end, allow about five minutes for students to practise the sentences in pairs.

Answers

Exercise 11: 1 morning 2 exercise 3 start 4 young
Exercise 12
O<u>K</u>, good <u>mor</u>ning, <u>eve</u>rybody!
To<u>day</u>, I <u>want</u> to <u>talk</u> to you about <u>three</u> <u>kinds</u> of <u>ex</u>ercise.
I <u>want</u> to <u>start</u> with <u>this</u> <u>question</u>.
<u>Which</u> <u>sport</u> is <u>bet</u>ter for <u>young</u> <u>men</u>? <u>Which</u> is <u>bet</u>ter for <u>women</u>?

SPEAKING TASK

👥👥 Ask students to read the speaking task and check understanding.

PREPARE

1 and 2 👤 Students work individually and complete their notes in the table. Encourage them to use the internet.

Allow 10–15 minutes for their research and note-taking. Students should use the names of the sports as the key words in the internet search. They can also narrow down their research by adding the key words from the table to the name of the sport. Monitor and help with the internet search.

3 and 4 👤 Students make notes individually. Encourage them to use the Glossary or a bilingual dictionary. Monitor and check the accuracy of the vocabulary noted by students. If necessary, give individual feedback on vocabulary and grammar.

PRACTISE

5 👤👥 Students record their presentations. Then they work in pairs and play the presentations to each other. Tell students to give each other feedback on grammar and vocabulary. Students should use the bullet points to help them evaluate each others' presentations.

PRESENT

6 👥👥 Students work in small groups and give their talks to the group. Remind them to take notes when they listen to other students. Monitor and note down any grammar mistakes that you hear. To give feedback, write the incorrect sentences on the whiteboard. Divide the class into teams and allow them five minutes to correct the sentences on paper. The team that corrects the most mistakes wins. At the end, ask for volunteers to present their talk to the class. Highlight the strengths of each speaker, e.g. organization, pronunciation or using extended answers.

Optional activity

👤👥 Personalize the task by asking students to prepare a presentation about their favourite sport (or their favourite football team). Students explain why their sport is better than other sports and encourage others to take it up. They can include specific information about where and when you can practise this sport, etc.

OBJECTIVES REVIEW

See Teaching tips, pages 10–11, for ideas about using the Objectives review with your students.

WORDLIST

See Teaching tips, pages 10–11, for ideas about how to make the most of the Wordlist with your students.

REVIEW TEST

See pages 114–115 for the photocopiable Review test for this unit and Teaching tips, pages 10–11, for ideas about when and how to administer the Review test.

ADDITIONAL SPEAKING TASK

See page 130 for an additional speaking task related to this unit.

If necessary, check understanding of the useful expressions in the Model language section. Allow students three or four minutes to make notes about the points in the box. Encourage them to use key words in their notes instead of complete sentences. Help with vocabulary for the task. Students then work in pairs and give their presentations to each other. Ask the listeners to write down any mistakes they hear while listening and allow students a minute to discuss the mistakes in pairs before swapping roles. Ask the listeners to record how long their partners speak for and check the times during the peer feedback. If necessary, discuss how students can extend their presentations by giving more details.

RESEARCH PROJECT

Create a class eBook outlining different sports

Divide the class into groups and ask each group to think about a different type of sport. Decide which aspect of the sports they should focus on, e.g. how to play, equipment, rules. Each group will then need to collect relevant information for their sport. Students can use the Cambridge LMS as a central place to put information and see what other members of the group have found out.

Tell the class they are going to create an eBook. You can find guides and eBook software by searching for 'create eBook'. The class will need to decide on a title for the eBook. Each group can add the information they have collected on their sport to the eBook.

6 JOBS

UNLOCK YOUR KNOWLEDGE

1, 2 and 3 👥 👥👥 Display the photograph on an interactive whiteboard. Students work in pairs and discuss the photograph. Encourage them to check the meaning of the adjectives in the Glossary. Allow three or four minutes for pair discussion, then discuss the questions as a class. Check understanding and pronunciation of *boring* /'bɔːrɪŋ/, *dangerous* /'deɪndʒərəs/, *difficult* /'dɪfɪkəlt/, *easy* /'iːzi/, *interesting* /'ɪntrəstɪŋ/ and *safe* /seɪf/.

> **Answers**
> **Exercise 1:** firemen /'faɪəmen/ / firefighters /'faɪəfaɪtəz/
> **Exercise 2:** dangerous, difficult, interesting

WATCH AND LISTEN

Video script

▶ In a forest in Minnesota, a fire starts and quickly spreads. At the Minnesota Fire Centre, Mary Locke takes the call and the fire rangers go into action. The helicopter crew sends information about the fire back to the Fire Centre. And then it's the turn of the crew of the CL2-15 to take off. The CL2-15 is no ordinary plane. It is a fire-fighting plane. The pilots have to be very experienced. They are going to pick up water from this lake. It can be a dangerous job. The CL2-15 is flying at 140 kilometres per hour now. The pilot must be very careful. If he makes a mistake, the plane will crash. It's time to open the water tanks on the plane. The plane picks up water from the lake. This is the most dangerous time for the crew. But the pilot does his job and picks up more than 5,000 litres of water. Then it's time to put out the fire.

The pilot has to fly low over the trees to hit the fire. He also needs to make the ground wet in front of the fire so it can't spread. The water drops on the fire.

It's a good hit! But the fire is a big one – the fire rangers have to go back to the lake. In just two minutes, the plane is ready again. The crew have to drop water 20 times to put out the fire. At last, it's time for the fire rangers to go home … until the next time.

PREPARING TO WATCH

UNDERSTANDING KEY VOCABULARY

1 👤 👥👥 Students work individually, then discuss their answers with a partner. Encourage students to use the Glossary. Check understanding and pronunciation of new vocabulary. You may want to draw students' attention to the fact that three out of the four verbs are phrasal verbs, i.e. they are made up of a verb plus a particle.

put out /pʊt aʊt/	to stop fire
pick up /pɪk ʌp/	to lift something
take off /teɪk ɒf/	to leave the ground and begin to fly
drop /drɒp/	to fall or to allow something to fall

> **Answers**
> 1 d 2 b 3 a 4 c

2 and 3 👥 Students complete Exercise 2 in pairs. If necessary, model the activity with the class. Monitor and give feedback on the pronunciation of the key vocabulary. Allow a few minutes for the speaking activity, then tell students to complete Exercise 3. Students complete the task in pairs. Remind them to use the Glossary. Check answers as a class.

> **Answers**
> **Exercise 3:** 1 put out 2 drop 3 take off 4 pick up

4 👥👥 Students complete the task individually, then check their answers with a partner. Encourage them to use the Glossary. Go over the answers as a class. Check understanding and practise pronunciation of key vocabulary, i.e. *speed* /spiːd/, *weight* /weɪt/, *time* /taɪm/, *water* /'wɔːtə/.

Answers

1 c kilometres per hour /ˈkɪləmiːtəz pər ˈaʊə/
2 b kilos /ˈkiːləʊz/
3 d minutes /ˈmɪnɪts/
4 a litres /ˈliːtəz/

WHILE WATCHING

UNDERSTANDING MAIN IDEAS

5 ▶ 👤👥 Students watch the video and complete the task individually. Then they check their answers with a partner. Encourage students to check the meaning of new vocabulary in the Glossary. Go over the answers as a class. Elicit the meaning of *helicopter* /ˈhelɪkɒptə/ (a type of aircraft that has two sets of large blades on top), *information* /ɪnfəˈmeɪʃən/ (facts about a situation) and *plane crew* /ˈpleɪn kruː/ (a group of people who work together on the aircraft). Encourage students to use the context to guess the meaning of these words.

Answers

1 takes off second
2 picks up water
3 takes off first
4 sends information
5 takes a call about the fire

UNDERSTANDING DETAIL

6 and 7 ▶ 👤👥 Students watch the video again and complete the task individually. Then they check their answers with a partner. Write the answers on the whiteboard and elicit the pronunciation of the numbers. Allow about five minutes for students to practise the questions and answers in pairs.

Answers

Exercise 6: 1 140 2 5,000 3 two 4 20

8 ▶ 👥 Students discuss the questions in pairs. If necessary, play the video one more time to allow them to check their answers. Ask students to scan the video script on page 217 and find the answers. Check the answers as a class.

Answers

1 c (*The pilots have to be very experienced. They are going to pick up water from this lake. It can be a dangerous job.*)
2 a (*The plane picks up water from the lake. This is the most dangerous time for the crew.*)

DISCUSSION

9 👤👥 Before the task, discuss with the class how making notes is useful for developing a talk and expanding length of turn. Discuss what information we usually include in notes, e.g. key vocabulary, main ideas, etc. Allow students about five minutes to read the questions and make notes. Students then discuss the questions in pairs. Monitor and help with note-making. At the end, ask students to share their ideas with the class.

Optional activity

👥 👥👥 Prepare sets of flashcards with different jobs. Make sure you include some very dangerous jobs and some relatively safe ones, e.g. *doctor, nurse, firefighter, police officer, soldier, taxi driver, teacher, shop assistant, singer, cleaner, cook, businessman/ businesswoman, pilot, baker, fisherman, student,* etc. Ask students to work in pairs and organize these jobs from the 'most dangerous' to the 'least dangerous'. Encourage them to negotiate the task by explaining their reasons behind their categorization in English. Monitor and give feedback. Write down any common mistakes and discuss them at the end. Allow up to ten minutes for the task. Then ask students to work with another pair and explain their ordering of jobs to each other. At the end, ask each pair to tell the class which jobs they thought to be the most and the least dangerous. Make sure students explain the reasons for their ordering.

LISTENING 1

PREPARING TO LISTEN

UNDERSTANDING KEY VOCABULARY

1 👤👥 Students complete the task individually, then check their answers with a partner. Encourage them to use the Glossary. Check understanding and pronunciation of the key vocabulary.

Answers

1 d 2 f 3 c 4 e 5 a 6 b

2 (🔊 6.1) 👥 Students predict the answers in pairs. Allow three or four minutes, then play the audio to allow students to check their answers. Drill the pronunciation with the class.

> **Answers**
>
> <u>law</u>yer (2) /ˈlɔɪə/
> <u>ban</u>ker (2) /ˈbæŋkə/
> engi<u>neer</u> (3) /endʒəˈnɪə/
> <u>pi</u>lot (2) /ˈpaɪlət/
> mu<u>si</u>cian (3) /myuːˈzɪʃən/
> <u>sci</u>entist (3) /ˈsaɪəntɪst/

3 👥 Students complete the task in pairs. Monitor and give feedback on pronunciation and vocabulary. Lead group discussion at the end.

Explanation box

👥 Display the Explanation box on an interactive whiteboard. Ask students to read the example sentences and elicit the difference between an opinion and advice. Elicit question forms using *should* (advice) and *I think you should* (opinion). Elicit statements and negative sentences.

> **Optional activity**
>
> 👥👥 Students work in pairs and give each other advice on how to improve their English. Monitor and correct expressions giving opinion and advice. At the end, ask students to share their ideas with the class. Make sure students use the expressions from the Explanation box. Write their ideas on the whiteboard, then discuss which ones are the most useful.

4 and 5 (🔊 6.2) 👥 Allow students to predict the answers in pairs. Then play the audio to allow them to check their answers. Students work in pairs and practise saying the dialogues. Allow about five minutes for practice. Monitor and give feedback on pronunciation.

> **Answers**
>
> 1 should 2 think 3 should 4 Should 5 think
> 6 should 7 think 8 should

PRONUNCIATION FOR LISTENING

6 (🔊 6.3) 👥👥 👥 Play the audio and pause after each sentence. Drill the sentences as a class. Allow students three or four minutes to practise saying the sentences in pairs.

> **Optional activity**
>
> (🔊 6.3) 👥 Play the audio and tell students to read the sentences in the Explanation box as they listen. Students work in pairs and underline the most stressed words in each sentence. Play the audio again to allow students to check their answers. Pause after each sentence and ask students to repeat. Check the pronunciation of *should* /ʃʊd/ and *think* /θɪŋk/. Tap on the desk to emphasize the rhythm. Allow a couple of minutes for students to practise the sentences in pairs.

> **Answers**
>
> <u>What</u> should I <u>do</u>?
> <u>Should</u> I <u>study</u> <u>Tur</u>kish?
> You should <u>work</u> <u>hard</u>.
> I <u>think</u> you should watch <u>videos</u> in <u>English</u>.
> I <u>don't</u> think you should <u>drink</u> a lot of <u>coffee</u>.

WHILE LISTENING

LISTENING FOR MAIN IDEAS

7 and 8 (🔊 6.4) 👥 👥👥 Students listen to the audio and complete Exercises 7 and 8. Then they check their answers with a partner. Check the answers as a class and ask students to explain their answers to Exercise 8. Write down useful lexical chunks on the whiteboard and elicit the meaning and the pronunciation.

go to medical /ˈmedɪkəl/ *school*	to study medicine, to study to be a doctor
become /bɪˈkʌm/ *a lawyer*	to study and learn so that you can work as a lawyer
a hard /hɑːd/ *life*	life that is not easy
to work hard	to work a lot
earn money /ɜːn ˈmʌni/	to get money for your work
to have good grades /greɪdz/	to receive very good grades at school
go to university /juːnɪˈvɜːsɪti/	to study at university

> **Answers**
>
> **Exercise 7:** musician, lawyer
> **Exercise 8:** 1 b 2 c

LISTENING FOR DETAIL

9 🔊 6.4 👥 Students discuss possible answers in pairs. Then play the recording again for them to check their answers. Check the answers as a class and draw students' attention to the sections containing the answers. With a weaker class, ask students to find the answers in the audio script on pages 217–218.

> ### Answers
> 1 next year (*Well, I'm going to college <u>next year</u>.*)
> 2 musicians (*There are <u>a lot of jobs in music</u>.*)
> 3 good (*It's <u>a good job</u>. It's not boring and you can earn good money and help people.*)
> 4 medical school (*... my mother thinks <u>I should go to medical school</u>.*)
> 5 good grades (*Well, you're a good student and <u>you have good grades</u>.*)
> 6 get a job (*But for now, I think <u>you should get a job</u>.*)

DISCUSSION

10 👥👥 Allow students about five minutes to make notes before the speaking practice. Draw their attention to the useful expressions and elicit example sentences from the class. Students discuss the task in pairs. Allow about five minutes for discussion. Then tell students to work with another pair and share their ideas. Monitor and give feedback on expressing opinion and giving advice.

◉ LANGUAGE DEVELOPMENT

VOCABULARY FOR JOBS

Explanation box

👥👥 Display the Explanation box on an interactive whiteboard. Check understanding of *suffix* /ˈsʌfɪks/ (a group of letters that you add to the end of a word to make another word). Circle the suffixes in the examples in the box.

1 and 2 👥 👥👥 Students complete the task in pairs. Encourage them to use the Glossary. Allow up to eight minutes for them to complete the task. Draw an ideas map on the whiteboard with the word *jobs* in the middle and three branches to represent each suffix. Ask students to write the jobs they came up with on the ideas map. Ask the rest of the

class to spell the words aloud. As a class, mark the stress on the words, then drill the pronunciation.

3 👥 Check understanding of *dream job* /driːm dʒɒb/ (a job you wish to have). Students discuss the questions in pairs. Monitor and make sure students answer the questions in complete sentences. Help students with the new structures, e.g. *I would like to* and *you have to*.

> ### Optional activity
> 👥👥👥 Prepare flashcards or photographs with people doing the jobs from the unit. Students take turns to pick a photograph. Then they describe the photograph to the class without mentioning the job. The rest of the class work in small teams. The team that guesses the job scores a point. Allow bonus points for spelling the job title aloud correctly. Keep the score on the whiteboard.

ADJECTIVES FOR PEOPLE

4, 5 and 6 👥 👥👥 Before the task, check understanding of *adjectives* and elicit examples. Elicit the difference between *body* /ˈbɒdi/ and *character* /ˈkærɪktə/. Students complete Exercises 4 and 5 individually, then check their answers with a partner. Encourage students to use the Glossary. Students then work in pairs and add more adjectives to the table in Exercise 4. Display the table on an interactive whiteboard and ask for volunteers to complete it. As a class, add more adjectives to the table. Check understanding and pronunciation.

> ### Answers
> #### Exercise 4
>
> | body | character |
> | --- | --- |
> | good-looking /ɡʊdˈlʊkɪŋ/ | clever /ˈklevə/ |
> | fit /ˈfɪt/ | friendly /ˈfrendli/ |
> | strong /ˈstrɒŋ/ | helpful /ˈhelpfəl/ |
> | slim /ˈslɪm/ | interesting /ˈɪntrəstɪŋ/ |
> | | kind /kaɪnd/ |
> | | polite /pəˈlaɪt/ |
>
> **Exercise 5:** 2 clever 3 kind 4 helpful 5 polite

7 👥 Students work in pairs and make sentences about the jobs in Exercise 1. Model the activity. Allow students about five minutes to say the sentences. Monitor and give feedback on sentence structure and pronunciation of key vocabulary.

Optional activity

Ask for volunteers to write their sentences from Exercise 7 on the whiteboard. Students work in pairs and discuss which statements they agree with and which ones they disagree with. Remind them to use the expressions for opinions, i.e. *I think + should* and *I don't think + should*. Allow up to eight minutes for discussion, then a lead class discussion at the end.

COLLOCATIONS FOR JOBS

8 Students complete the task individually, then check their answers with a partner. Remind them to use the Glossary to check the meaning of unknown words. Display the sentences on an interactive whiteboard and go over the answers as a class. Underline the collocations, i.e. *build houses*, *do experiments* /ɪkˈsperɪmənts/, *practise law* /ˈpræktɪs ˈlɔː/, *design roads*, *fly planes*, *design* /dɪˈzaɪn/ *houses*, *work on a farm* and *serve food* /sɜːv fuːd/. Check understanding of the collocations and drill the pronunciation as a class.

Answers

1 builder   2 scientist   3 lawyer   4 engineer   5 pilot
6 architect   7 farmer   8 waiter

LISTENING 2

PREPARING TO LISTEN

Lead-in

Students work in small groups and discuss any jobs they may have done in the past. Ask students to tell the group what job it was, how they got it, and what they had to do. If students have never worked before, ask them to talk about what jobs people in their family have. At the end, ask group members to tell the class about their partners' jobs. Elicit new vocabulary, e.g. *apply for a job*, *have experience* and *look for job*.

PREDICTING CONTENT

1 Students complete the task individually, then check their answers with a partner. Encourage students to check the meaning of new vocabulary in the Glossary. Check the answers as a class. Elicit the meaning of new vocabulary:

apply /əˈplaɪ/ *for a job*	to send your documents to a company in order to get a job
fitness instructor /ˈfɪtnəs ɪnˈstrʌktə/	a person who teachers sports at a sport centre
look for /lʊk fə/	to search for
exercise /ˈeksəsaɪz/	physical activity that you do to make your body stronger
to have experience /ɪkˈspɪərɪəns/	to have knowledge of something from doing it

Answers

1 University of Yukon / Sports Centre / Canada
2 fitness instructor
3 *has (have) experience* means the person knows something or can do something because they did it before.
4 a fit and strong person; a person who knows three or more sports; a person who can speak English and French; a person who has experience; a person who can teach sport and exercise; a person who is friendly and helpful

2 Divide the class into Students A and B. Student As open the book on page 195 and Student Bs open the book on page 197. Students work in their groups and check comprehension and the new vocabulary for the task. Encourage them to use the Glossary. Students then work in pairs of Student A and Student B and discuss the questions about the two applicants. Encourage students to answer the questions in complete sentences. At the end, ask for volunteers to give the answers using full sentences.

Answers

question	Student A	Student B
1	man	woman
2	Alan Green	Lucy Lau
3	Portland, US	Vancouver (Canada)
4	English and French	English, French and Cantonese
5	football, basketball, karate, judo	zumba, pilates, yoga, tennis

3 👥 Students work in the same pairs and show each other the descriptions of the candidates. With a larger class, ask the pairs to work together in groups of four. Encourage students to use *think + should* structures to express their opinions. Allow three or four minutes for discussion, then ask students to share their opinions with the class.

WHILE LISTENING

4 🔊 6.5 👤👥 Students listen to the audio and answer the question. Then they check their answer with a partner. Elicit words and phrases students heard which gave them the answer. If necessary, refer them to the audio script on page 218.

> **Answer**
> They choose Lucy Lau. (*I think we should choose Lucy. She teaches zumba, pilates and yoga – and these are very popular right now. [...] Would you like me to write to Lucy and <u>tell her the good news</u>?*)

LISTENING FOR DETAIL

5 🔊 6.5 👤👥 Before listening again, ask students to read the questions and check any unknown words in the Glossary. With a stronger class, ask students to predict the answers. Students then listen again and complete the task individually. Then they check their answers with a partner. During class feedback, discuss the correct answers. If necessary, tell students to look at the audio script on page 218 and underline the correct answer.

> **Answers**
> 1 a (*Which job is this? Is it for the fitness instructor? Or for the sports-centre nurse?*)
> 2 b (*But he's a student. I think a good fitness instructor should be a good teacher.*)
> 3 c (*Ah good! She's a sports scientist ... and she's a fitness instructor!*)
> 4 b (*But I think a fitness instructor has to be fit and strong.*)
> 5 a (*But if you want to be fit, you have to work hard. I think Alan can help people do that.*)
> 6 b (*But I think we should choose Lucy. She teaches zumba, pilates and yoga ...*)

DISCUSSION

6 👥 Students work in pairs and discuss whether they agree with Paul. Before the discussion, elicit expressions that are used to express opinion, e.g. *I think that, I believe that, in my opinion*, etc. Monitor and write down any common mistakes that you hear. At the end, write the mistakes on the whiteboard or say them aloud. Elicit the correct answers from the class.

CRITICAL THINKING

👥 At this point in each unit, students are asked to begin to think about the speaking task they will do at the end of the unit (*Choose a person for a job*). Give them a minute to look at the box.

APPLY

> **Optional activity**
> 👥 Remind students about the discussion between the two managers in Listening 2. Ask them about which criteria the managers were looking for in a fitness instructor. Draw students' attention to the Explanation box and elicit the answers, i.e. *a person with experience, someone who can teach tennis or volleyball, someone who can make the students work hard.* Check understanding of *criteria* /kraɪ'tɪərɪə/ (a set of standards by which we judge something).

1 👥 Students complete the task in pairs. Allow about five minutes for the activity. Encourage them to use the Glossary. Check the answers as a class.

> **Answers**
> 1 nurse (at the Sports Centre)
> 2 a person who has experience
> 3 a person who is helpful

ANALYZE

2 👥 Students complete the task in small groups. Encourage them to answer the questions in complete sentences. Allow about five minutes for discussion, then lead a class discussion at the end. Write down any new vocabulary on the whiteboard and elicit the meaning from the class.

Possible answers

1 A nurse has to: look after people in hospital; give people medicine; help people in hospital; talk to people in hospital; work at night; serve food and drink (sometimes).
2 A nurse should be: polite, clever, kind, strong, fit.

3 👤 👥 Students complete the task in pairs. Encourage them to use the Glossary. While monitoring, check understanding of the vocabulary in the table. Discuss students' answers as a class.

Optional activity

👤 👥 Ask students to think of a dream job they would like to do in the future. Students give a short presentation with photographs to illustrate it and the criteria needed to do the job. They work in groups and tell their group members about the job.

SPEAKING

PREPARATION FOR SPEAKING

HAVE/HAS TO

1 🔊 6.6 👤 👥 Students complete the task individually, then listen to the audio to check their answers. Play the audio again and ask students to repeat the sentences together. Ask students to work in pairs and practise saying the sentences.

Answers

1 has 2 has to 3 have 4 have 5 has 6 have to
7 has to 8 have to

Explanation box

👥 Draw students' attention to the Explanation box on page 116. Ask concept-checking questions about the example sentences. Some students may be confused by the other uses of *have*, i.e. as a verb meaning 'to have possession of something' or as an auxiliary verb in the Present perfect. If necessary, write three example sentences with these three different uses and elicit the differences in form and meaning. With a more advanced class, elicit synonyms of *have to* and *has to*, i.e. *must* and *should*. Ask students for example sentences.

2 and 3 👤 👥 Students complete Exercises 2 and 3 individually. Then they check their answers with a partner. Allow about five minutes for both tasks, then check the answers as a class.

Answers

Exercise 2
1 a noun phrase (*two jobs, a very good job, a difficult job*, etc.)
2 a verb (an infinitive)
Exercise 3
1 Students have to read a lot of books.
2 My teacher has to walk to school.
3 You don't have to study English.
4 Teachers don't have to work at night.
5 Do we have to learn this grammar?
6 What does a nurse have to do?

PRONUNCIATION FOR SPEAKING

4 and 5 🔊 6.6 👥 Students listen to the audio and discuss their answers to Exercises 4 and 5 in pairs. Check the answers as a class. Play the audio one more time and pause after each sentence to check the pronunciation of *has to*, *have to*, *has* and *have*. Ask students to repeat the sentences. Students work in pairs and practise the sentences.

Answers

Exercise 5: 1 a 2 d 3 b 4 c

6 and 7 👤 👥 Before the speaking task, model the answers using *have to* and *has to*. Give students two or three minutes to make notes. Students prepare their notes individually, then tell each other about the jobs. Monitor and make sure students use the expressions *have to* and *has to* correctly. Allow about five minutes for the task, then ask students to change partners. Students choose another job from Exercise 6 and repeat the task.

SPEAKING TASK

👥 Ask students to reread the speaking task. If necessary, ask them to read the job advertisement from the Critical thinking section on page 114. Discuss any unknown vocabulary as a class.

PREPARE

1 👥 Divide the class into Students A, B and C. Students work in small groups with students of the same letter. Ask them to read the applications and highlight the key information that appears in them. Encourage students to check the meaning of the new words in the Glossary or an online dictionary. If necessary, ask students to find information about where the applicants are from, what experience they have, and why they want the job.

PRACTISE

2 👥👤 Students work in groups of three consisting of Student A, B and C. Model the first question and elicit the answer. Students practise asking and answering the questions about their applicants. With a weaker class, students work individually and read the questions. Allow up to ten minutes to complete the answers. Monitor and help with reading comprehension.

Answers

question	Inesh	Morena	Darren
1	Yogyakarta/ Indonesia	São Paulo/ Brazil	Manchester/ England
2	Indonesian, Chinese, Spanish, English	Portuguese, Spanish, English	English (can't speak French)
3	yes – studying to be a nurse in a big hospital in Jakarta	no	no
4	no	yes – nurse in a children's hospital	yes – nurse in a big hospital
5	be polite and friendly – because nurses have to help doctors and work with patients	be fit and strong – because nurses have to work hard	play football, basketball and go to the gym – because a sports-centre nurse should do sports

DISCUSS

3 👥 Students work in groups of three. Each group should consist of a Student A, B and C. Students discuss who should get the job and why. Before they begin, draw their attention to the useful expressions and elicit example sentences from the class. Monitor and write down any common mistakes.

4 👥 Ask each group to present their decision to the class. Students have to give reasons for their decision. At the end, write the mistakes you noted during monitoring on the whiteboard or say them aloud. Elicit the correct answers from the class.

OBJECTIVES REVIEW

See Teaching tips, pages 10–11, for ideas about using the Objectives review with your students.

WORDLIST

See Teaching tips, pages 10–11, for ideas about how to make the most of the Wordlist with your students.

REVIEW TEST

See pages 116–117 for the photocopiable Review test for this unit and Teaching tips, pages 10–11, for ideas about when and how to administer the Review test.

ADDITIONAL SPEAKING TASK

See page 131 for an additional speaking task related to this unit.

Ask students to read the job advertisement and check understanding of any new vocabulary. Divide the class into groups A, B, C and D and allow time to read the roles. Monitor and help with any new vocabulary. Students A and B interview Students C and D for the advertised job. With an advanced class, tell students to add more questions to the role cards. After the interviews, Students A and B discuss who they would select for the job and ask each pair of the interviewers to present their decision to the class.

RESEARCH PROJECT

Create a training video for an interview

Ask students to think about different ways people should prepare for interviews. They could use the tools on the Cambridge LMS to share their ideas. They could think about how to dress, how to greet the interviewer, what questions the interviewer might ask and how you might answer these questions.

Tell students they are going to create a short video which teaches people how to prepare for an interview. Different groups in the class could present one aspect of this (e.g. how to dress). Ask them to plan the video by creating a script. They will also have to think about who will direct and record the video, who will do the editing and who will do the presenting. The class could upload their video to the Cambridge LMS or a video-sharing website.

7 HOMES AND BUILDINGS

UNLOCK YOUR KNOWLEDGE

1 👥 Display the photograph on an interactive whiteboard. Students complete the task in pairs. Encourage them to use the Glossary to check the meaning of the words in the box. Check understanding and the pronunciation of the words in the box, i.e. *African* /ˈæfrɪkən/ (of or from Africa), *Asian* /ˈeɪʒən/ (of or from Asia), *European* /ˌjʊərəˈpiːən/ (of or from Europe), *faraway* /ˌfɑːrəˈweɪ/ (a long way away), *interesting* /ˈɪntrəstɪŋ/ (unusual, exciting), *normal* /ˈnɔːməl/ (ordinary or usual), *traditional* /trəˈdɪʃənəl/ (following a custom) and *unusual* /ʌnˈjuːʒuəl/ (different from others of the same type in a way that is surprising, interesting or attractive).

2 👥 Model the task before students begin. Use the example sentence from the book. Encourage students to use the Glossary or a bilingual dictionary. Monitor and check that students are using the correct vocabulary. During class feedback, display the house on an interactive whiteboard. Ask for volunteers to label different parts of the house on the photograph. Ask the class to help the writers spell the words, e.g. *windows*, *doors*, *roof*, *walls*, etc.

Background note

The photograph shows a Himalayan monastery called Taktsang Goemba ('Tiger's Nest') located in the Paro Valley in Bhutan. It is one of Bhutan's most sacred religious sites.

WATCH AND LISTEN

Video script

▶ Today, Mumbai in India is an international centre. The number of people who live there has grown a lot. Many of these people live in slums. For example, the Dharavi Slum, where over one million people live in an area smaller than two square kilometres. It is home to more people than any other place on the planet. The number of homes in the slum grew and grew. In the small streets of the slum, there is a whole city. A lot of small businesses, shops and schools can be found in the spaces between the houses. The businesses in Dharavi earn 350 million dollars a year.

Krishna has his own business. He sells satellite TV to the people in Dharavi. Krishna has so many contacts in Dharavi that he has become an important person in the community. Today, he is visiting a family. Sushila, her husband and three children all live and eat in this very small space. Every year, when there is a lot of rain during the monsoon, their home becomes full of water. To stop these problems, the family has decided to pull down their home and build a new one. Krishna has many people building the new house. Some weeks later, the walls are finished, so the painting can now begin. Krishna asks Sushila's family to see their new home. They are very pleased with the work and soon start to make it look like a home again.

PREPARING TO WATCH

Optional lead-in

▶ 👤 👥 Select two or three scenes from the video before the class. Write down the timing positions so that you can easily find the scenes during the activity. Display the first scene, by pausing the video, so that the whole class can see it easily. Play *I Spy* with the class. A student chooses an object they can see in the scene from the video and says 'I spy with my little eye something beginning with ...' and names the letter the object begins with. The other students guess what object the student is thinking of. Model the question, i.e. *Is it a/an ...?* and do the first *I Spy* turn yourself. The student who guesses the object takes over from the speaker.

UNDERSTANDING KEY VOCABULARY

1 👤 👥 Students complete the task individually, then check their answers with a partner.

Students check their answers in the Glossary. During group feedback, use concept-checking questions to check understanding of the new vocabulary and elicit the pronunciation of the new words.

Answers

1 crowd /kraʊd/ 2 bakery /ˈbeɪkəri/
3 painting /ˈpeɪntɪŋ/ 4 slum /slʌm/ 5 narrow /ˈnærəʊ/
6 crowded /ˈkraʊdɪd/

2 ▶ 👤 👥 Students watch the video without the sound and complete the task. Then they check their answers with a partner. Check the answers as a class.

Answers

1 f 2 c 3 g 4 e 5 a 6 b 7 d

3 👥 Students discuss the question in pairs. Ask them to use the information from Exercises 1 and 2, in addition to what they saw while watching without sound.

Answer

b

WHILE WATCHING

UNDERSTANDING MAIN IDEAS

4 ▶ 👥 👥 Students watch the video and check their answer. During class feedback, elicit which answers include details (d, e) and which ones are not mentioned (a, c).

UNDERSTANDING DETAIL

5 ▶ 👥 Ask students to work in pairs. Students read the statements and predict the answers. Then play the video again and ask students to check their answers. Allow time for students to discuss their answers, then check as a class.

Answers

1 T (Many of these people live in slums.)
2 F (A lot of small businesses, shops and schools can be found in the spaces between the houses.)
3 T (The businesses in Dharavi earn 350 million dollars a year.)
4 F (Krishna has his own business. He sells satellite TV to the people in Dharavi.)

5 T (Sushila, her husband and three children all live and eat in this very small space. Every year, when there is a lot of rain during the monsoon, their home becomes full of water.)
6 T (Krishna has many people building the new house.)
7 F (Sushila, her husband and three children all live and eat in this very small space.)
8 F (They are very pleased with the work ...)

DISCUSSION

6 👥 👥 Ask students to think of ideas for and against living in the slum versus for and against living in an apartment. On the whiteboard, draw a 'for and against' table, with two rows for each type of living (see example in Listening 2, page 131). Allow students up to eight minutes to make notes about the discussion question. Students work in pairs and discuss it. Monitor and help students with grammar and vocabulary for the task. Lead class discussion at the end. Ask each pair to explain their point of view to the class. As a class, complete the table on the whiteboard.

LISTENING 1

PREPARING TO LISTEN

Optional lead-in

👥 👥 To review colours and places, prepare one set of flashcards with colours, e.g. *red, orange, blue, green, white*, etc., and another set with places, e.g. *school, hospital, restaurant, café, train station, cinema, electronics shop, bakery*, etc. Students work in pairs and discuss which colours are the most suitable for each building. Allow five or six minutes for discussion, then ask the pairs to explain their choices to the class.

UNDERSTANDING KEY VOCABULARY

1, 2 and 3 👥 Students complete Exercises 1 and 2 in pairs. Encourage them to use the Glossary. Lead class feedback and check understanding and pronunciation of the key vocabulary, i.e.

psychologist /saɪˈkɒlədʒɪst/	someone who studies how people think
architect /ˈɑːkɪtekt/	a person who designs buildings
restaurant /ˈrestrɒnt/	a place where meals are prepared and served to customers

manager /ˈmænɪdʒə/	the person who is responsible for managing a place
clean /kliːn/	not dirty
dirty /ˈdɜːti/	unwashed or stained
sad /sæd/	unhappy
thirsty /ˈθɜːsti/	needing to drink
hungry /ˈhʌŋgri/	wanting or needing food
same /seɪm/	exactly like another
fresh /freʃ/	new, recently done
healthy /ˈhelθi/	good for your health
different /ˈdɪfərənt/	not the same
change /tʃeɪndʒ/	to become different
way /weɪ/	the manner in which something happens

Students then work in pairs and ask and answer the questions from Exercise 2. If necessary, point out that one answer (*Yes, it is*) can be used twice and that the answer to item 8 will depend on students' opinions, so either *Yes, it can* or *No, it can't* is possible. Monitor and check the pronunciation of the key vocabulary.

> **Answers**
> **Exercise 1:** 1 b 2 c 3 a
> **Exercise 2**
> 1 dirty
> 2 sad
> 3 Yes, it does.
> 4 Yes, they do.
> 5 Yes, it is.
> 6 Yes, it is
> 7 Yes, they are.
> 8 Yes, it can. / No, it can't.

PRONUNCIATION FOR LISTENING

4 (◀) **7.1** 👤👥 Ask students to look at the six phrases and identify what the red letters have in common (they are consonants) and what the blue letters have in common (they are vowels). Ask students to speculate how these letters might be pronounced when they occur together, then play the audio and ask the class to answer the question. Draw students' attention to the Explanation box. Ask for volunteers to pronounce the example sentences in the box and elicit which sounds

are linked. Play the audio again and ask students to repeat the sentences as a class. At the end, allow three or four minutes for students to work in pairs to practise saying the sentences and linking words. Monitor and give feedback on linking words.

> **Answer**
> c (We pronounce the red and blue letters together.)

WHILE LISTENING

LISTENING FOR MAIN IDEAS

5 (◀) **7.2** 👥 Students read the sentences and predict the answers in pairs. Encourage them to use the Glossary to check the meaning of unknown words. Before listening, check understanding of *walls* /wɔːlz/ (vertical structures, often made of stone or brick, which divide the rooms in a house). Students listen and check their predictions. Go over the answers as a class.

> **Answers**
> 1 a 2 a 3 b 4 b

LISTENING FOR DETAIL

6 and 7 (◀) **7.2** 👥 Display the Skills box on an interactive whiteboard. Give students a minute to read the box, then elicit the meaning of *reason* /ˈriːzən/ (something which provides an excuse or explanation). Elicit examples of reasons by asking questions beginning with *why*. Students work in pairs and match the questions with reasons. Then they listen to the audio and check their answers. Check answers as a class. If necessary, tell students to scan the audio script on pages 218–219 and find the correct answers.

> **Answers**
> 1 b 2 d 3 c 4 a 5 e

DISCUSSION

8 👤👥 Give students four or five minutes to make notes about the discussion questions. Students then work in pairs and discuss the questions. Monitor and give feedback on linking words. Write down any common mistakes you hear during monitoring and elicit the correct answers at the end of the task.

⊙ LANGUAGE DEVELOPMENT

VOCABULARY FOR ROOMS

1, 2 and 3 👥 Students work in pairs and complete Exercises 1, 2 and 3. Encourage students to use the Glossary. Allow 10–12 minutes for the tasks. Then tell students to check their answers with another pair – allow five minutes for this. At the end, check the answers as a class and check understanding of the new vocabulary. Practise pronunciation of the new words as a class.

Answers

Exercise 2
a lecture hall /'lektʃə hɔːl/
b classroom /'klɑːsruːm/
c language lab / language centre /'læŋgwɪdʒ læb / 'læŋgwɪdʒ 'sentə/
d bedroom /'bedruːm/
e living room /'lɪvɪŋ ruːm/
f computer centre /computer lab /kəm'pjuːtə 'sentə / kəm'pjuːtə læb/
g bathroom /'bɑːθruːm/
h seminar room /'semɪnɑː ruːm/

Exercise 3
1 d
2 b (h possible)
3 h (b possible)
4 e
5 a
6 f (b possible)
7 c (d possible)
8 g

4 👥 Students complete the task in pairs. Monitor and discuss with each pair whether their answers have changed and if so, how.

5 👤👥 Students complete the task in pairs, then check their answers with another pair. Lead group feedback and discuss why the words fit into one category and not the other.

Answers

1 bedroom, living room, bathroom
2 lecture hall, classroom, language lab, computer centre, seminar room

Optional activity

👥 👥👥 Ask students to work in pairs and add more nouns to the two vocabulary groups in Exercise 5. Encourage students to use the Glossary or a bilingual dictionary. Allow up to ten minutes for the task. Then ask students to work with another pair and compare their lists. Monitor and check whether students use the vocabulary correctly. At the end, display Exercise 5 on an interactive whiteboard and ask for volunteers to add new words to each group. Ask the rest of the class to spell the new words for the writers. Check understanding of the meaning and pronunciation.

ADJECTIVES FOR FURNITURE

6 and 7 👥 Display the photographs on an interactive whiteboard. Before students begin, model the questions and answers with a stronger student. Students work in pairs and take turns asking and answering questions about the furniture in the photographs. Then they complete Exercise 7. Check answers as a class. Ask volunteers to name the pieces of furniture in the photographs. Drill pronunciation of the new vocabulary.

Answers

a bed /bed/ b coffee table /'kɒfi teɪbl/ c sofa /'səʊfə/ d chair /tʃeə/ e bookcase /'bʊk keɪs/ f study desk /'stʌdi desk/ g armchair /'ɑːmtʃeə/ h lamp /læmp/

8 👥 Ask students to underline adjectives in the phrases in Exercise 6. Tell them to check the meaning of these adjectives in the Glossary. Students complete the task in pairs, then check their answers with another pair. Monitor and check understanding of the adjectives. As a class, elicit the meaning of the adjectives and ask students for examples of other furniture or objects that can be described using these adjectives. Elicit pronunciation of the adjectives, i.e. *comfortable* /'kʌmfətəbl/, *glass* /glɑːs/, *leather* /'leðə/, *plastic* /'plæstɪk/, *wooden* /'wʊdən/, *brown* /braʊn/, *soft* /sɒft/ and *metal* /'metəl/. Notice that *comfortable* and *furniture* /'fɜːnɪtʃə/ are often mispronounced, so it may be useful to drill the correct pronunciation as a class.

Answers

glass, leather, plastic, wooden, metal

Optional activity

👤👥👥 Tell students that they are going to prepare an ideas map of their house. Start by drawing an ideas map of your own house/apartment on the whiteboard as an example. Use *there is* and *there are* expressions as you explain. The model ideas map should have the words *my home* in the middle, and each branch should represent different rooms. Branching out from each room should be examples of typical furniture in the rooms. When you finish, erase the ideas map and tell students to make their own ideas maps. Students work on their ideas maps for 10–12 minutes. Encourage them to use the Glossary or online dictionaries. Monitor and check the vocabulary and spelling. Then students work in small groups and explain the ideas maps of their homes to the group.

LISTENING 2

PREPARING TO LISTEN

UNDERSTANDING KEY VOCABULARY

1 👤👥👥 Students complete the task individually, then check their answers with a partner. Encourage students to use the Glossary. Check answers as a class and elicit the meaning of the key vocabulary. Ask students for the opposites (antonyms) of the words in the box. The opposites are highlighted in the sentences. Elicit and drill pronunciation of any difficult vocabulary.

> **Answers**
>
> 1 cheap /tʃiːp/
> 2 quiet /kwaɪət/
> 3 comfortable /ˈkʌmfətəbl/
> 4 far /fɑː/

> **Language note**
>
> Some students may confuse *quiet* /kwaɪət/ (silent) and *quite* /kwaɪt/ (a little / somewhat). Ask for a volunteer to write the two words on the whiteboard and tell the class to spell them out to help the writer. Say the two words aloud a few times to help students notice the difference in pronunciation. Elicit example sentences from the class to show the difference in meaning.

2 👥👥 Students complete the task in pairs. If necessary, tell them to use the Glossary. Check the answers as a class. Elicit the meaning and the pronunciation of *modern* /ˈmɒdən/ (designed and made using the most recent ideas and methods).

> **Answers**
>
> 1 adjectives
> 2 a very b quite c not very

WHILE LISTENING

LISTENING FOR MAIN IDEAS

3 🔊 7.3 👥👥 👤 Display the map on an interactive whiteboard. Before students listen to the audio, ask them to work in pairs and describe to each other what they can see on the map, i.e. places and types of building. Check understanding of the buildings and places by referring to the map. Students listen to the audio and answer the questions individually. Then they check their answers with a partner. Check answers as a class. If necessary, check understanding of *office* /ˈɒfɪs/, *town centre* /taʊn ˈsentə/, *windows* /ˈwɪndəʊz/ and *train station* /ˈtreɪn ˈsteɪʃən/.

> **Answers**
>
> 1 b 2 c 3 b

LISTENING FOR DETAIL

Skills note

👥👥👥 Depending on the class level, students may not be familiar with note-taking. If necessary, elicit basic note-taking principles before the task. Students should not try to write down the complete sentences, but rather note down the key words they hear in the discussion. Tell students not to get distracted with spelling the words they hear, but to just write them down while listening. They can correct their spelling afterwards.

4 and 5 🔊 7.3 👤👥👥 Before students listen again, ask them to identify the town centre, the park and the train station on the map displayed on the interactive whiteboard. Students listen and complete the task individually. Then allow them five minutes to compare their notes with a partner. If necessary, play the audio again to help them check their answers. With a weaker class, students may need to listen for the second time while looking at the audio script on page 219. Check answers as a class. Display the table on an interactive whiteboard and ask for volunteers to complete it.

Answers

place	+	−
town centre	• good place • near good roads	• very old buildings • cold in winter, hot in summer • not comfortable • expensive
park	• quiet • not far from a big road / near a big road	• (quite) far from the town centre
train station	• good for travel	• not cheap / expensive

1 big 2 yellow

DISCUSSION

6 👤👥 Allow students four or five minutes to make notes about the discussion question. Students complete the task in pairs. Monitor and help with grammar and vocabulary. Write down any common mistakes you can hear during monitoring. At the end, correct the mistakes as a class.

Optional activity

👥👥👥 Prepare a handout with a photograph of a building by a famous architect, such as Frank Gehry (e.g. Dancing House (Prague), Ray and Maria Stata Center (Cambridge, MA) or the Guggenheim Museum (Bilbao)). Alternatively, display the photograph on an interactive whiteboard. Students work in pairs and discuss: *What materials are used to make the building? What is this building probably used for?* and *Would you like to live in a building designed by this architect, and why/why not?*. Monitor and help with vocabulary. Allow up to eight minutes for discussion, then ask students to share their ideas with another pair. At the end, ask each group to present their ideas to the class.

CRITICAL THINKING

👥👥👥 At this point in each unit, students are asked to begin to think about the speaking task they will do at the end of the unit (*Discuss ideas for a new building*). Give them a minute to look at the box.

UNDERSTAND

1 and 2 👥👥 👥👥👥 Display the photographs on an interactive whiteboard. Students discuss the questions in pairs. Allow five or six minutes for the tasks. Ask students to give reasons for their answers in Exercise 2. If necessary, model the answers. Monitor and encourage students to answer in complete sentences and to support their opinions.

Answers
1 Photograph c (Ithaa)
2 Photograph a (At.mosphere)
3 Photograph b (The Rock)

APPLY

3 👤👥 Before the task, draw students' attention to the Skills box on page 132. Display it on the interactive whiteboard and give students a minute to read it. Ask them whether they have ever made a table with reasons 'for' and 'against'. Some students may remember using a similar table in Listening 2; others may have used one in a writing class. Elicit what information we put in the column *for* and what information we put in the column *against*, and what symbols are used to represent 'for' (+) and 'against' (−). Students complete the task individually, then check their answers with a partner. Tell students to use the Glossary to check the meaning of any new vocabulary. Discuss answers as a class. Display the table on an interactive whiteboard and ask for volunteers to explain their reasons for each building. Complete the table as a class.

4 👥👥 If possible, students should work with new partners. Students discuss the question in pairs. While monitoring, ask students to explain their reasons to you.

Optional activity

👥👥 👥👥👥 With a more advanced class, students can use the table to discuss the pros and cons of living in an apartment versus living in a house. Allow students up to ten minutes to complete the table with their reasons. Students then work with another pair and present the reasons to each other. Each group has to decide whether they would prefer to live in an apartment or in a house. Monitor and make sure students give their reasons in complete sentences and support their ideas. Help with grammar and vocabulary for the task. At the end, each group presents their choice to the class and gives the reasons.

SPEAKING

PREPARATION FOR SPEAKING

1 and 2 (◀7.4) 👤👥 Students listen to the audio, then complete Exercise 2 individually. Allow about seven minutes for the task, then ask students to check their answers with a partner. Encourage them to use the Glossary if necessary. Check answers as a class. Display the table on an interactive whiteboard and elicit the answers from students. Check understanding of *give a reason, give an opinion, agree or disagree* and *ask for an opinion*.

| Answers

• **give a reason**
  It's near some good roads.
  Because the buildings in the town centre are very old.
  They are cold in winter and hot in summer.
  They're not comfortable places.
  It's quiet and it's not far from a big road.
  It's quite far from the town.
  It's good for travel.
  The buildings near the train station aren't cheap.
  Big windows are good.
• **give an opinion**
  It's a good place.
  I don't think we should go there.
  The train station is good.
  I think we should go to the park.
  I think we should have big windows.
• **agree or disagree**
  I'm not sure.
  Yes, I agree.
• **ask for an opinion**
  What about here?
  What do you think?
  Why not?
  What about here?
  What do you think?
  What about here?
  What about the design?
  What about you?

ASKING FOR AN OPINION

3 👤👥 Students complete the task individually, then check their answers with a partner.

| Answers

1 you 2 blue 3 think 4 Indian food

4 👥👥👥 Ask students to work in pairs and answer questions 1, 2 and 4 in Exercise 3 with their own ideas. Allow them three or four minutes to make notes. Before they start, ask for a pair of volunteers to model the questions and answers. Ask students to stand up and ask their questions to five other students. Monitor and give feedback on the intonation.

GIVING AN OPINION

> **Language note**
>
> 👥👥👥 Students are going to practise using *should* to make suggestions or give opinions. Before the task, give example sentences similar to the target language in Exercise 5 and elicit the meaning of *should* /ʃʊd/ (used to say when we give advice). Check understanding and elicit the form *should* + verb (without *to*).

5 👥 If possible, ask students to work with new partners. Students complete the task in pairs. If necessary, tell them to use the Glossary. Ask students to take turns and practise saying their sentences. Monitor and give feedback on sentence stress. If necessary, correct the pronunciation of the key vocabulary.

AGREEING AND DISAGREEING

6 👥 Students complete the task in pairs. Check the answers as a class. Practise expressions for giving opinions and agreeing and disagreeing as a class. Give an opinion from Exercise 5 and point to students to answer using expressions of agreement or disagreement from Exercise 6. Drill the expressions for a couple of minutes.

| Answers

1 D 2 A 3 D 4 A

7 👥 Divide the class into Students A and B. Tell them to read their roles and practise the dialogues for three or four minutes. Monitor and give feedback on vocabulary and pronunciation. Make sure students use the expressions introduced in the section correctly. Write down any common mistakes you can hear while monitoring. Discuss the mistakes as a class and elicit the correct answers. Students then change their roles and practise the dialogue again.

SPEAKING TASK

PREPARE

1 👥 Display the map of Green Town on an interactive whiteboard. Tell students that they are going to discuss the best location for a restaurant in Green Town. As a class, ask students to describe the things they can see on the map, e.g. *roads*, *island*, *city centre*, *beach*, *sea*. Then students complete the task in pairs. Check answers as a class.

> ### Answers
> 1 open a new restaurant (in Green Town)
> 2 near the sea
> 3 Green Town is a small town that is popular with tourists. / It's a tourist town.
> 4 b
> 5 possible places to open your restaurant

PRACTISE

2, 3 and 4 👥 Students complete the activities in pairs. Tell students to use the Glossary if necessary. Monitor and check understanding of the vocabulary. Encourage students to discuss the questions using complete sentences. Allow about ten minutes for the task. Write down any common pronunciation mistakes and elicit the correct answers at the end of the task.

5 👤 Students practise saying their answers from Exercises 2–4. Monitor and give feedback on pronunciation and sentence stress.

> ### Optional activity
> 👤👥 Ask students to record their answers. Students first go over their answers and underline the most stressed words in each sentence. Allow them to practise the sentence stress for three or four minutes. Monitor and check whether the stress pattern is correct. Students record themselves saying the sentences. Students listen to their recordings in pairs and give each other feedback on sentence stress and pronunciation. At the end, ask for volunteers to play their recordings to the class. If possible, highlight the strengths, e.g. word pronunciation, intonation or sentence stress.

PRESENT

6 and 7 👥👥👥 Students work with new partners and complete the task. Monitor and write down any common mistakes in pronunciation and grammar. At the end, write the mistakes on the whiteboard or say them aloud and elicit the correct answers from the class. Ask students to share their ideas with the class.

OBJECTIVES REVIEW

See Teaching tips, pages 10–11, for ideas about using the Objectives review with your students.

WORDLIST

See Teaching tips, pages 10–11, for ideas about how to make the most of the Wordlist with your students.

REVIEW TEST

See pages 118–119 for the photocopiable Review test for this unit and Teaching tips, pages 10–11, for ideas about when and how to administer the Review test.

ADDITIONAL SPEAKING TASK

See page 132 for an additional speaking task related to this unit.

If necessary, check understanding of the useful expressions in the Model language section. Ask students to work individually and prepare a list of changes they would like to make in their college. Ensure students focus on the changes related to the physical place, e.g. *We should have more computers in the lab*. Students then work in pairs and share their ideas. Monitor and help with vocabulary for the task. Encourage students to use the model language. Ask students to choose one idea from each list. Students work with another pair and discuss their ideas. Tell students to choose the most interesting idea. At the end, students tell the class which idea they chose and explain why.

RESEARCH PROJECT

> ### Plan and present your ideal home
> Ask each student what would constitute their ideal home. They could think about rooms, size, garden, location and interior design (e.g. furniture, colours). They could note down their ideas on the Cambridge LMS. Ask them to create or find images of some of the things in their ideal home.
>
> Each student presents their ideal home to the rest of the class. This can turn into a friendly competition where the class votes for the best house. Students could use an online voting system. Search for 'voting software' to view some of these.

8 FOOD AND CULTURE

Learning objectives

Before you start the *Unlock your knowledge* section, ask students to read the Learning objectives box so that they have a clear idea of what they are going to learn in this unit. Tell them that you will come back to these objectives at the end of the unit when they review what they have learnt. Give them the opportunity to ask you any questions that they might have.

UNLOCK YOUR KNOWLEDGE

1, 2 and 3 👥 Students discuss the photograph in pairs. Monitor and help with vocabulary for the task. Allow four or five minutes for pair discussion, then ask the pairs to share their answers with the class.

Possible answers

1 pastries, cakes, desserts

WATCH AND LISTEN

Optional lead-in

👥👥👥 Display the video stills on an interactive whiteboard. Ask students to work in pairs and describe the stills to each other. Ask them to write down nouns for what they see in the video stills. Encourage them to use the Glossary or a bilingual dictionary. Allow four or five mintues for the task, then ask students to share their answers with the class. Write down the new vocabulary on the whiteboard. Elicit the spelling and the pronunciation from the class.

Possible answers

market /ˈmɑːkɪt/
people /ˈpiːpl/
food stalls /fuːd stɔːlz/
rice fields /raɪs fiːldz/
rice /raɪs/
family /ˈfæmli/
supper /ˈsʌpə/
dinner /ˈdɪnə/

Video script

▶ China is famous all over the world for its food. And in its capital city, Beijing, you can find many night markets, where they cook chicken, duck, vegetables and noodles.

China has many traditional dishes. Chinese people love to eat together in restaurants.

When they cook at home, Chinese people like to eat a lot of vegetables. They fry them quickly in different sauces. The most popular Chinese food is rice.

These people are planting rice in the mountains. A quarter of the world's rice comes from China. These fields were made 500 years ago and they are still growing rice here today. It is difficult to use machines in the rice fields, so the farmers use animals to help them. They collect and then dry the rice, and then it is ready to cook. Chinese people steam the rice until it is hot and sticky. Family meals are important and everybody enjoys chatting and eating together.

PREPARING TO WATCH

UNDERSTANDING KEY VOCABULARY

Language note

Notice that a few of the food names in the exercise are often mispronounced by students. In *lamb*, we don't pronounce the final *b*; *vegetables* is pronounced /ˈvedʒtəblz/.

1 👤👥 Students complete the task individually, then check their answers with a partner. Finally, students check their answers in the Glossary. During group feedback, use concept-checking questions to check understanding of the new vocabulary and elicit the pronunciation of the new words.

Answers

a chicken /ˈtʃɪkɪn/ b lamb /læm/ c rice /raɪs/
d cheese /tʃiːz/ e beans /biːnz/ f fish /fɪʃ/ g bread /bred/ h vegetables /ˈvedʒtəblz/ i noodles /ˈnuːdlz/

USING YOUR KNOWLEDGE TO PREDICT CONTENT

2 👥👥👥 Students discuss the question in pairs. Allow three or four minutes for pair discussion. Students then compare their answers with another pair. Monitor and check pronunciation of the food names. If necessary, help with vocabulary. Tell students that they will find out the answers while watching the video.

WHILE WATCHING

UNDERSTANDING DETAIL

3 ▶ 👥 👥👥 Students watch the video and check their answers to Exercise 2.

> **Answers**
>
> a (chicken), c (rice), h (vegetables), i (noodles)

4 ▶ 👥 👤 Students work in pairs and predict the answers. Encourage them to use the Glossary if necessary. Before they watch the video again, elicit the meaning of *popular* /ˈpɒpjʊlə/ (liked and enjoyed by many people), *field* /fiːld/ (an area of land used for growing crops) and *meals* /miːlz/ (occasions when food is eaten). Students watch the video and complete the task individually. At the end, check answers as a class. With a weaker class, ask students to scan the video script on page 220 and underline the correct answers.

> **Answers**
>
> 1 b (*... in its capital city, Beijing, you can find many night markets ...*)
> 2 a (*The most popular Chinese food is rice.*)
> 3 a (*A quarter of the world's rice comes from China.*)
> 4 c (*These fields were made 500 years ago ...*)
> 5 a (*Family meals are important ...*)

DISCUSSION

5 👤 👥👥 👥👥👥 Allow students three or four minutes to work individually and make notes about the questions. Encourage students to think of reasons for their opinions. Students then work in pairs and tell each other about the food and culture in their country. Allow about seven minutes for discussion, then ask students to work with another pair. Students tell the group about the food and culture in their partner's country. If students are all from the same country, ask them to compare their answers. Do they all say the same things? Monitor and help with vocabulary and pronunciation. Write down any common mistakes that you hear while monitoring and elicit the correct answers from the class at the end.

LISTENING 1

PREPARING TO LISTEN

UNDERSTANDING KEY VOCABULARY

1 and 2 👤 👥👥 Students complete Exercises 1 and 2 individually, then check their answers with a partner. Encourage students to use the Glossary. Lead class feedback at the end and check understanding and pronunciation of the key vocabulary.

> **Answers**
>
> **Exercise 1:** 1 the UK 2 farming / farmers / facts about farming
> **Exercise 2:** 1 rich /rɪtʃ/ 2 fruit /fruːt/ 3 meat /miːt/
> 4 spend /spend/ money /ˈmʌni/ on 5 grow /grəʊ/
> 6 feed /fiːd/ 7 facts /fækts/ 8 population /pɒpjʊˈleɪʃən/
> 9 million /ˈmɪljən/ 10 half /hɑːf/

PRONUNCIATION FOR LISTENING

3 🔊 8.1 👤 👥👥 Display the Explanation box on an interactive whiteboard. Allow a couple of minutes for students to read the information, then ask for volunteers to say the example sentences aloud. Correct the pronunciation of the numbers if necessary. With a weaker class, drill the example sentences following the highlighted stress pattern. Students then listen and answer the questions individually. Allow a couple of minutes for students to check their answers with a partner. Check the answers as a class.

> **Answers**
>
> 1 70 /ˈsevənti/; 17 /sevənˈtiːn/; 17
> 2 60 /ˈsɪksti/; 16 /sɪksˈtiːn/; 60
> 3 13 /θɜːˈtiːn/; 30 /ˈθɜːti/; 13
> 4 15 /fɪfˈtiːn/; 50 /ˈfɪfti/; 15; 50

> **Optional activity**
>
> 🔊 8.1 👥👥 Play the audio one more time and drill the stress pattern as a class. Students work in pairs and practise saying the dialogues following the stress pattern from the recording. Students practise the dialogues for three or four minutes. Monitor and give feedback on the pronunciation of the numbers. At the end, ask for volunteers to present their dialogues to the class. With a more advanced class, students can write similar dialogues in pairs and act them out in front of the class.

WHILE LISTENING

LISTENING FOR DETAIL

4 and 5 🔊 8.2 👤👥 Students listen to the audio and answer the questions individually. Then they check their answers with a partner. If necessary, encourage students to use the Glossary. At the end, display the audio script from page 220 on an interactive whiteboard and ask students to underline the correct answers to the questions.

Answers

Exercise 4
1 F (*There are many more people who can't grow their own food.*)
2 T (*... people in cities are richer than people in the country.*)
3 T (*This means that food for people becomes food for animals. And that means that food becomes expensive ...*)
4 T (*... modern cities are big and they are becoming bigger.*)
5 F (*More than half the people in the world live in cities.*)
Exercise 5: c

6 and 7 🔊 8.2 👤👥 Before the listening task, review numbers. Write down different numbers on the whiteboard and ask students to say them aloud, e.g. *million, thousand, hundred, fifty, half, twenty-five, quarter*, etc. Correct the pronunciation if necessary. Students then listen and complete Exercise 6 individually. Encourage them to use the Glossary to check the meaning of any new words. Then they check their answers with a partner. Draw their attention to the useful expressions in Exercise 7. Monitor and encourage students to discuss the answers using complete sentences and the expressions from the box. At the end, check the answers as a class.

Optional activity

👤👥 With a more advanced class, ask students to close their books and take notes while they listen. Explain that during lectures, we often write down important numbers and use key words to note down what these numbers refer to. Students listen and take notes. Allow students a couple of minutes to compare their notes with a partner. Monitor and check the quality of the notes. Students then use their notes to complete Exercise 6. If necessary, give advice on how students can improve their note-taking skills, e.g. listen to radio programmes or podcasts on the internet, and take notes while they listen.

Answers

1 4/four
2 60/sixty
3 30/thirty
4 50/fifty
5 ½ /half
6 75/seventy-five

DISCUSSION

8 👤👥 Before the discussion, elicit the meaning of *vegetarian* /ˌvedʒɪˈteərɪən/ (a person who does not eat meat). Give students four or five minutes to make notes about the discussion questions. Students work in pairs and discuss the questions. Monitor and help students with grammar and vocabulary. Write down any common mistakes you hear during monitoring and elicit the correct answers at the end of the task.

Optional activity

👤 Ask students to bring to class their favourite snack, e.g. biscuits, candy, chips, granola bars, juice. Students have to tell the class about their favourite snack, what it is, when they usually eat it, and why they like it. They should teach the class two new words that they learned by reading the packaging.

⊙ LANGUAGE DEVELOPMENT

COUNTABLE AND UNCOUNTABLE NOUNS

Explanation box

Prepare flashcards or slides to illustrate the example sentences in the Explanation box. Display them on an interactive whiteboard and ask questions, i.e. *Are there any apples?*, *Is there any rice?*, etc. Elicit the correct answers from students. Draw their attention to the Explanation box and check understanding of *how much* /haʊ mʌtʃ/ and *how many* /haʊ ˈmeni/. Elicit examples of countable and uncountable nouns.

1 👤👥 Students complete the task individually, then check their answers with a partner. Encourage students to use the Glossary. Allow up to ten minutes for the task. Then check their answers. Display the table on an interactive whiteboard and ask students to complete it. Ask the class to add five more examples to each column.

Answers

countable nouns	uncountable nouns
apple /ˈæpl/, banana /bəˈnɑːnə/, beans, lemon /ˈlemən/, noodles, oranges /ˈɒrɪndʒɪz/, peppers /ˈpepəz/, vegetable	beef /biːf/, bread, cheese, chicken, fish, lamb, milk /mɪlk/, rice

2 and 3 👥 Students complete Exercises 2 and 3 in pairs. Display the exercises on an interactive whiteboard and correct the answers as a class.

Answers

Exercise 2
1 There are some <u>peppers</u> on the <u>plate</u>.
2 There isn't <u>any</u> <u>fish</u> in the <u>bowl</u>.
3 How much <u>rice</u> is <u>there</u>?
4 There aren't <u>any</u> <u>lemons</u> on the <u>table</u>. / There are some <u>lemons</u> on the <u>table</u>.
5 How many <u>apples</u> are <u>there</u>?
Exercise 3
1 Are there <u>any</u> <u>bananas</u>?
2 How many <u>apples</u> <u>are</u> there?
3 Is there <u>any</u> <u>chicken</u>?
4 How much <u>rice</u> <u>is</u> there? / How many <u>bags</u> of <u>rice</u> <u>are</u> there?
5 How many <u>peppers</u> <u>are</u> there?

Optional activity

👥👥👥 Students work in pairs and mark the most stressed words in the sentences in Exercises 2 and 3. Check the answers as a class and drill the sentence stress as a group. Allow three or four minutes for students to practise saying the sentences in pairs. Monitor and give feedback on sentence stress.

Answers

See above.

VOCABULARY FOR FOOD

4 👥👥👥 Students complete the task in pairs. Monitor and check pronunciation of the new words. Encourage students to use the Glossary or refer to the photographs. Students compare their answers with another pair.

Answers

Answers may vary. If so, ask students to explain their reasons.
candy (S) /ˈkændi/
cheeseburger (F) /ˈtʃiːzbɜːgə/
chocolate (S) /ˈtʃɒklət/
fried chicken (F) /fraɪd ˈtʃɪkɪn/
fries (F) /fraɪz/
ice cream (S) /aɪsˈkriːm/
nuts (H) /nʌts/
oranges (H) /ˈɒrɪndʒɪz/
pizza (F) /ˈpiːtsə/
salad (H) /ˈsæləd/
tomatoes (H) /təˈmɑːtəʊz/

Optional activity

👥 Students work in pairs and divide the words into syllables and underline the stressed syllable in each word. Monitor and help with the task if necessary. Allow four or five minutes for the task and check the answers as a class. Drill the pronunciation of the new vocabulary. Then allow students two or three minutes to practise saying the words in pairs.

5 👤👥👥👥 Allow students two or three minutes to read the expressions in the box and make notes about themselves. Students then work in pairs and interview each other about the food they like. Monitor and check pronunciation of the new vocabulary, and encourage students to answer in complete sentences and to give reasons. Write down any common mistakes you hear during monitoring and discuss them as a class. Then ask students to interview five other students in the class and make notes about which food they like and dislike. At the end, ask for volunteers to share with the class who likes what food, and why.

Optional activity

👥👥👥 Prepare slips of paper with the food vocabulary from the Language development section. Divide the class into teams. Students take turns to choose a slip of paper and draw the food item on the whiteboard. Keep the scores on the whiteboard. The team that guesses the word correctly scores a point. The teams score bonus points by spelling the words correctly. The person who correctly guesses the word takes over. Play until all the words have been used. The team with the most points wins.

LISTENING 2

PREPARING TO LISTEN

PREDICTING CONTENT USING VISUALS

1 and 2 👥 Display the charts on an interactive whiteboard. Before the task, model the questions and answers. Students complete Exercise 1 in pairs. Monitor and help with interpreting the pie charts. Encourage students to use the Glossary. Students then discuss the questions in Exercise 2. Discuss answers as a class. Elicit the meaning of *pie chart* /ˈpaɪ tʃɑːt/ and *meals* /miːlz/.

> **Answers**
> **Exercise 2**
> 1 Four (because there are four parts on the chart)
> 2 Yes (because most people think food and family meals are important)
> 3 Two (because there are two parts on the chart)

WHILE LISTENING

LISTENING FOR MAIN IDEAS

3 (🔊 8.3) 👤👤 Students listen to the audio and answer the questions individually. Then they check their answers with a partner. Check answers as a class. If necessary, check understanding of *survey* /ˈsɜːveɪ/ (a study of an opinion or beliefs), *results* /rɪˈzʌlts/ (findings of a survey) and *surprised* /səˈpraɪzd/ (not expecting something).

> **Answers**
> 1 b 2 b 3 c

LISTENING FOR DETAIL

4 (🔊 8.3) 👥👤 Students work in pairs and guess whether the statements are true or false. Encourage students to check any new words in the Glossary. Then they listen and check their answers. With a weaker class, ask students to scan the audio script on page 220 and check their answers. At the end, check the answers as a class.

> **Answers**
> 1 F (*There were 20 students in my survey.*)
> 2 F (*... 15% come from Spain.*)
> 3 T (*You can see here that 'yes' is 70% and 'no' is 30%. That's six people!*)
> 4 F (*... again 'yes' is 70% (70% of 20 students = 14 students)*)
> 5 T (*... 80% of people think family meals are a good place to talk.*)
> 6 T (*... 20% of people think family meals are cheaper and healthier.*)

5 (🔊 8.3) 👥 Students label the diagrams, then listen again to check their answers. Display the charts on an interactive whiteboard and ask for volunteers to label them. If necessary, display the audio script from page 220 and underline the answers in the script.

> **Answers**
> Q1: a England b Italy c/d Spain/Egypt
> Q2: a yes b no
> Q3: a yes b no
> Q4: a a good time to talk b cheaper and healthier

DISCUSSION

6 👤👥 Allow students four or five minutes to make notes about the discussion questions. Students then complete the task in pairs. Monitor and help with grammar and vocabulary for the task. Write down any common mistakes you hear during monitoring. At the end, correct the mistakes as a class.

CRITICAL THINKING

👥 At this point in each unit, students are asked to begin to think about the speaking task they will do at the end of the unit (*Report the results of a survey*). Give them a minute to look at the box.

REMEMBER

1 and 2 👥 Before the task, draw students' attention to the Skills box. Check their understanding of *pie chart* and elicit from students when and why we use pie charts. Also check understanding of *questionnaire* /ˈkwestʃəˈneə/ and *survey* /ˈsɜːveɪ/. Students complete Exercises 1 and 2 in pairs. Encourage them to use the Glossary or a bilingual dictionary to check the meaning of unknown words in the questionnaire in Exercise 2. Monitor and encourage students to answer in complete sentences and to give reasons for their opinions. If necessary, model the answers. Allow five or six minutes for the tasks. At the end, ask students to share their answers with the class.

> **Answers**
> **Exercise 1:** an international food festival

APPLY

3 👥 Divide the class into Groups A and B. If you have a large class, you could have several Group As and several Group Bs. Allow students up to ten minutes to prepare the pie charts. Students can use computer programs such as Excel or Word, or they can draw the pie charts on flip charts. Monitor and help with the interpretation of the numbers. Make sure the pie charts are accurate (although see note on Q2 in answers on the right). Once the pie charts are ready, have students work in A+B pairs. Students tell each other about their pie charts. If necessary, model the task by using one of the pie charts from Listening 2. At the end, display the model pie charts on the right on an interactive whiteboard and ask students to compare them with their own.

Answers

Q1

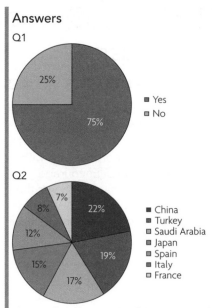

- ■ Yes
- ▫ No

Q2

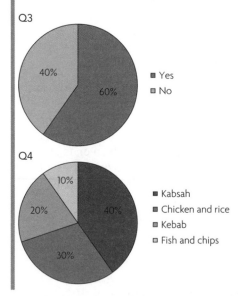

- ■ China
- ■ Turkey
- ▫ Saudi Arabia
- ▫ Japan
- ▫ Spain
- ■ Italy
- ▫ France

The pie chart for question 2 is more complicated than the others. Unless students are good at maths, the segments in their charts only need to approximately reflect the values that are required.

Q3

- ■ Yes
- ▫ No

Q4

- ■ Kabsah
- ■ Chicken and rice
- ▫ Kebab
- ▫ Fish and chips

Optional activity

👥 With a more advanced class, ask students to find a pie chart on the internet. The pie chart can be related to the topic of 'food and culture', or it can be related to students' interests. Monitor the internet search and advise students to add *pie chart* to the keywords they search for. Ask students to print out their pie charts or display them on their laptops/tablets. Students work in small groups and explain the pie charts to each other. Lead group discussion at the end and ask for volunteers to tell the class about their partner's pie chart.

SPEAKING

PREPARATION FOR SPEAKING

INTRODUCING A REPORT

1 ◀) **8.4** 👥 Students work in pairs and organize the introduction. Then they listen and check their answers.

> **Answers**
>
> 5 My questions were on the topic of 'Food and culture'.
> 3 This afternoon, I'm going to tell you about the results of my survey.
> 4 There were 20 students in my survey.
> 2 I'm Sofia.
> 6 I think this is an interesting topic.
> 1 Hello!

2 ◀) **8.5** 👥 Students work in pairs and complete the missing words. Then they listen and check their answers. If necessary, ask students to check their answers in the audio script on page 221.

> **Answers**
>
> 1 morning 2 34 3 traditional 4 interesting
> 5 everybody 6 fast 7 50 8 good

PRONUNCIATION FOR SPEAKING

3 ◀) **8.6** 👤👥 Students listen and complete the task individually. Then they check their answers with a partner. Play the audio again and check the answers. Pause after each sentence and ask the class to repeat following the stress pattern from the recording. If necessary, gently tap on your desk to emphasize the stressed syllables.

> **Answers**
>
> 1 I'm <u>go</u>-ing to <u>tell</u> you a-bout the re-<u>sults</u> of my <u>sur</u>-vey.
> 2 There were <u>fif</u>-teen <u>stu</u>-dents in my <u>sur</u>-vey.
> 3 My <u>to</u>-pic was <u>food</u> and <u>cul</u>-ture.

TALKING ABOUT THE RESULTS

4 and 5 ◀) **8.7** 👤👥 Ask students to work in pairs and scan the audio script for Listening 2 on page 220. Students complete Exercise 4 in pairs, then check their answers with another pair. Then students listen to the audio and complete Exercise 5. Allow time for them to compare their answers with a partner. Check the answers as a class.

> **Answers**
>
> **Exercise 4:** four
> **Exercise 5**
> a 1, 3, 4, 6, 7, 8
> b 2, 5

6 ◀) **8.7** 👥 Students complete the sentences in pairs. Tell them to predict as much as they can. If necessary, encourage them to use the Glossary. Then they listen again and check their answers. Allow a few minutes for students to compare their answers with a partner. Check the answers as a class. Play the recording again and ask the class to repeat the sentences as they hear them. Allow three or four minutes for students to practise saying the sentences in pairs. Monitor and give feedback on sentence stress and pronunciation of the new words.

> **Answers**
>
> 1 h 2 g 3 b 4 c 5 e 6 d 7 a 8 f

7 and 8 👥 Students complete Exercises 7 and 8 in pairs. Allow four or five minutes for the tasks, then check the answers as a class.

> **Answers**
>
> **Exercise 7:** 1 c 2 b 3 d 4 a
> **Exercise 8:** You can see here that …

9 👥 If possible, ask students to work with new partners. Students complete the task in pairs. Refer the students to the pie charts in the Critical thinking section on page 151. Model the task using the example in the Student's Book. Allow students four or five minutes to make notes before they practise speaking. Monitor and give feedback on grammar and pronunciation.

SPEAKING TASK

👥👥👥 Tell students that they are going to prepare a survey and then report the results of the survey to their classmates.

PREPARE/PRACTISE

1, 2, 3 and 4 👥👥 Students work in pairs and complete Exercises 1–4. Monitor and help with the writing stages of the survey. Make sure students prepare their survey correctly before they interview other students. Allow them up to ten minutes to prepare the survey, 15–20 minutes for the interviews, and ten minutes to tally the results. Monitor and make sure all students are on task. To make the activity more controlled and to ensure a variety of responses, divide the class into three groups (A, B and C) and assign them topics, e.g. *fast food*, *sweets* and *traditional food*.

5 👥👥 Students work in pairs and prepare a pie chart for each question from their survey. Allow students to use appropriate software to make the pie charts. If necessary, find students who know how to make pie charts on the computer and ask them to demonstrate to the class.

6 and 7 👤 Students prepare their presentation individually. Allow 10–12 minutes for preparation. Monitor and help students with the vocabulary for the task. If necessary, write down common grammar, vocabulary and pronunciation mistakes and discuss them with the class at the end.

DISCUSS

8 👥👥👥 Students work in small groups, preferably with new partners. If students were divided into groups as suggested above, then make sure that each new group has at least one A, B and C student. Students present the results of their survey to their groups. Monitor and write down any common mistakes you hear. Elicit the correct answers from the class at the end.

Optional activity

👤 Ask students to prepare a video presentation of their survey results with pie charts and any other visuals, e.g. photographs of the food or their classmates. Students show their videos to the class. Monitor and provide feedback at the end.

OBJECTIVES REVIEW

See Teaching tips, pages 10–11, for ideas about using the Objectives review with your students.

WORDLIST

See Teaching tips, pages 10–11, for ideas about how to make the most of the Wordlist with your students.

REVIEW TEST

See pages 120–121 for the photocopiable Review test for this unit and Teaching tips, pages 10–11, for ideas about when and how to administer the Review test.

ADDITIONAL SPEAKING TASK

See page 133 for an additional speaking task related to this unit.

Allow students three or four minutes to make notes to answer the questions. Encourage students to make notes using key words. Monitor and help with any vocabulary. Students work in pairs and discuss the questions. At the end, ask for volunteers to tell the class about their partner's favourite food.

RESEARCH PROJECT

Create an online cookery course

Show the class some cookery videos from a video-sharing website. Divide the class into groups and tell them that each group needs to select a recipe which they can make. Students could use a recipe known to them or choose a simple one from a cookbook or website. Each group could share its recipe with the rest of the class using the tools on the Cambridge LMS.

Tell students that each group will make a video demonstrating how to make their recipe and then upload the videos to the Cambridge LMS or a video-sharing website to create a cookery course.

9 ANIMALS

Learning objectives

Before you start the *Unlock your knowledge* section, ask students to read the Learning objectives box so that they have a clear idea of what they are going to learn in this unit. Tell them that you will come back to these objectives at the end of the unit when they review what they have learnt. Give them the opportunity to ask you any questions that they might have.

UNLOCK YOUR KNOWLEDGE

1, 2, 3 and 4 👥 Display the photograph on an interactive whiteboard. Students discuss the questions in pairs. Encourage them to use the Glossary or a bilingual dictionary to look up the name of the animal. Allow four or five minutes for pair discussion, then elicit the name of the animal and the descriptions from the class. Write the new vocabulary on the whiteboard and ask the class to spell the new words for you.

Answers

1 lion cubs
2 Africa
3 Lion cubs can still be dangerous, even though they're small. Fully grown lions are very dangerous. (Other possible adjectives: *cute, cuddly, furry, hungry, tired*)

WATCH AND LISTEN

Optional lead-in

▶ 👤👥👥 Play the video without the sound. Ask students to write down the names of the animals that they see in the video, i.e. *red panda* /rɛd ˈpændə/ and *rhino* /ˈraɪnəʊ/. Then ask students to work in pairs and brainstorm what they know about these animals. Ask them to use ideas maps to make notes about them. Encourage them to use the Glossary or a bilingual dictionary. Monitor and help with the brainstorming. At the end, ask students to share their ideas with the class. Draw ideas maps with the information about the animals on the whiteboard and complete them with the information from students. Students complete their ideas maps at the end of the class with the information they learnt from the video.

Video script

▶ Today, busy cities are everywhere, and people live in every part of the world. But what about animals? Where do they live when people build their cities? Where do they go? To answer these questions, we're going to Nepal in Asia to look at two different animals. We are travelling from Darjeeling to the Kathmandu valley and then to Chitwan National Park. Our first animal lives in green forests. This is a red panda. It's a very rare animal. Some people say there are only 10,000 red pandas in the wild. Red pandas are rare because people hunt them or because cities are getting bigger and they have nowhere to live. At night, the red pandas come down from the trees to eat. They eat leaves, flowers, eggs and fruit. In the morning, they return to the trees to sleep. They can fall out of the trees when they sleep, so it's important to find a good branch. The forest is the red panda's world. They can't live in cities like this. But the red panda is safe because no one can hunt them there. Let's look at another animal in a different part of the Chitwan National Park.

Look at the river. That's not a branch in the water – it's a one-horned Asiatic rhino. Rhinos often relax in the river on a hot day. Rhinos are dangerous animals – they can kill people easily. But in fact, there are now only 3,000 of these animals in India. Hunters look for rhinos. They kill them for their horns. A hunter can sell a rhino horn for 100,000 dollars or more. But these rhinos here are safe because they are protected in Chitwan National Park. The government in India sends police and soldiers to look after the rhinos. People can be a problem for animals – but we also look after them.

PREPARING TO WATCH

UNDERSTANDING KEY VOCABULARY

1 👤👥 Students complete the task individually, then check their answers with a partner. Remind them to use the Glossary to check the meaning of the key vocabulary. Allow two or three minutes for the task. Display the picture on an interactive whiteboard and ask for volunteers to label it. Elicit the pronunciation of the new words. Explain that nouns that end with *f*, like *leaf*, change the ending to *-ves* in plural, e.g. *leaves*.

Answers

a leaf /liːf//leaves /liːvz/
b branch /brɑːntʃ/
c flower /ˈflaʊə/
d fruit /fruːt/
e eggs /egz/

2 👥 Students complete the task in pairs. Encourage them to use the Glossary or a bilingual dictionary. Allow two or three minutes for the task, then elicit the new vocabulary from the class. Write the new words on the whiteboard and ask the class to spell them. Elicit the pronunciation. If possible, display photographs of these animals using the internet.

> **Possible answers**
>
> bird /bɜːd/, monkey /ˈmʌnki/, tiger /ˈtaɪɡə/, snake /sneɪk/, deer /dɪə/, bear /beə/, wolf /wʊlf/, insects /ˈɪnsekts/

3 and 4 👤👥 Students complete the activities individually, then check their answers with a partner. Encourage them to use the Glossary. Check the answers as a class. Check understanding and the pronunciation of the key vocabulary. Ask students to make original sentences with the key vocabulary. Note that we do not pronounce the *b* in *climb*.

> **Answers**
>
> **Exercise 3**
> 1 d come down /kʌm daʊn/, climb up /klaɪm ʌp/
> 2 a kill /kɪl/, look after /lʊk ˈɑːftə/
> 3 b sell /sel/, buy /baɪ/
> 4 c return /rɪˈtɜːn/, leave /liːv/
> **Exercise 4:** 1 government /ˈɡʌvənmənt/
> 2 hunter /ˈhʌntə/ 3 horn /hɔːn/ 4 soldier /ˈsəʊldʒə/

WHILE WATCHING

UNDERSTANDING MAIN IDEAS

5 ▶ 👤👥 Students watch the video and complete the task. Then they compare their answers with a partner. Check the answers as a class. Discuss why the other answers are incorrect.

> **Answers**
>
> 1 b (*To answer these questions, we're going to Nepal in Asia to look at two different animals.*)
> 2 c (*Some people say there are only 10,000 red pandas in the wild. [...], there are now only 3,000 of these animals in India.*)

UNDERSTANDING DETAIL

6 ▶ 👥 Students work in pairs and make predictions about the answers. Remind them to use the Glossary to check the meaning of unknown words. Students then watch the video one more time and check their answers. Ask them to look at the video script on page 221 and check their answers. At the end, check the answers and correct the false statements as a class.

> **Answers**
>
> 1 F (*Some people say there are only <u>10,000 red pandas</u> in the wild.*)
> 2 F (*They eat <u>leaves, flowers, eggs and fruit</u>.*)
> 3 F (*They <u>can't live in cities</u> like this.*)
> 4 T (*Rhinos often relax in the river on a hot day.*)
> 5 T (*... there are now only 3,000 of these animals in India.*)
> 6 F (*<u>Hunters</u> look for rhinos. They kill them for their horns.*)
> 7 T (*A hunter can sell a rhino horn for 100,000 dollars or more.*)
> 8 F (*<u>The government</u> in India sends police and soldiers to look after the rhinos.*)

DISCUSSION

7 👥 👥👥 Allow students two or three minutes to work in pairs and make notes about the questions. Monitor and make sure students think about reasons to support their opinions. Ask them to change partners and discuss the questions in pairs. Monitor and check that students explain their opinions. At the end, ask students to share their opinions with the class.

LISTENING 1

PREPARING TO LISTEN

USING YOUR KNOWLEDGE

1 👥 Display the photographs of the orangutans in Exercise 2 on an interactive whiteboard. Elicit the name of the animal: *orangutan*. Note that both pronunciations are common: /əˈræŋətæn/ and /əˈræŋətæŋ/. Students discuss the questions in pairs. Monitor and help with vocabulary. At the end, discuss students' ideas as a class and draw an ideas map on the whiteboard with the information from students.

UNDERSTANDING KEY VOCABULARY

2 and 3 👤👥 Students complete the tasks individually, then check their answers with a partner. Encourage students to use the Glossary. Allow up to ten minutes to complete the task. At the end, check the answers as a class. Check understanding and pronunciation of the new vocabulary.

> **Answers**
>
> **Exercise 2:** 1 orangutan /əˈræŋətæn/ or / əˈræŋətæŋ/
> 2 leaves /liːvz/ 3 tree /triː/ 4 jungle /ˈdʒʌŋɡl̩/
> 5 hands /hændz/ 6 stick /stɪk/
> **Exercise 3:** 1 long /lɒŋ/ 2 climb /klaɪm/ 3 wet /wet/
> 4 use /juːz/ 5 brain /breɪn/

PRONUNCIATION FOR LISTENING

4 👥 Draw students' attention to the Explanation box on page 163. Allow them a couple of minutes to read the information, then ask for volunteers to say the example words aloud. Correct the pronunciation if necessary. Students complete the task in pairs. Check understanding of *consonants* /ˈkɒnsənənts/. Check the answers as a class.

> **Answer**
>
> Consonants

5 🔊 **9.1** 👤👥 Students listen and complete the task individually. Then they check their answers with a partner. With a weaker class, play the audio again and ask students to repeat the words as a class. Check the answers. Allow students a couple of minutes to practise the words in pairs. Monitor and correct their pronunciation if necessary.

> **Answers**
>
> N hands, Y brains, N climb, Y world, Y wild,
> Y ground, Y umbrella

> **Optional activity**
>
> 👥 With a more advanced class, prepare flashcards with words which contain silent consonants, e.g. *comb* /kəʊm/, *bomb* /bɒm/, *bridge* /brɪdʒ/, *black* /blæk/, *ghost* /ɡəʊst/, *school* /skuːl/, *whistle* /ˈwɪsl̩/, *watch* /wɒtʃ/, *answer* /ˈɑːnsə/, etc. Students work in pairs and underline the silent consonants. Then they check their answers with another pair. Check the answers as a class and elicit the pronunciation of the words on the flashcards. If necessary, drill the pronunciation as a class.

WHILE LISTENING

LISTENING FOR MAIN IDEAS

6 🔊 **9.2** 👤👥 Before listening, ask students to predict the answers and discuss them as a class. Students listen to the audio and answer the questions individually. Then they check their answers with a partner. If necessary, encourage students to use the Glossary. Display the audio script from page 221 and highlight the relevant passages.

> **Answers**
>
> 3 what orangutans eat (*They're omnivores, so they can eat meat, fruit and vegetables, but they usually eat fruit.*)
> 2 what kind of places orangutans live in (*It's a good name for them, because orangutans are 'arboreal'. That means they live in trees.*)
> 4 why orangutans are special (*... they are very clever. They are good toolmakers.*)
> 1 what the name *orangutan* means (*... let me start with the name.*)

LISTENING FOR DETAIL

Explanation box

👥 Display the Explanation box on an interactive whiteboard. Elicit the meaning of *definition* /defɪˈnɪʃən/ and ask students when and why we use definitions. Students work in pairs, read the example sentences in the box, and underline expressions that can be used to give a definition, i.e. *is a kind of, means, that means* and *so*. With a more advanced class, ask students to make their own definitions of simple objects around the class.

7 🔊 **9.2** 👤👥 Students listen, then discuss the answers with a partner. Do not give the answers at this stage, but allow students to check how much they understood.

> **Optional activity**
>
> 👤👥 With a stronger class, ask students to close their books and take notes while they listen. Tell them to write down any technical words they hear and the definitions. Explain that they should not worry about the spelling of the technical words, as they will have a chance to correct the spelling after listening. Explain that when we take notes, we often use the equals symbol (=) to indicate a definition, e.g. *falcon = bird*. Students listen and take notes. Then they compare their notes with a partner. Students use their notes to complete Exercise 8.

8 👥 Students work in pairs and match the sentence halves. Encourage them to use their notes. Ask students to scan the audio script on page 221 and find the highlighted words from Exercise 7. Display the script on an interactive whiteboard and highlight the correct answers as a class. Elicit the expressions used to introduce definitions and underline them in the script.

> **Answers**
>
> 1 d orangutan /əˈræŋətæn/ (... the word orang _means_ 'man', and the word hutan _means_ 'forest'. So 'orangutan' _means_ 'the man in the forest'.)
> 2 b arboreal /ɑːˈbɔːrɪəl/ (... orangutans are 'arboreal'. _That means_ they live in trees.)
> 3 e omnivore /ˈɒmnɪvɔː/ (They're omnivores, _so_ they can eat meat, fruit and vegetables ...)
> 4 a primate /ˈpraɪmeɪt/ (... a primate _is a kind of_ animal that can use its hands to climb trees.)
> 5 c toolmaker/ˈtuːlmeɪkə/ (They are good toolmakers. _That means_ they can make things to help them.)

DISCUSSION

9 👤👥 Before the discussion, give students three or four minutes to make notes about the questions. Students work in pairs and discuss the questions. Monitor and help them with grammar and vocabulary. Write down any common mistakes you hear during monitoring and elicit the correct answers at the end of the task.

⊙ LANGUAGE DEVELOPMENT

VOCABULARY FOR ANIMALS

1 👤👥 Display the diagram on an interactive whiteboard. Students complete the task individually, then check their answers with a partner. Encourage students to use the Glossary. If possible, have students search the internet for images of the animals and show them to the class. Allow up to ten minutes for the task, then discuss the answers as a class. Elicit the meaning of _insect_ /ˈɪnsekt/ (a type of very small animal with six legs and usually with wings), _mammal_ /ˈmæməl/ (any animal of which the female feeds her young on milk from her own body) and _reptile_ /ˈreptaɪl/ (an animal that produces eggs and uses the heat of the sun

to keep its blood warm). Check the meaning and pronunciation of the new vocabulary, i.e. _cockroach_ /ˈkɒkrəʊtʃ/, _bear_ /beə/ and _lizard_ /ˈlɪzəd/. If necessary, display photographs of the animals on an interactive whiteboard.

> **Answers**
>
> 1/2 locust /ˈləʊkəst/, wasp /wɒsp/
> 3/4 cat /kæt/, horse /hɔːs/
> 5/6 snake /sneɪk/, crocodile /ˈkrɒkədaɪl/

> **Optional activity**
>
> 👥 Draw students' attention to the Explanation box. Allow them a minute to read it. Discuss briefly whether students find vocabulary trees / ideas maps useful. Elicit the organization of the vocabulary trees in Exercise 1. Divide the class into three groups. Assign each group one of the vocabulary trees from Exercise 1. Ask each group to add more words to their vocabulary tree. Allow four or five minutes for the task. Encourage students to use the Glossary or an online dictionary. When they have finished, display the vocabulary trees from Exercise 1 on an interactive whiteboard and ask representatives from each group to add more animals to each category. Ask the rest of the group to help the writer with the spelling. Each group should explain the new vocabulary to the class. Elicit the pronunciation of the new words.

DEFINITIONS

2 👤👥 Students complete the task individually, then check their answers with a partner. Check answers as a class and check understanding of _blood_ /blʌd/, _herd_ /hɜːd/ and _tusk_ /tʌsk/.

> **Answers**
>
> 1 a 2 a 3 a 4 b 5 b

3 👥👥 Students complete the task in pairs and guess the animals. Ask them not to use the Glossary or the internet. Students should be able to guess the meaning of the difficult words, like _burrows_ /ˈbʌrəʊz/ and _swarm_ /swɔːm/, by reading the definitions. At the end, display the text on an interactive whiteboard and ask volunteers to underline the difficult words and their definitions in the text. Check answers as a class.

> **Answers**
>
> 1 dhub lizard 2 locust

4 and 5 👤👥 Before the task, draw students' attention to the box with useful expressions.

Use these expressions to model the task and ask students to guess the animal you are describing. Students then choose an animal from Exercise 1 and prepare their definition following the model. To avoid repetition during the task, prepare slips of paper with names of animals. Students then draw the names of the animals that they will work on. Allow four or five minutes for students to make notes. Monitor and encourage students to use key words in their notes and make sure they do not write the whole definition. When they are ready, ask them to close their books and use only their notes. Students then work in pairs and read out their definition to each other. Their partner has to guess which animal they are describing.

Optional activity

👥 👥👥 Students work in pairs, if possible with partners from the same country. Ask them to prepare vocabulary ideas maps of animals in their country. The ideas map should have three branches: *water*, *land* and *air*. Students write examples of each type of animal in the ideas map. Encourage them to use the Glossary or a bilingual dictionary. Monitor and help with vocabulary. Allow up to ten minutes to complete the ideas maps, then ask students to work with another pair (if possible, the other pair should be from a different country). Students tell each other about different animals in their countries. Monitor and encourage students to expand their answers by giving details, like what the animals eat, in what environment they live, etc. When they have finished, ask for volunteers to present their ideas maps to the class and discuss them.

LISTENING 2

PREPARING TO LISTEN

USING YOUR KNOWLEDGE

1 and 2 👥 Display the photographs on an interactive whiteboard. Students complete Exercises 1 and 2 in pairs. Encourage them to use the Glossary. Monitor and make sure students answer the questions in Exercise 2 in complete sentences. When they have finished, discuss the answers as a class and elicit the pronunciation of *bald eagle* /bɔːld ˈiːgl/ and *oryx* /ˈɔrɪks/. Allow students to speculate about where the animals live and what they eat. Tell them that they will hear more about these animals in the listening.

Answers

Exercise 1
1 photographs b, c
2 photographs a, d
Exercise 2: See audio script 9.3.

UNDERSTANDING KEY VOCABULARY

3 👥 Before the task, check understanding of *noun*, *verb* and *adjective*. Elicit examples. Students complete the task in pairs. Encourage them to use the Glossary. Monitor and check the understanding of the new vocabulary. When they have finished, display the table on an interactive whiteboard and ask for volunteers to make original sentences with the words from the table. Write the sentences on the whiteboard.

Answers

nouns	verbs	adjectives
fish /fɪʃ/	cut /kʌt/	hard /hɑːd/
grass /grɑːs/	jump /dʒʌmp/	long /lɒŋ/
rabbit /ˈræbɪt/	run /rʌn/	sharp /ʃɑːp/

4 👥 Students work in pairs. Tell them to take turns to ask and answer the questions. Monitor and give feedback on the pronunciation of the key vocabulary. Check the answers at the end.

Answers

2 fish 3 grass 4 rabbit 5 cut 6 jump 7 hard

WHILE LISTENING

LISTENING FOR MAIN IDEAS

5 (◄) 9.3 👤👥 Students listen to the audio and answer the questions individually. Then they check their answers with a partner. Display the photographs on an interactive whiteboard and check the answers as a class. Ask which words or phrases students heard that gave them the answers.

Answers

1 c 2 b 3 a 4 d

LISTENING FOR DETAIL

6 (◄) 9.3 👤👥 Tell students that they are going to listen again and take notes to answer the questions. Allow them two or three minutes to read the questions. Students may ask about the new vocabulary, e.g. *nest*, *beak* or *nomadic*. Tell them that they will hear the definitions of these words in the recording. With a stronger class, ask students to work in pairs and predict the answers. Students listen and make notes individually. Then allow them two or three minutes to compare their notes with a partner. Monitor and check students' notes. Students work in pairs and answer the questions using their notes. If necessary, ask them to scan the audio script on page 222 and find the answers. Check the answers as a class.

> **Answers**
> 1 US and Canada
> 2 the eagle's home / the place where the eagle lives
> 3 fish
> 4 cut (fish)
> 5 no (deserts)
> 6 Abu Dhabi / the UAE
> 7 grass and fruit
> 8 They travel around / don't live in one place.

7 Display the photographs on an interactive whiteboard. On the photographs, circle or point to *nest*, *beak*, *feathers* and *horns*, but do not say these words in English. Students work in pairs and find these words in English. Encourage them to use a bilingual dictionary or the Glossary. Monitor and help with vocabulary search. When students have finished, elicit the meaning and the pronunciation of *nest* /nest/, *beak* /biːk/, *feather* /ˈfeðə/ and *horns* /hɔːnz/.

DISCUSSION

8 Allow students four or five minutes to make notes about the discussion questions. Students complete the task in pairs. Monitor and help with grammar and vocabulary for the task. Write down any common mistakes you hear during monitoring. When students have finished, correct the mistakes as a class.

CRITICAL THINKING

At this point in each unit, students are asked to begin to think about the speaking task that they will do at the end of the unit (*Describe an animal*). Give them a minute to look at the box.

REMEMBER

1 Students discuss the questions in pairs, then discuss the questions as a class. Display the sample texts on an interactive whiteboard. Check understanding of *dictionary* /ˈdɪkʃənəri/, *translation* /trænsˈleɪʃən/ and *definition* /defɪˈnɪʃən/.

> **Answers**
> 1 (online) dictionaries   2 (online) translation tool
> 3 Students' own answers   4 (online) dictionary

APPLY

2 Students complete the task in pairs, then check the answers as a class. Display the texts on an interactive whiteboard and ask for volunteers to write the numbers 1–7 on the whiteboard. Check understanding of the expressions (a–g).

> **Language note**
>
> *Collocations* /kɒləˈkeɪʃənz/ are words or phrases that are often used with other words or phrases in a way that sounds correct to people who have spoken the language all their lives.

> **Answers**
> 1 b 2 e 3 a 4 d 5 g 6 f 7 c

Skills box

Students read the information in the Skills box and discuss which points they have done before and which problems they face when using dictionaries and translating. Note that many students at this level are often dependent on translation tools. To show them that we cannot completely rely on the translation tools, copy and paste a fragment from audio script 9.3 from page 222 into an online translation tool. Translate the text into students' mother tongue(s) and display the translation on an interactive whiteboard. Ask students whether there are any problems with the translation.

3 Students complete the task in pairs. Monitor and help them with the dictionary search and deciding which word is the correct translation. Check answers as a class.

> **Answers**
> 1 a horse b lion c chicken/hen
> 2 a foal b cub c chick

SPEAKING

PREPARATION FOR SPEAKING

INTRODUCING A TOPIC

1 and 2 🔊 9.4 👤👥 Students listen and complete Exercise 1 individually. Then ask them to work in pairs and check their answers. Monitor and, if necessary, play the audio one more time. Check the answers as a class.

> **Answers**
> 1 today 2 tell 3 about 4 everybody 5 talk 6 about
> 7 this 8 here

USING QUESTIONS IN A TALK

3 🔊 9.5 👥 Before the task, draw students' attention to the Skills box. Allow them a minute to read the box. Elicit why speakers use questions in their talks. Students then work in pairs and complete the gaps with the questions. Then play the audio to check the answers.

> **Answers**
> 1 c 2 a 3 b

4 and 5 🔊 9.6 👥 Students work in pairs and complete the gaps with the questions. If necessary, ask them to check the meaning of new vocabulary in the Glossary. Then play the audio. Students listen and check their answers. When they have finished, ask the pairs to check their answers with another pair.

> **Answers**
> 1 c 2 d 3 e 4 a 5 b

6 🔊 9.6 👤👥 Students read the text and answer the questions individually. Then they compare their answers with a partner. Check the answers as a class. Elicit the function of *well* and *so*. *Well* /wel/ is used to introduce something you are going to say, often to show surprise or to continue a story. *So* /səʊ/ is used at the beginning of a sentence to connect it with something that has been said before. It is also used as a short pause to emphasize what we are saying.

> **Answers**
> 1 So 2 Well

PRONUNCIATION FOR SPEAKING

7 🔊 9.6 👤👥 Students listen to the first three sentences from the recording and follow the text in the exercise. Then stop the audio and discuss with students the purpose of the pauses (to help listeners to understand). Ask students to look at the audio script on page 222, listen to the audio and mark the pauses in the presentation. Allow a couple of minutes for students to check their answers with a partner.

> **Answers**
> OK, // hello, everybody. // My name's Luo Yan, // and I'm going to talk about // brown bears. // This is a photograph of a brown bear. // So, // where do these bears live? // Well, they live in forests and near rivers. // They often live in mountains. // And where can you see brown bears? // In a lot of countries! // Brown bears live in America // and Europe // and parts of Asia. // How do they live? // Well, // they sleep for the winter // and they hunt in the summer. // They have to eat a lot in the summer, // so bears are often hungry. // And so what do they eat? // Well, // they eat a lot of different things. // They like fruit, // fish, // vegetables, // nuts // and grass. // So why are they special? // Well, // they are very, very strong animals. // They can move rocks and trees and other big things easily.

> **Optional activity**
>
> 👥👥 👥 With a weaker class, practise saying the presentation with the class. Play the audio and pause after each sentence. Drill the sentence stress as a group. If necessary, tap gently on your desk to emphasize the stressed words. After group drill, allow students between two and four minutes to practise saying the presentation in pairs. Monitor and give feedback on pronunciation and sentence stress.

SPEAKING TASK

PREPARE

1 👥👥 Divide the class into three groups: A, B and C. Each group turns to the page with their assigned animal and reads the text.

2 and 3 👥👥 Students complete the tasks in small groups. Encourage them to use the Glossary and online dictionaries. Monitor and help with the dictionary search. Make sure students select the definitions that are related to the context in which they were given. Encourage students to find the pronunciation of the new words in online dictionaries. While monitoring, work with the groups to check understanding of the new words and the pronunciation.

PRACTISE

4 👥 Before the task, model the questions and answers using the examples from Listening 2. Students complete the task in pairs with partners from the same group. Monitor and make sure students answer in complete sentences.

> ### Answers
>
> **Group A (tigers)**
> 1 jungles and forests in India, China and South-East Asia
> 2 (other) animals
> 3 They hunt at night.
> 4 They can see in the dark, they are famous for their stripes.
> **Group B (ants)**
> 1 all over the world / in different countries
> 2 different kinds of food, e.g. fruit and vegetables
> 3 in a colony
> 4 They are very strong, they don't have lungs.
> **Group C (koalas)**
> 1 forests in Australia
> 2 leaves from trees
> 3 They sleep a lot, they live in trees.
> 4 They have pouches, they have waterproof fur.

5 and 6 👤 Students prepare their presentation individually. Allow 10–12 minutes for the internet search and note-making. Monitor and help with the text in Exercise 6. If necessary, ask for volunteers to read their text to the class as a model.

7 👥 Students practise their introductions in pairs. Monitor and write down any common mistakes that you hear. When they have finished, correct the mistakes as a class.

8, 9 and 10 👥👥 Students work in groups of three (A+B+C). They tell each other about their animals. Other students take notes. Allow 10–15 minutes for the presentations. Then students go back to their groups and compare notes. Allow between two and four minutes for them to complete the notes. Ask the groups to tell the class what they found out about the other groups' animals.

DISCUSS

11 👥👥 Discuss which of the animals were the most interesting, and why.

> ### Optional activity
>
> 👥 Students use the model presentation from *Preparation for speaking* and give a presentation about a popular animal from their country. Alternatively, students can make a video or a slide show about the animal and record themselves describing the animal.

OBJECTIVES REVIEW

See Teaching tips, pages 10–11, for ideas about using the Objectives review with your students.

WORDLIST

See Teaching tips, pages 10–11, for ideas about how to make the most of the Wordlist with your students.

REVIEW TEST

See pages 122–123 for the photocopiable Review test for this unit and Teaching tips, pages 10–11, for ideas about when and how to administer the Review test.

ADDITIONAL SPEAKING TASK

See page 134 for an additional speaking task related to this unit.

Allow students time to find a photograph of the animal on the internet. Give them about seven minutes to make notes to answer the questions. Monitor and help with vocabulary. Ask students to work in pairs and practise their presentation. Students then present their talk to the class. Monitor and provide feedback.

RESEARCH PROJECT

> ### Research and report on people's knowledge of animals
>
> Explain to students that they are going to research how much people know about animals and then present a survey. Ask them to think about questions which focus on knowledge of different animals, e.g. where they live and what they eat. Students could use the Cambridge LMS to share their ideas.
>
> Students can then use these questions in a survey (search for 'online survey' to find free online-survey software). The results can then be analyzed and the data presented to a local zoo / animal charity to highlight knowledge of various animals and areas where education needs to play more of a role.

10 TRANSPORT

UNLOCK YOUR KNOWLEDGE

Background note

The photograph shows a view of the Keizersgacht canal in Amsterdam, Holland.

1, 2 and 3 Display the photograph on an interactive whiteboard. Students discuss the questions about the photograph in pairs. Encourage them to use the Glossary or a bilingual dictionary to find out the names of the forms of transport in the photograph. Elicit the names from the class and write them on the whiteboard. Ask the class to spell the names as you write. Check understanding and the pronunciation of the means of transport.

Answers

1 The photograph was taken in Holland (The Netherlands). Students may be able to guess this from the canal, the bicycles and the style of architecture.
2 a cars, vans
  b bicycles/bikes, (canal) boats

WATCH AND LISTEN

Video script

▶ About 100 kilometres from the Arctic Circle is a village in Alaska. There are no roads in or out of town. In winter, the rivers are frozen and the ice is thin. Parts of the Tozitna River are less than five centimetres thick. Stan and Joey need to cross the river. Stan tests the ice to see if he can stand on it. The ice is very thin in places. The ice breaks. But Stan is safe. Stan and Joey hope that the dogs will run and jump over the hole in the ice. They are safe for now.

This is not the only kind of transport in Alaska, but other transport cannot travel over the ice. In another part of Alaska is the main town, called Bethel. All the supplies for the villages come through this town. These supplies are for the village of Akiachak. Akiachak is about 50 kilometres from Bethel. But there are no roads there. There is only one way to get to Akiachak – by hovercraft. When it is minus 40 degrees, boats and planes are useless. Over snow, ice and water, the hovercraft will follow the frozen river to Akiachak.

PREPARING TO WATCH

Optional lead-in

Display a map of North America with Alaska clearly indicated. Ask students to work in pairs and make notes about Alaska. They should use their background knowledge and make notes about the people, language, weather, etc. in Alaska. Then ask the pairs to share their ideas with the class. On the whiteboard, draw an ideas map with the word *Alaska* in the middle and add information from students to the ideas map.

UNDERSTANDING KEY VOCABULARY

1 Students complete the task in pairs. Encourage them to use the Glossary. Monitor and check the pronunciation of the words in the box. When they have finished, check the answers as a class. Display the video stills on an interactive whiteboard and ask students to identify the Alaskan forms of transport in the photographs.

Answers

dog sled /ˈdɒg sled/	a sledge pulled by dogs
hovercraft /ˈhɒvəkrɑːft/	a vehicle that travels quickly just above the surface of water or land
snowmobile /ˈsnəʊməbiːl/	a small motor vehicle for travelling on snow and ice

2 Display the map on an interactive whiteboard. Students complete the task in pairs. Encourage them to use the Glossary. Monitor and, if necessary, point out the footnotes with the definitions of the new words. Allow between two and four minutes for the task, then discuss students' answers as a class. Make sure students give reasons to support their answers. Check understanding and pronunciation of *ice* /aɪs/, *supplies* /sə'plaɪz/ and *road* /rəʊd/.

3 👥 👥👥 Students complete the task in pairs. Encourage them to use the Glossary. Allow five or six minutes for the task, then discuss the answers as a class. Encourage students to correct the false statements. Check understanding and pronunciation of the highlighted vocabulary, i.e. *frozen* /'frəʊzən/, *stand* /stænd/, *thin* /θɪn/, *thick* /θɪk/, *break* /breɪk/, *useless* /'juːsləs/ and *hole* /həʊl/.

Answers
1 T 2 F 3 F 4 T

WHILE WATCHING

UNDERSTANDING MAIN IDEAS

4 ▶ 👥 👥👥 Students work in pairs and guess the answers. Then they watch the video and check their answers. Allow two or three minutes after watching for students to compare answers with another pair and write them down. Check the answers as a class. Elicit the spelling of any new words in the answers.

Answers
1 There is snow. / It's snowy/snowing. / There is ice.
2 The rivers freeze / are frozen. / The water in the rivers freezes.
3 dog sled, hovercraft and snowmobile
4 a Because there are no roads.
  b Because they are useless. / Because it's very cold. / Because it's –40°C.

UNDERSTANDING DETAIL

5, 6 and 7 ▶ 👤 👥 Students predict the answers individually, then compare their ideas with a partner. Then they watch the video again and check their answers. Check the answers as a class. If necessary, ask students to scan the video script on page 222 and underline the correct answers.

Answers
1 T (*About 100 kilometres from the Arctic Circle is a village in Alaska. [...] In winter, ...*)
2 T (*Parts of the Tozitna River are less than five centimetres thick.*)
3 F (*Stan tests the ice to see if he can stand on it.*)
4 T (*... other transport cannot travel over the ice.*)
5 F (*These supplies are for the village of Akiachak. [...] There is only one way to get to Akiachak – by hovercraft.*)
6 F (*Over snow, ice and water, the hovercraft will follow the frozen river to Akiachak.*)

DISCUSSION

8 👥 👥👥 Students work in pairs and make notes about the question. Allow between four and six minutes for note-making and brainstorming. Then draw students' attention to the expressions in the box. Model the task by using them. Students work with another pair and discuss their ideas. Monitor and give feedback on vocabulary and pronunciation. Write down any common mistakes and elicit the correct answers at the end. Allow about seven minutes for discussion, then ask the groups to present their ideas to the class.

LISTENING 1

PREPARING TO LISTEN

UNDERSTANDING KEY VOCABULARY

> **Optional activity**
>
> 👥 👥👥 Prepare flashcards with the means of transport from the box in Exercise 1. Ask students to keep their books closed so that they do not repeat the private transport versus public transport categorization. Ask students to organize the flashcards into categories. Students work in pairs and discuss categories into which they want to organize the words. Monitor and discuss students' ideas in pairs. When they have finished, ask the pairs to present their categories to the class.

1 and 2 👤 👥 Students complete the task individually, then compare their answers with a partner. They then discuss Exercise 2 in pairs. Encourage students to use the Glossary. Lead class feedback at the end and check understanding and pronunciation of the key vocabulary. If necessary, drill the pronunciation of the vocabulary as a class.

Answers

private /ˈpraɪvət/	public /ˈpʌblɪk/
bicycle /ˈbaɪsɪkl/	bus /bʌs/
car /kɑː/	ferry /ˈferi/
motorbike	river taxi /ˈrɪvə ˈtæksi/
/ˈməʊtəbaɪk/	taxi /ˈtæksi/
	train /treɪn/
	tram /træm/
	underground
	/ˈʌndəɡraʊnd/

3 🧍👥 Students complete the task individually, then compare their answers with a partner. Encourage students to use the Glossary. Check the answers as a class. Check understanding and pronunciation of the key vocabulary. If necessary, drill the pronunciation of the new words.

Language note

Some students may find it difficult to distinguish the exact difference between *journey*, *trip* /trɪp/ and travel /ˈtrævəl/. *Journey* is used to refer to the distance travelled between places. *Trip* is used when you go somewhere for a short time, e.g. *a business trip*. *Travel* describes moving from one place to another over long distance.

Answers

1 ticket /ˈtɪkɪt/	a small piece of paper or card given to someone to show that they have paid for a journey
2 journey /ˈdʒɜːni/	the act of travelling from one place to another, especially in a vehicle
3 passenger /ˈpæsəndʒə/	a person who is travelling in a vehicle but is not driving or flying it

PRONUNCIATION FOR LISTENING

4 🔊 **10.1** 👥 Students work in pairs and practise saying the years in the box. Then they listen to the audio and check whether they said them correctly. Allow students a couple of minutes to take turns and practise saying the years. Then draw their attention to the Explanation box on page 181. Give them a minute to read the examples and elicit the rules for

pronouncing years. If necessary, write your own examples on the whiteboard and ask for volunteers to say the years.

5 and 6 🔊 **10.2** 🧍👥 Students listen and complete the task individually. Then they check their answers in pairs. Check the answers as a class. Ask for volunteers to pronounce the years. Allow a couple of minutes for students to practise saying the years in pairs. Students discuss Exercise 6 in pairs. Explain that with the years after 2010, both pronunciations are acceptable. To check understanding, write examples of years after 2010 on the whiteboard and elicit both pronunciations from the class.

Answers

Exercise 5: 1 1435 2 1749 3 1949 4 1953 5 2015
Exercise 6: The year 2015 can be pronounced *twenty fifteen* or *two thousand and fifteen*.

Background note

Most of the years in Exercises 4 and 5 are significant dates in history.

1238	Islamic calendar; year of the Prophet Muhammad's birth
1868	Start of Meiji era in Japan
1923	Turkey became a republic under Ataturk.
1996	On or near the birth date of the average for students for this course
2015	The year after publication of this course, when students will most likely reach Unit 10
1949	China became the People's Republic of China.
1953	Egpyt became a republic.

PREDICTING CONTENT USING VISUALS

7 and 8 👥 👥 Display the photographs on an interactive whiteboard. Students work in pairs and discuss the questions in Exercises 7 and 8. Allow two or three minutes for discussion. With a more advanced class, ask students to make notes with their answers. Students then work with another pair and discuss their predictions. Monitor and help with vocabulary to describe the photographs, but do not explain the photographs in detail.

WHILE LISTENING

Skills box

👥 Draw students' attention to the Skills box. Check understanding of *take notes*. Ask students to work in small groups and discuss when we take notes, whether note-taking is important at college or university and why, what information we usually write down, and how we can organize the notes. Display the questions on an interactive whiteboard. Allow students four or five minutes for discussion, then ask the groups to share their ideas with the class. Emphasize that students should focus on numbers and recurring key words. With a more advanced class, discuss different organizational methods for the notes, e.g. bullet points, table, ideas map.

LISTENING FOR MAIN IDEAS

9 ◀) **10.3** 👤👥 Ask students to close their books and take notes while they listen. Remind them to focus on key words and numbers. Then ask students to work with a partner and compare their notes. Allow them two or three minutes to compare notes and find the spelling of any new words in the Glossary. Monitor and give feedback on the quality of the notes, the amount of information noted down, and the organization of the notes.

10 👥 Students work in pairs and answer the questions using their notes. Check answers as a class.

Answers

1 Transport for London and Oyster cards (the electronic tickets)
2 Looks after private and public transport in London / looks after people and passengers (who use transport)
3 8 million (3 million private, 5 million public)
4 1863
5 a kind of ticket / an electronic ticket

LISTENING FOR DETAIL

11 ◀) **10.3** 👤👥 Students use their notes to answer as many questions as they can. If necessary, ask them to use the Glossary to check the meaning of any new words in the task, e.g. *introduce* /ˌɪntrəˈdjuːs/ (to put something into use for the first time). Then they listen again and check their answers. Allow two or three minutes for students to compare their

answers with a partner. Display the task on an interactive whiteboard and ask for volunteers to give answers and then spell them aloud. Explain that being able to spell aloud correctly helps with listening and note-taking skills. With a weaker class, ask students to scan the audio script on pages 222–223 and underline the correct answers.

Answers

1 cars, taxis, buses, trains (*Three million people travel in private cars and taxis and another five million use the bus, trains …*)
2 over 150 years old (*… it's more than 150 years old. It opened in 1863.*)
3 2003 (*… in 2003 we introduced the Oyster card system of electronic tickets.*)
4 (Paper) tickets were slow and/or London was bigger and more people lived and worked there. (*… there was a problem – it was very slow.*)
5 online (*You can pay for your journeys online …*)

DISCUSSION

12 👤👥 Before the discussion, give students four or five minutes to make notes about the questions. Students work in pairs and discuss the questions. Monitor and help students with grammar and vocabulary. Write down any common mistakes you hear during monitoring and elicit the correct answers at the end of the task.

⊙ LANGUAGE DEVELOPMENT

VOCABULARY FOR TRANSPORT

1 and 2 👥 Students complete the tasks in pairs, then check their answers with another pair. Encourage students to use the Glossary. Allow 10–12 minutes for the tasks, then check their answers. Display the words from Exercise 1 on an interactive whiteboard and elicit pronunciation. Draw students' attention to the dependent prepositions, e.g. *go by, check in, take off, arrive at* and *depart from*. Check understanding of the new words.

Language note

Students may find some of the items in Exercise 2 confusing. Explain that some of the expressions are collocations, e.g. *ride a motorbike, board the boat* or *take a bus*. Other answers can be guessed by their dependent prepositions (see above).

Answers

Exercise 1: 1 i 2 j 3 f 4 e 5 d 6 c 7 a 8 g 9 b 10 h
Exercise 2: 1 ride /raɪd/ 2 reserve /rɪˈzɜːv/
3 arrives /əˈraɪvz/ 4 departs /dɪˈpɑːts/ 5 go /ɡəʊ/
6 board /bɔːd/ 7 take /teɪk/ 8 check in /tʃek ɪn/
9 takes off /teɪks ɒf/ 10 lands /lændz/

Optional activity

👥👥 With a more advanced class, work with collocations, i.e. groups of words that are often found together. Display the sentences from Exercise 2 on an interactive whiteboard and discuss the first two sentences with the class. Elicit the collocations (1) *ride / a motorbike* and (2) *reserve / a seat*. Students work in pairs and underline the collocations in the remaining sentences. Monitor and help with the task. Check the answers as a class. As a follow-up activity, prepare a memory game using the collocations. Divide the collocations into halves (see below) and write each half on one piece of paper. Students work in small groups and play the game using the 22 pieces of paper with the collocations. Students lay the pieces of paper on the table with the words facing down. Players take turns and uncover two pieces of paper at a time. If the halves match, they take the halves and score a point. If the halves do not match, the player puts the pieces of paper down back in the same place. Students play until they match all the collocations.

Answers

3 arrive / at platform
4 depart / from
5 go by / train
6 board / the boat
7 take the bus / to school
8 show your ticket / and your passport / check in / at the airport
9 the plane takes / off
10 the plane / lands

THE PAST SIMPLE

Explanation box

👥👥 Display the Explanation box on an interactive whiteboard. Give students a minute to read the example sentences. Ask for volunteers to underline the verbs in these sentences on the interactive whiteboard. Elicit the form and meaning of the verbs in the past form. Elicit the pronunciation of the regular past forms and make sure students do not pronounce the extra vowel at the end of *opened*, *lived*, *worked* and *introduced*. Ask for volunteers to make their own

sentences using the underlined verbs. Write the sentences on the whiteboard. Drill the sentences as a class. Correct the pronunciation of the regular past forms if necessary.

Language note

The pronunciation of the suffix -ed differs depending on the last sound of the verb. We pronounce it as /t/ after all voiceless consonant sounds except /t/ (i.e. /f, k, p, ʃ, tʃ, s, ks/), e.g. *work, introduce, check, finish, look, practise,* etc. We pronounce it as /d/ after all voiced consonant sounds except /d/ (i.e. /b, ɡ, j, l, m, n, r, v, z/), and all the vowels, e.g. *open, live, advise, believe, clean, control,* etc. We pronounce -ed as /ɪd/ if the verb ends in /t/ or /d/, e.g. *want, need, end, land,* etc.

3 👥 Students complete the task in pairs. Encourage them to use the Glossary, and monitor and check pronunciation of the irregular forms. Check the answers as a class.

Answers

4 make 5 take 6 can 7 put 8 go 9 come

Optional activity

👥👥 Play *Bingo* using the irregular verb forms. Each student prepares a piece of paper with a 3x3 grid. Students fill in their grid with the infinitive forms of nine verbs. They can choose any verbs they want. To play the game, read out the past forms of irregular verbs at random. If a student has a matching form, they cross it off their *Bingo* board. When they cross out all the verbs on their board, they shout out *Bingo!*.

4 and 5 👥👥 Students complete the exercises individually, then check their answers with a partner. Monitor and check pronunciation of the irregular verbs. Encourage students to use the Glossary. As a class, check the answers and drill the pronunciation and sentence stress of the sentences. Allow students two or three minutes to practise saying the sentences in pairs. Monitor and give feedback on the pronunciation of the past forms.

Answers

Exercise 4: 1 took /tʊk/ 2 went /went/ 3 had /hæd/
4 was /wɒz/ 5 walked /wɔːkt/
Exercise 5: b 5 c 1 d 2 e 4

6 and 7 👥 Students complete the exercises in pairs. Monitor and keep students on task. Allow four or five minutes for them to finish, then check the answers as a class.

> **Answers**
>
> **Exercise 6:** verbs in negative statements: *didn't have, couldn't find, didn't go*
> verbs in questions: *Did you take?, Could they ride?*
> **Exercise 7:** 1 *didn't/couldn't* 2 *Did/Could*

8 👥 Model the task with a stronger student. Students work in pairs and practise the dialogues. Monitor and give feedback on the pronunciation of the past verb forms and grammar in questions. Write down any grammar or pronunciation mistakes that you hear during the monitoring. When you have finished, write the mistakes on the whiteboard or say them aloud and elicit the correct answers from students.

LISTENING 2

PREPARING TO LISTEN

> **Optional activity**
>
> 👥 👥👥 Display photographs 2 and 3 from Exercise 1 on an interactive whiteboard. Ask students to work in pairs and discuss whether they have ever been in the situations in the photographs. Ask them to describe these situations to each other. Allow three or four minutes for discussion. Monitor and help with vocabulary for the task. Students then share their experiences with the class. Write down any key vocabulary on the whiteboard and check understanding.

USING YOUR KNOWLEDGE

1 and 2 👥 Students complete the exercises in pairs. Encourage students to use the Glossary. Monitor and check understanding of the new words. Encourage students to explain their answers to the questions in Exercise 2 in complete sentences. When they have finished, check the answers as a class and ask students to share their responses to Exercise 2 with the rest of the class.

> **Answers**
>
> **Exercise 1:** 1 sky bridge /ˈskaɪbrɪdʒ/
> 2 traffic jam /ˈtræfɪk dʒæm/ 3 travelator /ˈtrævəleɪtə/
> 4 sky train /ˈskaɪtreɪn/
> 5 metro railway /ˈmetrəʊ ˈreɪlweɪ/

UNDERSTANDING KEY VOCABULARY

3 👥👥 Students complete the task individually, then check their answers with a partner. Encourage them to use the Glossary to check the meaning of the key vocabulary. Monitor and check understanding and the pronunciation of the key words. Check the answers as a class. Drill the sentences as a group. Allow students two or three minutes to practise saying the sentences in pairs. Monitor and give feedback on the pronunciation of the key vocabulary.

> **Answers**
>
> | | |
> |---|---|
> | 1 transport system /ˈtrænspɔːt ˈsɪstəm/ | the different means of transport in a city or country that people can use |
> | 2 get stuck /get stʌk/ | to be unable to move forward |
> | 3 Commuters /kəˈmjuːtəz/ | people who regularly travel between home and work |
> | 4 destination /destɪˈneɪʃən/ | a place where someone is going |
> | 5 congestion /kənˈdʒestʃən/ | overcrowding, a lot of people and traffic in one place |

WHILE LISTENING

TAKING NOTES

4 🔊 **10.4** 👥👥 Before the listening task, ask students to work in pairs and predict the missing information. Explain that during exams, they can use grammar and logic to guess the missing information. For example, gap 2 is an adjective, and gaps 3 and 4 can be guesses using background knowledge. Students listen and complete the notes individually, then they check their answers with a partner. Check the answers as a class.

Display the task on an interactive whiteboard and ask for volunteers to fill in the gaps. Correct the spelling as a class.

Optional activity

👤👥 With a more advanced class, ask students to close their books and take notes in their notebooks. Students compare their notes, then use them to complete the task in Exercise 4. Allow time to compare notes. Monitor and give feedback on the quality of the notes. If necessary, point out the spelling mistakes and ask students to find the correct spelling in the Glossary.

Answers

1 Transport in cities (problems and solutions)
2 congested
3 expensive
4 pollution
5 it reduces congestion
6 they get stuck in traffic jams
7 it's too small
8 underground
9 sky trains / sky bridges
10 drive

LISTENING FOR DETAIL

5 and 6 🔊 **10.4** 👥 Students work in pairs and use their notes to answer the questions. Then they listen to the audio and check their answers. Allow students three or four minutes to compare their answers with a partner. If necessary, display the audio script from page 223 on an interactive whiteboard and underline the correct answers as a class.

Answers

1 Because everyone uses a car.
2 They are slow and expensive, and they cause pollution.
3 free cycles
4 Dubai
5 To reduce traffic congestion / make public transport better
6 London, Bangkok

DISCUSSION

7 👤👥 Allow students four or five minutes to make notes about the discussion questions. Students complete the task in pairs. Monitor and help with grammar and vocabulary. Write

down any common mistakes you hear during monitoring. When they have finished, correct the mistakes as a class.

CRITICAL THINKING

👥👥 At this point in each unit, students are asked to begin to think about the speaking task that they will do at the end of the unit (*Describe a solution to a transport problem*). Give them a minute to look at the box.

REMEMBER

1 👤👥 Before the task, draw students' attention to the Skills box. Allow them a minute to read the box. Check understanding of *flow chart* /ˈfləʊ tʃɑːt/ and elicit when and why we use flow charts, e.g. when we take notes in a lecture or when we organize a talk or to write down steps of doing something. Students complete the task individually, then compare their answers with a partner. Monitor and encourage students to use the Glossary. Display the flow chart on an interactive whiteboard and discuss the answers with the class. Check understanding of the key words, i.e. *problem* /ˈprɒbləm/, *solution* /səˈluːʃən/, *topic* /ˈtɒpɪk/ and *result* /rɪˈzʌlt/.

Answers

1 topic 2 problem 3 solution 4 result

APPLY

2 👥 Students complete the task in pairs. Monitor and encourage them to use the Glossary. Check the answers as a class.

Answers

1 d 2 a 3 b 4 c

3 and 4 👤👥 Students work individually and prepare flow charts with the information from Exercise 2. Then they work in pairs and tell each other about the problem and solution in their flow charts. Monitor and help with vocabulary. Encourage students to speak in complete sentences.

SPEAKING

PREPARATION FOR SPEAKING

1 👥 👥👥 Display the photographs on an interactive whiteboard. Ask students to work in pairs and make notes to answer the questions. Allow three or four minutes for note-taking. Monitor and help with the vocabulary to describe the photographs. Students share their ideas with the class. As they speak, write their ideas on the whiteboard in bullet points.

> **Suggested answers**
>
> dead fish / dirty rivers / people threw rubbish in the water / water pollution / oil spill / boats polluted the water, etc.

2 👥 Students complete the task in pairs. Encourage them to use the Glossary to check the meaning of new words. Monitor and help with the task if necessary. When students have finished, discuss the answers as a class.

> **Answers**
>
> 1 b 2 a 3 d 4 c

3 👥 👥👥 Students work in pairs and prepare a flow chart using the information from Exercise 2. Allow five or six minutes for the task. Monitor and check understanding of the vocabulary in the task. Students then change partners and tell their new partners about the information in the flow chart. Monitor, and encourage students to expand their answers by adding the information from the whiteboard (see Exercise 1 above). When they have finished, ask for volunteers to display their flow charts and to explain them to the class. If possible, encourage students to use the flow-chart tool in Word or other programs. Students can teach each other how to use this tool if necessary.

DESCRIBING A TOPIC

4 🔊 10.5 👤 👥 Ask students to fill in the gaps individually. Students then listen and check their answers. Allow a couple of minutes for students to compare their answers with a partner and check the meaning of new words in the Glossary. At the end, check understanding of the words in the box and elicit example sentences from students.

> **Answers**
>
> 1 population 2 This means that 3 This is because 4 can be 5 For example

5 🔊 10.6 👥 Students fill in the gaps in pairs. Then they listen and check their answers. Allow them a couple of minutes to compare their answers and check the meaning of new words in the Glossary. Check the answers as a class.

> **Answers**
>
> 1 Ships 2 sending goods 3 ships 4 For example 5 become dirty

> **Optional activity**
>
> 🔊 10.6 👥👥 👥👥 Play the audio one more time to drill the sentence stress and pronunciation. Pause after each sentence and ask students to repeat it together as they heard it on the recording. Emphasize the stressed syllables by tapping on a desk. Allow students two or three minutes to practise saying the extract in pairs. Monitor and give feedback on sentence stress and pronunciation of the individual words.

6 👤 👥 Students work individually and make notes to complete the sentences about trains. Allow them two or three minutes to make notes. Then they practise describing their topics in pairs. Monitor and give feedback on vocabulary and grammar. When they have finished, ask for volunteers to present their ideas to the class.

DESCRIBING A PROBLEM

7 🔊 10.7 👥 Students complete the gaps in pairs. Encourage them to use the Glossary. Students then listen and check their answers. Display the activity on an interactive whiteboard and ask for volunteers to fill in the gaps. Elicit the pronunciation of the past verb forms. If necessary, drill the pronunciation of the past verb forms.

> **Answers**
>
> 1 happened /ˈhæpənd/ 2 used /juːzd/ 3 were /wɜː/ 4 had /hæd/ 5 came /keɪm/ 6 killed /kɪld/ 7 were /wɜː/ 8 could not / couldn't /ˈkʊdənt/

PRONUNCIATION FOR SPEAKING

8 🔊 10.8 👥👥 👥👥 Students work in pairs and decide in which verbs we do not pronounce the vowel in the -ed suffix. Encourage students to practise saying the verbs aloud. Then they listen and check their answers. If necessary, play the audio one more time and pause after each word. Ask students to repeat the pronunciation.

9 and 10 (◀ **10.8**) 🎧 Students listen to the audio again and complete Exercise 9. They compare their answers with a partner. Then they complete the table headings in Exercise 10. Display the table on an interactive whiteboard and check the answers as a class. Drill the pronunciation of the past verb forms. Ask for volunteers to make example sentences with the new verbs.

Answers

Exercise 9: happened /d/   used /d/   visited /ɪd/
guessed /t/   added /ɪd/   hated /ɪd/
asked /t/   helped /t/   showed /d/   watched /t/
changed /d/   decided /ɪd/
Exercise 10: 1 /t/ 2 /d/ 3 /ɪd/

DESCRIBING A SOLUTION

11 🧍🎧 Students complete the task individually, then check their answers with a partner. Check the answers as a class. As a class, mark the most stressed words in the sentences and drill them together. Allow a minute for students to practise saying these sentences in pairs.

Answers

1 They <u>decided</u> to make <u>companies clean</u> the <u>rivers</u>.
2 The <u>companies</u> had to <u>buy modern ships</u>.
3 The <u>companies cleaned</u> the <u>rivers</u>.

12 🎧🎧 Students work in pairs and make notes to answer the questions. Allow three or four minutes for brainstorming and note-making. Monitor and help with vocabulary for the task. Students then work with another pair and discuss their ideas.

DESCRIBING RESULTS

13 (◀ **10.9**) 🧍🎧 Students listen and complete the task individually. Then they check their answers with a partner. Play the audio again and pause after each statement. Ask students to repeat the sentences as they heard them on the recording. Make sure students follow

the rhythm of the recording. Allow a couple of minutes for students to practise saying the sentences in pairs.

Answers

2 Why? Because the companies weren't happy that they had to clean the rivers.
8 I think it was a good solution.
5 But there was some good news.
7 That means there are more fish than before.
1 So, was it a good solution? Well, that's a very interesting question!
4 And they didn't want to pay to clean the rivers.
6 The fishermen are happier because the rivers are cleaner.
3 The old ships were cheap, but modern ships are expensive.

14 🎧 Students complete the task in pairs. Monitor and give feedback on the pronunciation of the key vocabulary and grammar. Monitor and write down any common mistakes you hear. Elicit the correct answers from the class at the end.

SPEAKING TASK

1 🎧🎧 Divide the class into Group A and Group B. Students discuss the questions in threes or fours with students from the same group. Monitor and help with grammar and vocabulary for the task. Allow four or five minutes for discussion, then ask the groups to share their ideas with the class.

Possible answers

2 a People cannot move quickly; people can be late (e.g. for work, for a meeting, etc.).
  b Parents can't see their children. / Young children go to bed before the parents come home. / Young children / families are unhappy.

PREPARE

2 and 3 🎧 Students work with a partner from the same group and answer the questions about the photographs. Encourage students to use the Glossary. Allow four or five minutes for the task, then ask students to prepare a flow chart about the traffic problems and solutions in the city they were assigned. Students can use Word or other software to make their flow charts.

Answers

A & B: 1 c 2 a 3 d 4 b

PRESENT

4 👥 Ask students to work with a new partner from the same group. Students use their flow charts to describe the problem and solution in their city. Monitor and give feedback on vocabulary and pronunciation. Write down any common mistakes you hear. Elicit the correct answers from the class at the end.

5 👥 Students work with a partner from another group and describe the problem and solution using their flow charts and photographs. Allow 10–15 minute for the task. Monitor and encourage students to expand their ideas.

DISCUSS

6 👥👥 Ask for volunteers to present their problem and solution to the class. Ask for two or three volunteers from each group. Then discuss the questions as a class.

> ### Optional activity
>
> 👤👥 Students record themselves (or make a video) describing the problem and solution. They could use the photographs from the book or the internet and use them in a video with a voiceover (their voice) explaining the transportation problem and the solution. Students prepare their recordings individually, then play them in small groups. Other students listen and write down any grammar or pronunciation mistakes they hear. Students give each other constructive feedback at the end. Ask for volunteers to show their movies to the class.

OBJECTIVES REVIEW

See Teaching tips, pages 10–11, for ideas about using the Objectives review with your students.

WORDLIST

See Teaching tips, pages 10–11, for ideas about how to make the most of the Wordlist with your students.

REVIEW TEST

See pages 124–125 for the photocopiable Review test for this unit and Teaching tips, pages 10–11, for ideas about when and how to administer the Review test.

ADDITIONAL SPEAKING TASK

See page 135 for an additional speaking task related to this unit.

If necessary, check understanding of the useful expressions in the Model language section. Students work in pairs and brainstorm different traffic problems in their city. Elicit ideas from the class and draw an ideas map on the whiteboard. Ask pairs to choose one of the problems from the brainstorming session. Allow students up to ten minutes to make a list of possible solutions. Students then discuss which of the solutions on their list is the best. Ask the pairs to present their problem and solution to the class.

RESEARCH PROJECT

> ### Research and share how transport may change in the future
>
> Divide the class into groups. Ask some groups to research different types of transport being used today. Ask the other groups to research future types of transport. They can do this by searching for 'proposed future transport' or looking at an online encyclopedia. Each group could think about what is good and bad about the different types of transport.
>
> Tell the class that they are going to use the tools on the Cambridge LMS to share the information which they have collected. Students could vote on which form of future transport they would most like to use. Students could use an online voting system. Search for 'voting software' to view some of these.

REVIEW TESTS ANSWERS AND AUDIO SCRIPTS

The *Review tests* are designed to be used after students have completed each unit of the Student's Book. Each *Review test* checks students' knowledge of the key language areas and practises the listening skills from the unit. The *Review tests* take around 50 minutes to complete, but you may wish to adjust this time depending on your class or how much of the Student's Book unit you covered.

Review tests can be given for homework as general revision. *Review test* audio is accessed from the Cambridge LMS. Use the *Additional speaking tasks* at the end of the Teacher's Book or in the Online Workbook to test your students' speaking skills. Photocopy one test for each student. Students should do the tests on their own. You can check the answers by giving students their peers' papers to mark, or correct the papers yourself. Keep a record of the results to help monitor individual student progress.

REVIEW TEST 1 ANSWERS

1 1 student (2) 2 teacher (2) 3 university (5) 4 car (1)
5 father (2) 6 home (1) 7 hotel (2) 8 presenter (3)
9 computer (3) 10 school (1)
2 1 T 2 F 3 T 4 F 5 F 6 T 7 T 8 T 9 F 10 T
3 1 He 2 his 3 I 4 Her 5 their
4 1 is 2 are 3 Are 4 is 5 am
5 1 F 2 T 3 T 4 F 5 T

REVIEW TEST 1 AUDIO SCRIPTS

◀) 1.1

1 student 2 teacher 3 university 4 car 5 father 6 home
7 hotel 8 presenter 9 computer 10 school

◀) 1.2

Hi! My name is Samira and I come from Egypt. I'm 19 years old and I'm a college student in Sydney. That's in Australia. I study business here. In the future, I want to be a successful businesswoman. I have two younger brothers and one older sister. My little brothers are still at school. They like football and video games. My sister is 22. She is a student at Cairo University. She wants to be a doctor. My parents live in Alexandria. My mother is a science teacher at a high school and my father is a hotel manager. They work very hard. In my free time, I like to draw. I love *manga*. I like Japanese culture and food. I hope to go there one day.

REVIEW TEST 2 ANSWERS

1 1 cold 2 snow 3 rainy 4 June 5 sunny
2 1 It's a cold day in winter.
2 There's snow in the mountains.
3 It's rainy in spring.
4 It's hot in June.
5 It's sunny but it's winter.
3 1 desert 2 red 3 dry 4 47 5 winter

4 1 c 2 a 3 b 4 b 5 c
5 1 mountains 2 forest 3 beautiful 4 inside 5 sky
6 1 January 2 August 3 July 4 September 5 February
7 1 T 2 F 3 F 4 T 5 T

REVIEW TEST 2 AUDIO SCRIPTS

◀) 2.1

1 It's a cold day in winter.
2 There's snow in the mountains.
3 It's rainy in spring.
4 It's hot in June.
5 It's sunny, but it's winter.

◀) 2.2

Today, I want to talk about the weather in Rub Al Khali. Do you know what Rub Al Khali means? It means 'the empty quarter' or 'an empty place'. It's the name of the desert in Saudi Arabia and the United Arab Emirates. It's a very big desert. In this photograph, you can see the sand. There is a lot of sand there. The sand is red and it looks like big mountains. Most people never visit this place because it's very hot and dry. The average temperature in the summer is 47 degrees centigrade. On a very hot day, it can be 56 degrees centigrade. But in the winter, the weather in Rub Al Khali is cooler, and people like to spend nights in the desert camping. From December to February, the nights in the desert can be very cold. In this photograph, you can see palm trees and houses. It's Liwa Oasis. It's green and sunny. There's a lot of water here for the farms and people. The weather in the oasis is good for people. It rains here a few times a year.

REVIEW TEST 3 ANSWERS

1 1 a 3 b 1 c 2
2 a 1 b 3 c 2
3 a 2 b 1 c 3
2 1 ↘ 2 ↘ 3 ↗ 4 ↘ 5 ↗
3 1 F 2 T 3 F 4 F 5 T 6 T
4 1 Sunday 2 Thursday 3 Friday 4 Saturday
5 Wednesday
5 1 at; in 2 on 3 at 4 in
6 1 She plays tennis every Monday.
2 I don't watch television at night.
3 Do you eat lunch at home?
4 What time do you get up every morning?
5 He doesn't walk to school.

REVIEW TEST 3 AUDIO SCRIPTS

◀) 3.1

1 **A:** What would you like to order?
B: Just a cup of tea, please.
A: And what about you?
C: I'll have coffee.
A: Anything else?
2 **A:** Hello! This is Dora's Gym. How can I help you?
B: I'd like more information about your programmes and membership fees.
A: Hold on a moment, please. I'll transfer your call.
B: Thank you. I'll wait.

3 A: I'm sorry for missing your lecture. Can you tell me about the assignment?

B: What happened?

A: Well, I woke up at seven … but then I closed my eyes and I fell asleep again. I woke up again at nine and it was too late.

B: Well, you missed the lecture and the assignment. What you have to do now …

🔊 3.2

1 What would you like to order?

2 And what about you?

3 Anything else?

4 How can I help you?

5 Can you tell me about the assignment?

🔊 3.3

Sam: Excuse me! My name's Sam and I'm doing a survey about young people's lifestyle in London. Can I ask you some questions?

John: Yes, of course.

Sam: What's your name?

John: I'm John.

Sam: First of all, how old are you?

John: I'm 23.

Sam: And are you from London?

John: No. I'm from Liverpool, but I moved here two years ago for work.

Sam: OK … do you go out to eat often?

John: Yes, I go out with friends quite often … usually we eat out in the evenings. I don't like cooking dinners or eating alone.

Sam: And what types of restaurant do you usually go to?

John: I like fast food. I know – it's unhealthy, but it's cheap and quick.

Sam: Mm-hmm. What about other places? Do you go anywhere else?

John: Sometimes we go to a cinema, and then we go and have some pizza. There is a great pizza place near my apartment.

Sam: And what about lunch … do you go out to have lunch?

John: No. That's too expensive. I make my own sandwiches and take them to work with me.

Sam: OK. And what about sport or entertainment? Do you go to the gym?

John: Not really. Again, it's very expensive and I don't like to exercise inside. I play football at the weekend and I jog in the park when it's sunny.

Sam: And do you go to the theatre a lot?

John: Not really … maybe once a year. I prefer the cinema.

Sam: OK. Thank you for your time.

REVIEW TEST 4 ANSWERS

1 1 This 2 There 3 here 4 this 5 Those

2 1 b 2 a 3 b 4 c 5 a

3 1 big 2 ground 3 cappuccino 4 three 5 get a map of the museum

4 A museum shop B stairs C café D lifts E toilets

5 1 F 2 T 3 T 4 F 5 F 6 T 7 F

6 1 Turkey 2 Europe 3 Italy 4 Asia 5 London 6 America 7 Spain 8 Moscow

REVIEW TEST 4 AUDIO SCRIPTS

🔊 4.1

A: So … have you decided where we can go during the long weekend?

B: I have some ideas. Here are some brochures I got from the tourist agency.

A: So … what's this?

B: This is a cycling trip along the river. We start in the city centre and then cycle in a group to the nearest town. There we have lunch and rest. Then we come back here.

A: That sounds a little bit boring. What about this one? This looks interesting.

B: Oh yeah … that's a day trip on a boat. You stop in small towns and walk around. Those are very quiet places.

A: Is there any food on the boat?

B: No. There's no food on the boat … just drinks. But you can get it on the way.

A: So what do you think?

B: I like the cycling tour better. It's good exercise and it can be interesting.

A: OK. We'll do that, then.

🔊 4.2

Welcome to Oxford and thank you for visiting our museum. It's a really big building and it will take you several hours to see all the rooms. I don't want you to get lost, so I will just quickly explain the layout of the museum. Please have a look at these maps. So … we are now on the ground floor in front of the main entrance. If you look at this map, you will see that the building has empty space inside. It's called a patio. There is a small garden and the museum café. They make delicious cappuccino. The museum has three floors, and you can use the lifts to move from one floor to another – they're here on the left. If you like exercise, you can use the stairs. There are two sets of stairs. One in Room A2 and the other in Room A5. You can use either. Now, the toilets are next to the information desk and on the right of the ticket office. At the information desk, you can get maps of the museum and more information about our future exhibitions. It's also a good meeting point if you get lost. Some of you may want to spend some time in our museum shop. We have beautiful souvenirs, books and posters. So please allow yourself some time for shopping. The museum shop is on the other side of the building, between Rooms A3 and A4.

REVIEW TEST 5 ANSWERS

1 1 F 2 T 3 T 4 F 5 F

2

/k/ country	/f/ phone	/ŋ/ strong
classes quick	find	doing running

3 1 running 2 cheap 3 easy 4 back 5 exercise 6 shoes 7 water 8 warm 9 places 10 night

4 1 slow 2 weak 3 unhappy/sad 4 thin 5 unhealthy

5 1 swimming 2 tennis 3 football 4 basketball 5 diving

6 1 I think baseball is ~~more~~ easier than volleyball.
2 In my opinion, yoga is **healthier** than running.
3 Tennis players are ~~more~~ **stronger** than golf players.
4 I think zumba is **better** than judo.
5 Skiing is more dangerous **than** kung fu.

REVIEW TEST 5 AUDIO SCRIPTS

◀ 5.1

A: Hi, Abdullah … what have you been doing today?

B: I went to the gym. You know, the one on the way from the university.

A: Yeah, I know that place. Why did you go there?

B: I wanted to find out what activities they have. I don't like just working out. I'd like to learn something new, like kung fu or judo.

A: And can they teach these at the gym?

B: Well, yes. They told me that they have judo classes every Monday and Wednesday. But you have to be quick and strong to do it. I'm not sure if I am.

A: Is there anything else you can do there?

B: Yes, they have yoga classes.

A: Yes, yoga is slower than judo.

B: That's right, and it will make me stronger. But it's on Tuesdays and Fridays at 8 a.m. I'm not sure …

◀ 5.2

classes … doing … find … quick … running

◀ 5.3

Thank you for having me here today. I want to talk to you about jogging, or running. Many people go jogging because it's cheap and easy. It's cheaper than going to a gym and it can keep you fit and healthy. But there are a few things you must think about before you start jogging. You may ask 'What's the problem?' Well, jogging can cause problems in your back. It's very important that you exercise a little before you run. Also, make sure that your running shoes are comfortable. Another thing is drinking water. After a long run, you can feel tired and sleepy. Drink a lot of water before and after jogging. In the winter, wear warm clothes and don't stay outside for too long. And don't run when it's snowing. Finally, make sure you're safe, so don't run in places you don't know or late at night. On the campus, we have a lot of paths for runners, and you can do it any time you want and as long as you want. The university campus has lights and security, so it's better if you stay on the campus. Now, let's talk about …

REVIEW TEST 6 ANSWERS

1 1 b 2 a 3 a 4 c 5 c
2 1 have to 2 have 3 has to 4 have to 5 has
3 1 learn 2 polite 3 interesting 4 clean 5 look 6 late
7 early 8 read 9 questions 10 work
4 1 T 2 F 3 T 4 T 5 F
5 1 c 2 a 3 e 4 b 5 d
6 1 I think you should work hard.
2 Students have to study every day.
3 I don't think you should watch movies at night.
4 What should I do?
5 Should I get a job?

REVIEW TEST 6 AUDIO SCRIPTS

◀ 6.1

A: Did you talk to your teacher?

B: Well, yeah. Like you told me, I went to see her to talk about which courses to take next year.

A: And what did she say?

B: She said I should get a job before I choose my major.

A: So she didn't say you should study medicine?

B: No, Mom, she didn't.

A: But what about your future? You have very good grades and you work so hard, you should be a doctor.

B: Ah … well, I was thinking that I should get a part-time job this year before I choose my major. It will give me time to think.

A: But what kind of job can you do? Work in a supermarket? Or a fast-food place? I don't think you should do that.

B: No. I've applied for a part-time job as a receptionist in a hospital. They say I can …

◀ 6.2

1 Doctors have to work at night.
2 Teachers have a lot of holidays.
3 A fireman has to be strong.
4 Scientists have to be clever.
5 My sister has a good job.

◀ 6.3

A: OK … now, let me introduce our next speaker today: Mr Charles Han. Mr Han works for the university HR department and so I thought he would be the best person to talk to you about job interviews. Please give him a warm welcome.

B: Thank you for inviting me to your Careers Day. As I understand, many of you have started applying for jobs. So if you find a job you like, you send your application, and then you have to go to a job interview. That's when the managers of the company want to meet you and learn more about you. How many of you have done job interviews before? Please raise your hands … Not many, I see. So, for me, the best candidate is polite, clever and interesting. You have to prepare for the interview, which means you should wear clean clothes, look good and healthy, and bring your documents with you. You should never be late for your interview. So make sure that the night before your interview, you go to bed early and don't oversleep. Another important thing is to read about the company you want to work for. Go online and read about them so that you can answer any questions they ask you. Also, find out the salary you would like to earn and don't be afraid to discuss it.

C: Sir!

B: Yes. Do you have a question?

C: Yes … I want to know what questions they will ask me.

B: That's a good question. You should think about the questions they will ask you and prepare yourself. The most popular questions are about your job experience. Where did you work before, and what did you do there? Another common question is 'Why you are interested in the job?' You should remember that …

REVIEW TEST 7 ANSWERS

1 1 F 2 T 3 T 4 F 5 F
2 1 feed 2 same 3 living 4 bed 5 small
3 1 a 2 b 3 a 4 b 5 c
4 1, 3, 4, 6, 8
5 1 lamp 2 chair 3 armchair 4 sofa 5 study desk
6 1 comfortable 2 quiet 3 cheaper 4 far 5 wooden
7 1 kitchen 2 bathroom 3 classroom 4 computer lab
5 language centre

REVIEW TEST 7 AUDIO SCRIPTS

🔊 7.1

A: Have you decided what colour you want to paint your room?

B: Not yet. I like green because it's very soft and calm.

A: Er … are you sure? It reminds me of a hospital building or a school. It's not a good colour for a bedroom.

B: Do you think so? What about blue? I think blue will look good in the bedroom. It'll be the same colour as the armchair and the curtains.

A: But it will be too much blue in one room. Why don't you paint the room yellow? It's clean and fresh. I think blue and yellow go well together.

B: OK. But what about the living room? Do you think we should paint that, too?

A: I think so. I'd like to paint it red.

B: Red? No, that's too strong. The room will look small and it will …

🔊 7.2

1 feed **2** same **3** living **4** bed **5** small

🔊 7.3

A: On today's show, I'd like to welcome Ellen Lee. Ellen has recently published a book about feng shui for college students. Ellen, can you tell us more about it?

B: Yes. My book is about using the principles of feng shui in students' dormitories or residences. I feel that college students can improve their grades and health by following feng shui.

A: So can you quickly explain what feng shui is?

B: It's an old Chinese study which says that the way our environment is organized can change the way we feel. So if we follow the principles of feng shui, we can improve our lives. We can use feng shui to decorate our homes, organize the furniture or even the gardens and outdoor space. There are rules for different rooms in the house – for example, in the bedroom you should make sure that your feet don't face the door.

B: And so how can college students apply these rules in their dorms?

A: The first rule is to keep your room clean, especially your desk. Clean up your desk before you study as it will help you concentrate. Another thing is to make sure your desk is facing the door. You can also improve the feng shui in your room by burning candles or putting plants in the corners. Green plants will keep you calm and ready to work hard. Finally, decorate your room with red and orange pillows and carpets. They will give you more energy to study.

B: This is very interesting. Can you tell us more about …

REVIEW TEST 8 ANSWERS

1 1 dinner 2 fish 3 beef 4 vegetable 5 noodles

2 1 13 2 Sunday 16th July 3 7 p.m. 4 Sarah
5 054 677 5638

3 1 more than five 2 between one and five
3 one or less 4 home 5 fast food 6 cafeteria
7 nuts and dried fruit 8 sweets 9 crisps
10 chocolate

4 1 some 2 any 3 much 4 any/many 5 many

5 1 Are there **any** bananas?
2 Is there **any/much** tea left?
3 How **much** water do you need?
4 There is **some** food in the kitchen. / There **isn't** any food in the kitchen.

5 How **much** beef do you need?

6 1 chicken 2 cheese 3 rice 4 bread 5 noodles

REVIEW TEST 8 AUDIO SCRIPTS

🔊 8.1

A: Hello. Is this the Han Kang restaurant?

B: Yes, it is. How can I help you?

A: I'm organizing a dinner for some guests at the university. They're from Korea. Do you think they'll enjoy your menu?

B: I think so. We have a lot of traditional dishes with fried beef and fish. But for special occasions, I'd recommend a Korean barbecue.

A: What is that?

B: It's a plate with small pieces of beef which you can grill at the table. We serve it with spicy sauces and vegetable dishes.

A: And do you serve noodles?

B: Yes, we have noodles with fish and vegetables.

A: That sounds great. I'd like to book a table for 13 people for a Korean barbecue.

B: When?

A: On Saturday the 15th of July.

B: Er … Saturday … We're very busy. What time do you want to come?

A: Seven o'clock in the evening.

B: We're already fully booked in the evening. Can I recommend Sunday?

A: The next day? Oh, that sounds fine. So it will be Sunday at seven.

B: That's right. Can I have your name and phone number, please?

A: Yes, it's Sarah with an H.

B: S-A-R-A-H?

A: That's correct. My phone number is 054 677 5638.

B: Let me check. It's 0-5-4 6-double 7 5-6-4-8?

A: No, no! It's 3-8 at the end.

B: OK. Anything else?

🔊 8.2

Chris: Hello, today we'd like to share with you the results of our survey about student eating habits. We were interested in this topic because food is very important, and we felt that many students don't eat healthily. I'll let Sam explain the pie charts.

Sam: OK, thank you, Chris. So, we interviewed 50 students on campus. The first pie chart shows how much fruit students eat. Unfortunately, most students – that is, 65% – eat one piece of fruit or less. But 15% eat five pieces of fruit or more. That's very good. The rest of the students – 20% – eat between one and five pieces. The second pie chart shows where students usually eat. As you can see, most of the students eat in the university cafeteria. Only 10% eat at home, and 15% eat fast food every day. The students said that the food in the cafeteria is more interesting and cheaper. It's good value for money. Finally, we asked about snack food. We know that all students eat snack food, especially when they study at night. The favourite snack food is chocolate. Almost 50% of students eat it during exams. Another 25% of students eat crisps and 15% eat sweets. Only 10% of students snack on nuts and dried fruit, which are the healthiest snacks. So, to summarize this …

REVIEW TEST 9 ANSWERS

1 1 T 2 T 3 F 4 T 5 F 6 T 7 F 8 F 9 T 10 F
2 1 b, c 2 c, d 3 a, c 4 a 5 d 6 a 7 b
3 1 leaves 2 wet 3 brain 4 climbed 5 jungle
4 1 crocodile 2 snake 3 whale 4 bear 5 lion
5 1 b 2 a 3 d 4 e 5 c

REVIEW TEST 9 AUDIO SCRIPTS

◀)) 9.1

A: I've just finished the writing assignment. What about you?
B: No. I've been trying to finish it for three days now. I find it really difficult.
A: What's the problem?
B: Well, I wanted to write about penguins, and so I started to read about them, but now I have too much information, and we only have to write 500 words.
A: Let's see if I can help you with it. Mm … so you want to write about the Emperor penguin. But why?
B: I saw this great documentary on television and got really interested. Did you know that they can't fly, but they're excellent divers? They can stay under water for up to 20 minutes.
A: Can they swim very fast?
B: Not that fast, only 10 kilometres per hour.
A: Do you have any other amazing facts about them?
B: Well … let me look at my notes … did you know that they can drink salt water? Just like seals and sea lions.
A: Really? It seems you have some interesting facts about them. Why don't you …

◀)) 9.2

A: Hello, everybody! Today on *Amazing Animals* we have a special guest from Mongolia. Bolormaa is a student at Manchester University, but she's originally from Ulan Bator in Mongolia. Welcome to our podcast.
B: Thank you for having me here. I love to talk about my country.
A: So, what animals can people see in Mongolia?
B: Well, the most popular animals in Mongolia are horses. In fact, they are called Mongol horses. You can recognize them immediately. They are short and very strong. These horses can be found everywhere around my country. They are very different from the typical Arabian horses you see here, for example.
A: And what other animals can people see in Mongolia?
B: I think our camels are very interesting. My uncle, who lives close to the Gobi desert, has a few camels. Mongolian camels have two humps. Unfortunately, they are in danger of dying out. I have read that there are only two million left in the world.
A: Really? That's very bad. Do you know what causes this?
B: I believe it's because of the growing human population. The camels are losing their natural environment. They don't have enough food and water.
A: Is it true that camels carry water in their humps?
B: No, it's not. In fact, a camel's hump is made of fat, which changes into energy when it's needed.
A: And how do they survive the cold winters?
B: That's a good question. The winters in Mongolia are extremely cold; in January, for example, it can be minus 30 degrees at night. During this season, the camels grow a woolly coat which protects them from the cold. In the spring, they lose the hair because the summers are very hot. Camel hair is used to …

REVIEW TEST 10 ANSWERS

1 1 T 2 T 3 F 4 T 5 F
2 1 2014 2 1997 3 2007 4 1979 5 1832
3 1 Cycle 2 blue 3 rent 4 2010 5 health
6 49% (forty-nine percent)
7 47,000 (forty-seven thousand) 8 credit card
9 7 (seven) 10 bikes
4 1 plane 2 boat 3 train 4 car 5 bicycle/bike
5 1 arrive 2 traffic jam 3 takes off 4 destination
5 ticket
6 1 had 2 opened 3 went 4 wanted 5 came

REVIEW TEST 10 AUDIO SCRIPTS

◀)) 10.1

A: Have you decided which transport solution you will talk about?
B: No. I wanted to talk about electric cars, but now I've changed my mind. What about you?
A: I think I'll talk about electric buses. Last year, when I was in Seoul, I saw an electric bus – it was really interesting.
B: Was it like a trolleybus? You know, a bus which uses an electric connection.
A: No. It was very different. It's called OLEV – O-L-E-V – and it means an 'online electric vehicle'.
B: But how is it different from other electric vehicles?
A: It doesn't use any fuel and it doesn't need to stop to get electricity. It can do it while it's moving.
B: Do you know how it works?
A: From what I understand, the bus uses WiFi to get electricity.
B: It seems like an interesting solution. It can help with the air pollution in big cities.
A: I think so. It can be used as public transport. I have read that some cities in Europe and America want to try this solution, but there are still few problems with …

◀)) 10.2

1 2014 **2** 1997 **3** 2007 **4** 1979 **5** 1832

◀)) 10.3

A: … another transport solution introduced in London is Barclays Cycle Hire, or BCH. Has anyone seen these bikes? Yes?
B: Are they blue?
A: That's right. The blue bikes you see in London are part of the Barclays Cycle Hire programme. People can rent a bike on the street, travel to their destination, then return the bike in another place in the city. The programme was introduced in 2010. The aim is to make people walk and cycle more. This is good for their health and for the environment. Our research shows that 49% of our members said they are now more interested in cycling, and during the 2012 Olympic Games, people hired around 47,000 bicycles in one day – that is, of course, the biggest number in one day.
B: I wanted to ask … how can people hire these bikes?
A: It's very easy. First of all, anyone with a credit card and a PIN can hire a bike. If you have a credit card, you can rent a bike for 24 hours or seven days. Another way is to go to our website and sign up to be a member. This way, you can buy a one-year membership and use the bikes any time and anywhere you want in the city. Now, let me tell you more about …

Name: .... **Date:** ....

LISTENING (20 marks)

LISTENING 1

1 (◀ **1.1**) Listen and write the number of syllables you hear next to each word.
1 mark for each correct answer.

1 student _____

2 teacher _____

3 university _____

4 car _____

5 father _____

6 home _____

7 hotel _____

8 presenter _____

9 computer _____

10 school _____

LISTENING 2

2 (◀ **1.2**) Listen to the recording. Are the sentences true (T) or false (F)?
1 mark for each correct answer.

1 Samira is Egyptian. _____

2 She is 18 years old. _____

3 She lives in Australia. _____

4 She wants to be a hotel manager. _____

5 She has two older brothers and a younger sister. _____

6 Her brothers love football. _____

7 Her sister wants to become a doctor. _____

8 Her parents live in Alexandria. _____

9 Her parents are both science teachers. _____

10 She wants to visit Japan. _____

LANGUAGE DEVELOPMENT (15 marks)

3 Circle the correct words. 1 mark for each correct answer.

1 *He / His* is 19 years old.

2 This is *his / he* car.

3 *I / My* want to be a businessman.

4 *She / Her* teacher is from Australia.

5 Is it *their / they* house?

4 Complete the sentences with the correct form of the verb *be* from the box. Some words can be used more than once. 1 mark for each correct answer.

| are   is   am |

1 My name _____ Sue.

2 Her parents _____ Chinese.

3 _____ you a student?

4 Her older brother _____ a doctor.

5 I _____ from Hong Kong.

5 Are the sentences true (T) or false (F)? 1 mark for each correct answer.

1 'Brother' is a type of an **occupation**. _____

2 China is a **country**. _____

3 My mother and father are my **parents**. _____

4 Someone who plays a lot of basketball is a **businessman**. _____

5 **Scientists** study how things work. _____

TOTAL _____/ 35

Name: .... **Date:** ....

LISTENING (20 marks)

LISTENING 1

1 (◀) **2.1** Listen and circle the words you hear. 1 mark for each correct answer.

1 It's a *cold / hot* day in winter.

2 There's *sand / snow* in the mountains.

3 It's *rainy / sunny* in spring.

4 It's hot in *June / July*.

5 It's *sunny / rainy*, but it's winter.

2 (◀) **2.1** Listen again and underline the most stressed words in each sentence in Exercise 1. 1 mark for each correct sentence.

LISTENING 2

3 (◀) **2.2** Listen and complete the sentences below with the words in the box. There are some words you will not need. 1 mark for each correct answer.

47 57 desert dry forest red spring wet white winter

1 Rub Al Khali is a _____.

2 The sand there is _____.

3 The weather is hot and _____.

4 In summer, it's usually about _____ °C.

5 People camp in Rub Al Khali in _____.

4 (♦ 2.2) Listen again and choose the correct ending (a, b or c). 1 mark for each correct answer.

1 The talk is about
   a people in Rub Al Khali.
   b farms in Liwa Oasis.
   c the weather in Rub Al Khali.

2 Rub Al Khali means
   a 'an empty place'.
   b 'a hot place'.
   c 'a sandy place'.

3 It gets colder in the desert
   a in summer.
   b between December and February.
   c in spring.

4 Liwa Oasis is very
   a sandy and hot.
   b green and sunny.
   c cold and windy.

5 It rains there
   a in winter.
   b in autumn.
   c a few times a year.

LANGUAGE DEVELOPMENT (15 marks)

5 Complete the sentences with the words from the box. You will not need all the words.
1 mark for each correct answer.

beautiful forest inside mountains sea sky

1 You can see snow on top of these _____. They are very high.
2 The trees in the _____ change colour in autumn.
3 It's a _____ day – we should go to the beach.
4 I like to stay _____ when it rains. I don't like to get wet.
5 There are no clouds in the _____.

6 Correct the spelling mistakes in the names of the months. 1 mark for each correct answer.
1 Janaury 2 Ogust 3 Julay 4 Setpember 5 Ferbruary

7 Are the sentences true (T) or false (F)? 1 mark for each correct answer.
1 The sky is blue. _____
2 Grass is white. _____
3 Snow is black. _____
4 Tomatoes can be red or green. _____
5 Trees can be red and yellow in the autumn.

TOTAL _____ / 35

Name: .... **Date:** ....

LISTENING (20 marks)

LISTENING 1

1 (🔊 **3.1**) Listen to three conversations in different places. Write 1, 2 or 3.
1 mark for each correct answer.

1 Which conversation is

a at university? _____

b in a café? _____

c on the phone? _____

2 Which conversation is between

a two friends and a waiter? _____

b a lecturer and a student? _____

c a person and a receptionist? _____

3 Which conversation has somebody who wants to ask

a about gym membership? _____

b what people want to eat and drink? _____

c about an assignment? _____

2 (🔊 **3.2**) Listen to the questions from the conversations again. Do they have falling or rising intonation? Write ➚ if it is rising and ➘ if it is falling. 1 mark for each correct answer.

1 What would you like to order? _____

2 And what about you? _____

3 Anything else? _____

4 How can I help you? _____

5 Can you tell me about the assignment? _____

LISTENING 2

3 (🔊 **3.3**) Listen to the recording. Are the statements true (T) or false (F)? 1 mark for each correct answer.

1 John is from London. _____

2 He doesn't like to cook for himself. _____

3 He doesn't like to eat fast food. _____

4 He eats lunch in a café every day. _____

5 He plays football at the weekends. _____

6 He likes to go jogging in the park. _____

LANGUAGE DEVELOPMENT (15 marks)

4 Correct the spelling mistakes in the days of the week. 1 mark for each correct answer.

1 Sanday   2 Thersday   3 Fraiday   4 Saterday   5 Wenesday

5 Complete the sentences with the prepositions from the box. Some prepositions can be used more than once. 1 mark for each correct answer.

at   in   on

1 Amal gets up _____ 7.45 _____ the morning.
2 Yen goes to cinema with friends _____ Tuesdays.
3 My English classes start _____ nine.
4 I prefer to study _____ the evening.

6 Unscramble the words to make sentences. 1 mark for each correct sentence.

1 every Monday / plays / tennis / She / .

_____

2 at night / don't / watch / I / television / .

_____

3 eat lunch / at home / you / Do / ?

_____

4 do / What time / morning / you / get up / every / .

_____

5 to school / He / walk / doesn't / .

_____

TOTAL _____/ 35

Name: ....   **Date:** ....

LISTENING (20 marks)

LISTENING 1

1 (◀)) **4.1** Listen to two students and complete the sentences with the correct direction words. 1 mark for each correct answer.

1 _____ is a cycling trip along the river.

2 _____ we have lunch and rest.

3 Then we come back _____.

4 What about _____ one?

5 _____ are very quiet places.

2 (◀)) **4.1** Listen again and choose the correct answer (a, b or c). 1 mark for each correct answer.

1 What are the students talking about?
   a their summer holiday
   b plans for a long weekend
   c activities in their city

2 The cycling trip
   a has a lunch break.
   b is not with other people.
   c starts at the river.

3 The boat trip
   a is half a day.
   b takes a day.
   c is in the morning.

4 There is
   a food and drink on the boat.
   b just food on the boat.
   c no food on the boat.

5 The students choose
   a the cycling trip.
   b the boat trip.
   c to stay at home.

LISTENING 2

3 (◀)) **4.2** Listen to the recording and circle the correct words. 1 mark for each correct answer.

1 The museum is in a very *big / small* building.

2 The speaker is on the *ground / first* floor.

3 The tourists should try the *ice cream / cappuccino* in the café.

4 The museum has *two / three* floors.

5 The information desk is a good place to *buy tickets to the museum / get a map of the museum*.

4 (◀ **4.2**) Listen again. Look at the map and match the letters (A–E) with the places below. 1 mark for each correct answer.

> café   lifts   museum shop   stairs   toilets

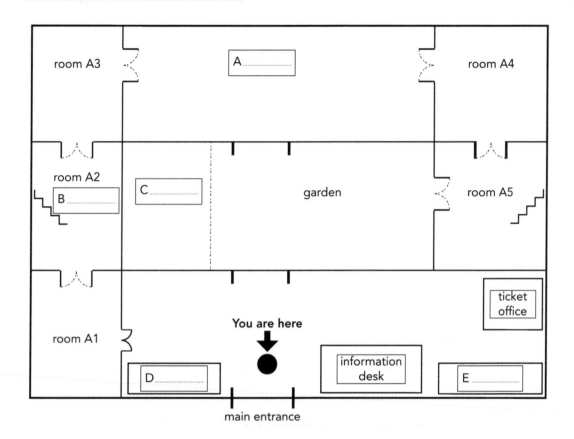

LANGUAGE DEVELOPMENT (15 marks)

5 Are the sentences true (T) or false (F)? 1 mark for each correct answer.

1 A library is a good place to keep your money. _____

2 You need to go to the station to take a train. _____

3 Use a bridge to cross a river. _____

4 You can study in the supermarket. _____

5 People buy milk in the park. _____

6 You can get money from the bank. _____

7 Planes take off and land at the port. _____

6 Unscramble the names of the places. 1 mark for each correct answer.

1	TYRUKE	_____	5	DNOLON _____
2	UEEROP	_____	6	CAMIREA _____
3	LYIAT	_____	7	NIASP _____
4	AASI	_____	8	COWSOM _____

TOTAL _____/ 35

REVIEW TEST 5

Name: .... Date: ....

LISTENING (20 marks)

LISTENING 1

1 (◀ 5.1) Listen to the recording. Are the statements true (T) or false (F)?
1 mark for each correct answer.

1 Abdullah does judo at the gym. _____

2 The judo classes are on Mondays and Wednesdays. _____

3 You have to be quick and strong to do judo. _____

4 Yoga will not make you stronger. _____

5 Yoga classes are on Thursdays and Fridays. _____

2 (◀ 5.2) Listen and put the words in the correct column of the table.
1 mark for each correct answer.

| classes | doing | find | quick | running |

/k/ c̲ountry	/f/ p̲h̲one	/ŋ/ stron̲g̲

LISTENING 2

3 (◀ 5.3) Listen and complete the gaps with the words from the talk. 1 mark for each correct answer.

I want to talk to you about jogging, or (1) _____ . Many people go jogging because it's
(2) _____ and (3) _____. But jogging can cause problems in your (4) _____. It's very
important that you (5) _____ a little before you run. Also, make sure that your running
(6) _____ are comfortable. Drink a lot of (7) _____ before and after jogging. In the winter, wear
(8) _____ clothes. Finally, don't run in (9) _____ you don't know or late at (10) _____.

LANGUAGE DEVELOPMENT (15 marks)

4 Write the adjectives with the opposite meaning. 1 mark for each correct answer.

1 fast   _____
2 strong   _____
3 happy   _____
4 fat   _____
5 healthy   _____

5 Correct the spelling mistakes in the sports. 1 mark for each correct answer.

1 swiming   _____
2 tenis   _____
3 foodball   _____
4 bascketball   _____
5 diveing   _____

6 Correct the comparative forms. 1 mark for each correct sentence.

1 I think baseball is more easier than volleyball.
2 In my opinion, yoga is healthy than running.
3 Tennis players are more strong than golf players.
4 I think zumba is best than judo.
5 Skiing is more dangerous kung fu.

TOTAL _____ / 35

Name: .... **Date:** ....

LISTENING (20 marks)

LISTENING 1

1 (🔊 6.1) Listen and choose the correct answer (a, b or c). 1 mark for each correct answer.

1 Who are the speakers?
   a a teacher and a student
   b a mother and daughter
   c two friends

2 What advice did the teacher give to the student?
   a that she should get a job
   b that she should choose a major now
   c that she should study medicine

3 What does the mother want her daughter to do?
   a She wants her to study medicine.
   b She wants her to get a job.
   c She wants her to work in a supermarket.

4 What is the student's decision?
   a She will study to be a doctor.
   b She will stop studying.
   c She will follow the teacher's advice.

5 Where has she applied for a job?
   a in a shop
   b in a fast-food restaurant
   c in a hospital

2 (🔊 6.2) Listen and complete the sentences with the correct form of *have* or *have to*. 1 mark for each correct answer.

1 Doctors _____ work at night.

2 Teachers _____ a lot of holidays.

3 A fireman _____ be strong.

4 Scientists _____ be clever.

5 My sister _____ a good job.

LISTENING 2

3 🔊 **6.3** Listen and complete the notes taken by a student. 1 mark for each correct answer.

Job interview – managers meet you and (1) _____ more about you

Best candidate = (2) _____ , clever and (3) _____

Prepare for the interview:
- wear (4) _____ clothes
- (5) _____ good and healthy
- bring documents
- don't be (6) _____ (go to bed (7) _____)
- (8) _____ about the company online
- find out about the salary

Interview (9) _____ :
- your job experience = Where did you (10) _____ before? / What did you do?
- Why are you interested in the job?

LANGUAGE DEVELOPMENT (15 marks)

4 Are the statements true (T) or false (F)? 1 mark for each correct answer.
1 Nurses work in hospitals. _____
2 Waiters have to have a university degree. _____
3 Policemen often work at night. _____
4 Lawyers have to study for many years. _____
5 Builders work in banks. _____

5 Match the sentence pairs. 1 mark for each correct answer.

1 He is very helpful.	a I think I will start running every day.
2 I want to get fit.	b She always smiles and talks to everyone.
3 This actor is very good-looking.	c He helped me fix my computer.
4 My teacher is very friendly.	d He didn't say 'Hello' when I walked in.
5 This waiter is not very polite.	e Everyone wants to look like him.

6 Unscramble the words to make sentences. 1 mark for each correct sentence.
1 should / I / work hard / you / think / .
2 study / have to / Students / every day / .
3 I / you / at night / should / don't / watch movies / think / .
4 I / should / do / What / ?
5 I / a job / Should / get / ?

TOTAL _____ / 35

REVIEW TEST 7

Name: .... **Date:** ....

LISTENING (20 marks)

LISTENING 1

1 (🔊 **7.1**) Listen to the recording. Are the statements true (T) or false (F)? 1 mark for each correct answer.

1 The student wants to paint her room white. _____

2 Her friend does not like green. _____

3 The armchair and the curtains are blue. _____

4 The students also want to paint the kitchen. _____

5 The students agree that red is the best colour for the living room. _____

2 (🔊 **7.2**) Listen and circle the words you hear. 1 mark for each correct answer.

1 fed / feed

2 same / seem

3 living / leaving

4 bad / bed

5 small / smell

LISTENING 2

3 (🔊 **7.3**) Listen to the radio programme and choose the correct answer (a, b or c).
1 mark for each correct answer.

1 Who is Ellen Lee?

  a a book author

  b a college student

  c a radio presenter

2 How can feng shui help students?

  a It can make them happy.

  b It can help improve their grades.

  c It can help them get slim.

3 Where does feng shui come from?

  a China   b Sweden   c Fiji

4 Feng shui is about

  a gardening.

  b organizing your space.

  c furniture in bedrooms.

5 We can guess that 'dorms' means

  a classrooms.

  b a place where students eat.

  c a place where students work and sleep.

4 (🔊 **7.3**) Listen again and tick (✓) the five tips you hear. 1 mark for each correct answer.

1 Change your bed so that your feet don't face the bedroom door. ☐

2 Change your dining-room table so you can see the kitchen. ☐

3 Keep your room clean. ☐

4 Make sure your desk is tidy when you study. ☐

5 Paint the walls green. ☐

6 Put plants in your room. ☐

7 Keep the windows open in the summer. ☐

8 Use red and orange to decorate the room. ☐

LANGUAGE DEVELOPMENT (15 marks)

5 Match the pictures with the words in the box. You will not need all the words. 1 mark for each correct answer.

> armchair bookcase chair lamp sofa study desk

1 _____

2 _____

3 _____

4 _____

5 _____

6 Complete the sentences with the words from the box. You will not need all the words. 1 mark for each correct answer.

> cheaper comfortable far near noisy quiet wooden

1 My sofa is not very _____. I need to buy a new one.
2 I like my room to be _____ when I study, so I switch off the music.
3 This bed seems expensive. Can we find a _____ one?
4 My office is not _____ from home. I usually walk there.
5 I'd like a _____ bookcase. I don't like plastic ones.

7 Correct the spelling mistakes in the rooms. 1 mark for each correct answer.
1 kitcken
2 batheroom
3 clasrum
4 combuter lap
5 language sentre

TOTAL _____ / 35

Name: ....   **Date:** ....

LISTENING (20 marks)

LISTENING 1

1 🔊 8.1 Listen and complete the sentences with the words you hear. 1 mark for each correct answer.

1 The caller is organizing a _____ for university guests.
2 The restaurant offers Korean dishes, like fried beef and _____.
3 Guests can grill the _____ at the table.
4 The barbecue is served with spicy sauces and _____ dishes.
5 The caller also asks if they serve _____.

2 🔊 8.1 Listen again and complete the notes about the booking. 1 mark for each correct answer.

Korean barbecue
Number of guests: (1) _____
Date: (2) _____
Time: (3) _____
Name: (4) _____
Phone number: (5) _____

LISTENING 2

3 🔊 8.2 Listen and label the pie charts with the words from the box. 1 mark for each correct answer.

between one and five   cafeteria   chocolate   crisps   fast food
home   more than five   nuts and dried fruit   one or less   sweets

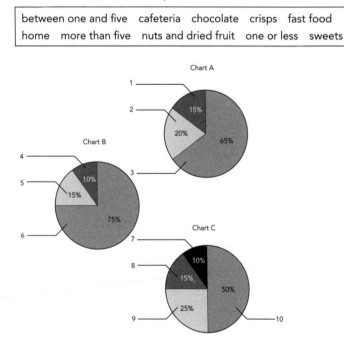

LANGUAGE DEVELOPMENT (15 marks)

4 Complete the sentences with the words from the box. Some words can be used more than once. 1 mark for each correct answer.

any   many   much   some

1 There is _____ milk in the fridge.

2 Are there _____ oranges?

3 How _____ sugar do you take?

4 There aren't _____ lemons left.

5 How _____ apples should I buy?

5 Correct the sentences. 1 mark for each correct sentence.

1 Are there some bananas?

2 Is there many tea left?

3 How many water do you need?

4 There is any food in the kitchen.

5 How many beef do you need?

6 Label the food pictures. 1 mark for each correct answer.

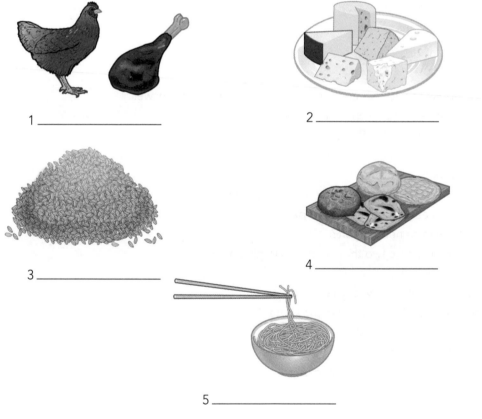

1 _____

2 _____

3 _____

4 _____

5 _____

TOTAL _____/ 35

Name: .... Date: ....

LISTENING (20 marks)

LISTENING 1

1 (🔊 9.1) Listen to the recording. Are the statements true (T) or false (F)?
1 mark for each correct answer.

  1 The conversation is between two students. _____

  2 One student is having problems writing the assignment. _____

  3 They have to write 700 words. _____

  4 The student saw a programme about penguins on television. _____

  5 Most penguins can fly. _____

  6 Penguins are excellent divers. _____

  7 Penguins can stay under water for over 20 minutes. _____

  8 Penguins are fast swimmers. _____

  9 Penguins can drink sea water. _____

  10 Seals can't drink sea water. _____

LISTENING 2

2 (🔊 9.2) Listen and choose the correct answers. 1 mark for each correct answer.

  1 Which TWO cities does the presenter mention?
    a Cairo   b Manchester   c Ulan Bator   d Montreal

  2 Which TWO words are used to describe the Mongol horses?
    a long   b tall   c short   d strong

  3 Which TWO other animals are mentioned in the programme?
    a Arabian horses   b eagles   c camels   d pandas

  4 How many Mongolian camels are left?
    a two million   b millions   c two thousand   d 20 million

  5 What do camels carry in their humps?
    a water   b water and fat   c a woolly coat   d fat

  6 What is the temperature in Mongolia in the winter?
    a –30°C   b –13°C   c 30°C   d –40°C

  7 The summers in Mongolia are
    a windy.   b very hot.   c rainy.   d very cold.

LANGUAGE DEVELOPMENT (15 marks)

3 Complete the sentences with the words from the box. You will not need all the words.
1 mark for each correct answer.

brain climbed jungle leaves stick wet

1 The _____ on this tree are yellow and dry. I think it needs water.

2 My dog fell into the river and now he's all _____.

3 The average human _____ weighs about 1.5 kg.

4 My cat _____ a tree and now she doesn't want to come down.

5 I don't like walking in the _____. There are too many insects.

4 Unscramble the names of the animals. 1 mark for each correct answer.
1 DICCOROLE   _____
2 NASKE   _____
3 HAWLE   _____
4 ARBE   _____
5 IOLN   _____

5 Match the sentence halves. 1 mark for each correct answer.

1 A cockroach	a for a baby horse.
2 A 'foal' is the name	b is a kind of insect.
3 Wolves have two long teeth	c That means that they eat meat.
4 Mammals are animals	d called 'fangs'.
5 Frogs are carnivorous.	e with warm blood.

TOTAL _____/ 35

Name: .... **Date:** ....

LISTENING (20 marks)

LISTENING 1

1 (◀ **10.1**) Listen to the recording. Are the statements true (T) or false (F)? 1 mark for each correct answer.

  1 The students have to prepare a talk about a solution to a transport problem. _____

  2 One of the students saw the electric bus in Seoul. _____

  3 The electric bus is called OLEF. _____

  4 The bus gets electricity through WiFi. _____

  5 Some cities in Europe and America are using this bus. _____

2 (◀ **10.2**) Listen and write the years that you hear. 1 mark for each correct answer.

  1 _____

  2 _____

  3 _____

  4 _____

  5 _____

LISTENING 2

3 (◀ **10.3**) Listen and complete the sentences with words that you hear. 1 mark for each correct answer.

  1 'BCH' means 'Barclays _____ Hire'.

  2 The BCH bikes are _____.

  3 People in London can _____ a bike in one place, then return it in another part of the city.

  4 The BCH programme started in _____.

  5 Cycling is good for people's _____ and for the environment.

  6 _____ of the members of the programme are now more interested in cycling.

  7 The biggest number of bikes that people have hired in one day is about _____.

  8 To hire a bike, you need a _____ and a PIN.

  9 People can rent the bikes for 24 hours or _____ days.

  10 People who have one-year membership can use the _____ any time.

LANGUAGE DEVELOPMENT (15 marks)

4 Label the transport pictures. 1 mark for each correct answer.

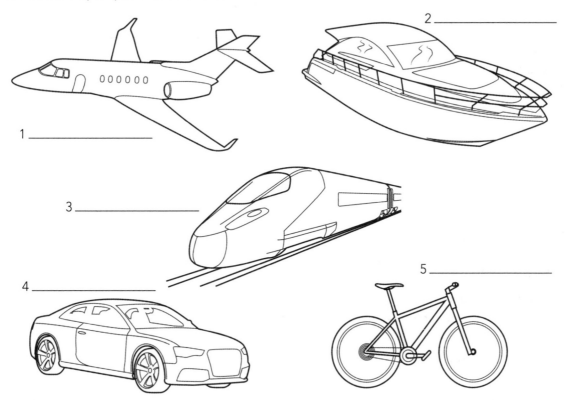

1 _____

2 _____

3 _____

4 _____

5 _____

5 Complete the sentences with the words and phrases from the box. You will not need all the words. 1 mark for each correct answer.

| arrive   check in   destination   reserve   takes off   ticket   traffic jam |

1 I leave Exeter at 7 a.m. and I _____ at King's Cross at 9.30.

2 Sorry for being late! There was a terrible _____ on my way to work.

3 His flight _____ at 10.30 p.m. He should be at the airport at eight.

4 A: What's your _____ ?

   B: I'm going to Edinburgh.

5 Can I have a return _____ to Cambridge, please?

6 Complete the sentences with past simple of the verbs from the box. 1 mark for each correct answer.

| come   go   have   open   want |

1 I _____ a terrible journey to work yesterday – there was so much traffic!

2 Dubai Metro _____ in 2009.

3 We _____ on holiday to France last year.

4 I _____ to take a taxi, but I couldn't find one.

5 I _____ here by bus.

TOTAL _____ / 35

ADDITIONAL SPEAKING TASK 1

1 Work with a classmate you don't know very well and interview each other.
Use the questions in the box.

> Where do you come from?
>
> How old are you?
>
> What is your hometown?
>
> What do you do?
>
> What do you like to do in your free time?
>
> What do you want to do in the future?

2 Tell the class about your partner.

MODEL LANGUAGE

TALKING ABOUT PEOPLE

Introducing your talk

I'm going to tell you about (*name*).

Giving personal details

This is (*name*).

He's/She's (*age*).

He's/She's from (*country*).

He's/She's a(n) (*occupation*).

He's/She's from (*city*).

He/She has (*number of brothers/sisters*).

He/She wants to (*verb*).

(*Name*) is a famous (*occupation*).

Using possessive adjectives

His/Her family is from (*country/city*).

His/Her father is a(n) (*occupation*).

My mother is a(n) (*occupation*).

Our family lives in (*city*).

ADDITIONAL SPEAKING TASK 2

Prepare a short presentation about weather in your country. Use the ideas below.
Make sure you speak for a minimum of one minute.

> Describe the weather in your country. Make sure you mention
>
> 1 how many seasons there are
> 2 what the weather is like in each season
> 3 what people usually do in each season
> 4 what your favourite season is, and why.

MODEL LANGUAGE

TALKING ABOUT PLACES AND WEATHER

Organizing your talk

I'm going to talk about two photographs of a place in (season).
Here's my first photograph.
Here is another photograph of (place) in (season).

Talking about seasons

There's a lot of rain in (spring/autumn/winter/summer) in (country).
(Country) gets a lot of (snow/rain) in (spring/autumn/winter/summer).
In the rainy/dry season, …
In (country), (season) begins in (month) and ends in (month).
(Season) in (country) is from (month) to (month).

Describing weather

It's sunny/rainy/windy/cloudy/stormy.
There are clouds in the sky.
The wind is strong today.
There is snow in the mountains.

Describing things in a photograph

There's a forest. / There's a river.
There are buildings. / There are a lot of people.
There isn't any sand. / There are no trees.

ADDITIONAL SPEAKING TASK 3

Find someone who
- likes to eat out.
- posts photographs online.
- doesn't go to the cinema.
- goes to the gym.
- runs every day.
- doesn't drink coffee.
- cooks food for their family.
- doesn't watch TV.
- plays computer games every night.

MODEL LANGUAGE

TALKING ABOUT LIFESTYLES

Asking permission to do a survey

Excuse me! Can I ask you some questions?

Excuse me! Can I have a few minutes of your time?

I'd like to ask you some questions.

Asking questions about lifestyle

Do you live with your parents?

Do you work or study?

What do you study?

Do you have a busy lifestyle?

How do you relax?

Do you (play football)?

When do you (go to the gym / go out with your friends)?

Talking about lifestyle

I study (*subject*).

I go to the gym every week.

I have lunch with friends every weekend.

She plays tennis on Mondays.

He chats online.

They play computer games.

I go to the cinema every Friday.

ADDITIONAL SPEAKING TASK 4

> Give directions from the college to your house.
> - Draw a simple map with the directions from the college to your house.
> - Label the map with important places.
> - Use the map to give instructions to your house.

MODEL LANGUAGE

ASKING FOR AND GIVING DIRECTIONS

Asking for directions

Where's the (library)? Is it near the (supermarket)?

Can you tell me the way to the (library)?

I'm looking for the (library). Is it near here?

Excuse me, where's the (library)?

I can't find the (library) – is it near the (bank)?

Giving directions

It's between the (bank) and the (bookshop).

It's there, on the left/right.

It's (opposite / next to) the (restaurant).

It's (behind / in front of) the (bank).

Go (across / out of) the square and turn (left/right).

Go along Tower Street and over the bridge.

Go down Fort Street.

Then turn (right/left).

Go across the road and through the park.

Go straight on.

The supermarket is on the (right/left), next to the bus station.

The university library is behind the student's union on Park Street.

The bank is next to the café and opposite the gym on South Road.

ADDITIONAL SPEAKING TASK 5

Prepare a short presentation about your favourite sport. Use the ideas below.
Make sure you speak for a minimum of one minute.

> Describe a sport that you are interested in. You should mention
> 1 how you became interested in this sport.
> 2 why it is interesting.
> 3 what equipment you need to do it.
> 4 what skills you need to do it.
> Discuss if this sport is good for young or old people.

MODEL LANGUAGE

TALKING ABOUT SPORT

Introducing your talk

Today, I want to talk to you about three kinds of sport/exercise.

I want to start with these questions: Which sport is better for young men? Which is better for women?

Describing sports

There are (two players/teams).

You can do it alone.

There are (12) players in a team.

There are no winners or losers.

You score (points/goals).

You can play it (outside/inside).

Comparing sports

I think (sport) is better for (older people).

(Women) are (tougher/stronger/fitter/weaker) than men.

(Zumba) is faster than (pilates).

(Pilates) is slower than (zumba).

(Zumba) is good for (your heart).

You can (get fit).

(Free diving) is harder than (running).

(Yoga) is easier for woman.

(Zumba) is healthier than (walking).

> **ARE YOU LOOKING FOR A PART-TIME JOB ON THE CAMPUS?**
> We are looking for a hard-working, helpful and polite student to help in the college library. You should be able to work at least ten hours per week during the week. You should be able to speak English fluently.

Interviewers

Student A: Librarian	**Student B: Library assistant**
You have selected two students to interview for a part-time job in the library. During the interview, you want to find out from the students • what they study • why they chose this subject • why they want to work in the library • how many hours per week they can work, and on which days.	You have been asked to help during the job interviews for a part-time position. You want to find out from the students • their strengths and weaknesses • how they would describe themselves • if they can speak foreign languages • if they like reading books.

Interviewees

Student C: Name _____	**Student D: Name** _____
You have applied for a part-time job in the library. You are a science student and you don't read books for fun. You want to be a doctor in the future. You can work in the afternoons, but you can't work during the exam period.	You are a second-year language student. You are studying French and you can speak English fluently. You love to read books and spend a lot of time in the library. You can only work at weekends because you have a lot of coursework during the week.

MODEL LANGUAGE

Discussing criteria for a job

I want a person who (has experience / is polite / can speak languages).

We want a person who can (make students work hard).

We are looking for a person who (works in a big hospital / has a degree / likes children).

He/She has to be (helpful/polite/clever/friendly).

He/She doesn't have to be (strong/slim/fit/interesting).

I (don't) think he/she should be (interesting / strong).

He/She has to be able to (speak English / work long hours).

Discussing candidates

He's/She's from (*city*) in (*country*).

He/She speaks / can't speak (*language*).

He's/She's a student in …

He/She thinks it's important to … because a (nurse) …

ADDITIONAL SPEAKING TASK 7

What changes would you like to make in your college?
- Make a list of things you would like to change in your college.
- Work with a partner and tell each other about your ideas.
- Choose one idea from each list and discuss it with another pair.
- Decide which idea is the most interesting and share it with the class.

MODEL LANGUAGE

PHRASES FOR A DISCUSSION

Asking for an opinion
What do you think?
What about here?
Why not?
What about the walls?
What colour do you think we should paint the walls?

Giving an opinion
I think we should (go to the park).
I think we should have (big windows).
I don't think we should (paint the walls blue).
I think it should be …
The walls should be (yellow/blue).

Agreeing
Oh, I see.
Yes, that's true.
Yes, you're right.
I agree.

Disagreeing
I'm not sure.
I don't agree.

Describing places
It's near some (good roads / restaurants / shops).
The buildings are very old.
They are (not) comfortable places.
The buildings are very expensive.
It's quite far from town.

ADDITIONAL SPEAKING TASK 8

1 Make notes to answer these questions.

1 Do you like to cook? If yes, what kind of food do you like to cook?
2 What do you usually eat for dinner?
3 Are there any types of food you don't like? Why?
4 What is your favourite type of food? What do you like about it?
5 Do you like to eat in restaurants?

2 Work with a partner and discuss your answers.

MODEL LANGUAGE

PRESENTING SURVEY RESULTS

Introducing your presentation
This afternoon, I'm going to tell you about the results of my survey.
There were (20) students in my survey.
My questions were on the topic of (food and culture).
I think this is an interesting topic.

Organizing the presentation
My (first/second/third/last) question was …
So my conclusion is that …

Talking about the results
You can see here that (50%) of the students come from (England) and (15%) come from (Spain).
You can see that half of the students are from (England).
You can see here that 'yes' is 70% and 'no' is 30%.
You can see here that the results are interesting.
First, 80% of people think that …
Secondly, 20% of people think that …

ADDITIONAL SPEAKING TASK 9

1 Prepare a short presentation about your favourite animal. Use these questions to help you.

1 What is your favourite animal?

2 What does it look like?

3 Where does it live?

4 What does it eat?

5 What is special about it?

6 Why do you like it?

7 Can people keep it in their homes?

2 Bring photographs of the animal to class.

MODEL LANGUAGE

GIVING A PRESENTATION ABOUT AN ANIMAL

Introducing your topic

Good morning! I'm (name) and today I'm going to tell you about (a bird from my country).

I'm going to tell you about the animal in this photograph here. So this is (an Arabian oryx).

Describing an animal

You can see here that they live (in forests / in mountains / near rivers).

(Brown bears) live in (America and Europe).

You can see them in many countries, for example …

They eat (fish / small animals / fruit / vegetables / nuts / grass).

They sleep for the winter and hunt in the summer.

They are famous for (their horns).

They can run and jump very fast.

They are very (strong/small/big/weak/fast/slow).

They are (brown/white/orange/black).

ADDITIONAL SPEAKING TASK 10

1 Choose a traffic problem in your city.

2 What are solutions to this problem?

3 Which solution is the best?

....

MODEL LANGUAGE

PRESENTING A PROBLEM AND SOLUTION

Introducing the topic

I'm going to start with some facts about (life in the cities).

Presenting cause and effect

The population of cities grows more quickly than in the countryside. This means that cities become really congested.

This is because everyone uses cars to travel around the city, and this can be a problem.

Being in a car for a long time can be dangerous because drivers suffer from tiredness and road rage.

Presenting solutions

Firstly, the plan is to reduce traffic congestion by making public transport better.

They have to introduce more buses.

The plan for the future is to (make the metro system bigger).

They should build sky bridges and travelators to connect stations.

Adding more information

What is more …

Also, …

Another solution is …

ACKNOWLEDGEMENTS

Author acknowledgements

I would like to give special thanks to all the Cambridge University Press editors for their continuous encouragement and comments. Many thanks go to my colleagues, Claudia Kiburz, Julie Rose, and Christine Thorne for their creativity and enthusiasm for teaching. Finally, I would like to thank my husband, Robert Ryan, for his endless support.

Sabina Ostrowska

Publisher acknowledgements

The publishers are extremely grateful to the following people and their students for reviewing and trialling this course during its development. The course has benefited hugely from your insightful comments, advice and feedback.

Mr M.K. Adjibade, King Saud University, Saudi Arabia; Canan Aktug, Bursa Technical University, Turkey; Olwyn Alexander, Heriot Watt University, UK; Harika Altug, Bogazici University, Turkey; Laila Al-Qadhi, Kuwait University, Kuwait; Tahani Al-Taha, University of Dubai, UAE; Valerie Anisy, Damman University, Saudi Arabia; Anwar Al-Fetlawi, University of Sharjah, UAE; Ozlem Atalay, Middle East Technical University, Turkey; Seda Merter Ataygul, Bursa Technical University Turkey; Kwab Asare, University of Westminster, UK; Erdogan Bada, Cukurova University, Turkey; Cem Balcikanli, Gazi University, Turkey; Gaye Bayri, Anadolu University, Turkey; Meher Ben Lakhdar, Sohar University, Oman; Emma Biss, Girne American University, UK; Dogan Bulut, Meliksah University, Turkey; Sinem Bur, TED University, Turkey; Alison Chisholm, University of Sussex, UK; Dr. Panidnad Chulerk , Rangsit University, Thailand; Sedat Cilingir, Bilgi University, Istanbul, Turkey; Sarah Clark, Nottingham Trent International College, UK; Elaine Cockerham, Higher College of Technology, Muscat, Oman; Asli Derin, Bilgi University, Turkey; Steven Douglass, University of Sunderland, UK; Jacqueline Einer, Sabanci University, Turkey; Basak Erel, Anadolu University, Turkey; Hande Lena Erol, Piri Reis Maritime University, Turkey; Gulseren Eyuboglu, Ozyegin University, Turkey; Sam Fenwick, Sohar University, Oman; Peter Frey, International House, Doha, Qatar; Muge Gencer, Kemerburgaz University, Turkey; Dr. Majid Gharawi and colleagues at the English Language Centre, Jazan University, Saudi Arabia; Jeff Gibbons, King Fahed University of Petroleum and Minerals, Saudi Arabia; Maxine Gilway, Bristol University, UK; Dr Christina Gitsaki, HCT, Dubai Men's College, UAE; Neil Harris, Swansea University, UK; Vicki Hayden, College of the North Atlantic, Qatar; Joud Jabri-Pickett, United Arab Emirates University, Al Ain, UAE; Ajarn Naratip Sharp Jindapitak, Prince of Songkla University, Hatyai, Thailand; Aysel Kilic, Anadolu University, Turkey; Ali Kimav, Anadolu University, Turkey; Bahar Kiziltunali, Izmir University of Economics, Turkey; Kamil Koc, Ozel Kasimoglu Coskun Lisesi, Turkey; Ipek Korman-Tezcan, Yeditepe University, Turkey; Philip Lodge, Dubai Men's College, UAE; Iain Mackie, Al Rowdah University, Abu Dhabi, UAE; Katherine Mansfield, University of Westminster, UK; Kassim Mastan, King Saud University, Saudi Arabia; Elspeth McConnell, Newham College, UK; Lauriel Mehdi, American University of Sharjah, UAE; Dorando Mirkin-Dick, Bell International Institute, UK; Dr Sita Musigrungsi, Prince of Songkla University, Hatyai, Thailand; Mark Neville, Al Hosn University, Abu Dhabi, UAE; Shirley Norton, London School of English, UK; James Openshaw, British Study Centres, UK; Hale Ottolini, Mugla Sitki Kocman University, Turkey; David Palmer, University of Dubai, UAE; Michael Pazinas, United Arab Emirates University, UAE; Troy Priest, Zayed University, UAE; Alison Ramage Patterson, Jeddah, Saudi Arabia; Paul Rogers, Qatar Skills Academy, Qatar; Josh Round, Saint George International, UK; Harika Saglicak, Bogazici University, Turkey; Asli Saracoglu, Isik University, Turkey; Neil Sarkar, Ealing, Hammersmith and West London College, UK; Nancy Shepherd, Bahrain University, Bahrain; Jonathan Smith, Sabanci University, Turkey; Peter Smith, United Arab Emirates University, UAE; Adem Soruc, Fatih University Istanbul, Turkey; Dr Peter Stanfield, HCT, Madinat Zayed & Ruwais Colleges, UAE; Maria Agata Szczerbik, United Arab Emirates University, Al Ain, UAE; Burcu Tezcan-Unal, Bilgi University, Turkey; Scott Thornbury, The New School, New York, New York, USA; Dr Nakonthep Tipayasuparat, Rangsit University, Thailand; Susan Toth, HCT, Dubai Men's Campus, Dubai, UAE; Melin Unal, Ege University, Izmir, Turkey; Aylin Unaldi, Bogaziçi University, Turkey; Colleen Wackrow, Princess Nourah bint Abdulrahman University, Riyadh, Saudi Arabia; Gordon Watts, Study Group, Brighton UK; Po Leng Wendelkin, INTO at University of East Anglia, UK; Halime Yildiz, Bilkent University, Ankara, Turkey; Ferhat Yilmaz, Kahramanmaras Sutcu Imam University, Turkey.

Special thanks to Peter Lucantoni for sharing his expertise, both pedagogical and cultural.

Special thanks also to Michael Pazinas for writing the *Research projects* which feature at the end of every unit. Michael has first-hand experience of teaching in and developing materials for the paperless classroom. He has worked in Greece, the Middle East and the UK. Prior to his current position as Curriculum and Assessment Coordinator for the Foundation Program at the United Arab Emirates University he was an English teacher for the British Council, the University of Exeter and several private language institutes. Michael is also a graphic designer, involved in instructional design and educational eBook development. His main interests lie in using mobile technology together with attractive visual design, animation and interactivity. He is an advocate of challenge-based language learning.

Text and Photo acknowledgements

Dictionary

Cambridge dictionaries are the world's most widely used dictionaries for learners of English. Available at three levels (Cambridge Essential English Dictionary, Cambridge Learner's Dictionary and Cambridge Advanced Learner's Dictionary), they provide easy-to-understand definitions, example sentences, and help in avoiding typical mistakes. The dictionaries are also available online at dictionary.cambridge.org. © Cambridge University Press, reproduced with permission.

Corpus

Development of this publication has made use of the Cambridge English Corpus (CEC). The CEC is a multi-billion word computer database of contemporary spoken and written English. It includes British English, American English and other varieties of English. It also includes the Cambridge Learner Corpus, developed in collaboration with Cambridge English Language Assessment. Cambridge University Press has built up the CEC to provide evidence about language use that helps to produce better language teaching materials.

Typeset by Integra.